Lewis Carroll's *Alice* Novels:

The Study Guide Edition

By Francis Gilbert

This edition first published in 2017 by FGI publishing:
www.francisgilbert.co.uk;
fgipublishing.com
Copyright © 2016 Francis Gilbert
FGI Publishing, London UK, sir@francisgilbert.co.uk
British Library Cataloguing-in-Publications Data
A catalogue record for this book is available from the British Library.

ISBN-13: 978-1494758646
ISBN-10: 1494758644

Dedication
For Year 7.

Acknowledgments
First, huge thanks to Jason Bristow for initially working with me to develop a Scheme of Work on *Alice in Wonderland*; some of the ideas developed then are here in the "Teaching Points" sections; Second, gratitude must go to Erica Wagner, for always supporting me with my writing and teaching. Third, I'm very grateful to all the students, teachers, lecturers and other lively people who have helped me write this book.
Also by Francis Gilbert:
I'm A Teacher, Get Me out Of Here (2004)
Teacher on the Run (2005)
Yob Nation (2006)
Parent Power (2007)
Working The System: How To Get The Very State Education For Your Child (2011)
The Last Day Of Term (2012)
Gilbert's Study Guides on: *Frankenstein, Far From The Madding Crowd, The Hound of the Baskervilles, Pride and Prejudice, The Strange Case of Dr Jekyll and Mr Hyde, The Turn of the Screw, Wuthering Heights* (2013)
Dr Jekyll & Mr Hyde: The Study Guide Edition (2014)
Romeo and Juliet: The Study Guide Edition (2014)
Charlotte Brontë's Jane Eyre: The Study Guide Edition (2015)
Austen's Pride and Prejudice: The Study Guide Edition (2015)
Mary Shelley's Frankenstein: The Study Guide Edition (2015)
The Turn of the Screw: The Study Guide Edition (2015)

Contents

Introduction

This study guide takes a different approach from most study guides. It does not seek to tell you about the story and characters in a boring fashion, but attempts to show how it is the author's techniques and interests that inform every single facet of these classic novels. Most study guides simply tell you *what* is going on, and tack on bits at the end which tell you *how* the writer created suspense and drama at certain points in the book, informing you a little about *why* the writer might have done this.

This study guide starts with the *how* and the *why*, showing you right from the start *how* and *why* the writer shaped the key elements of the book. It also poses questions constantly to get you thinking for yourself; it is your personal opinion, backed up by argument and evidence, which really counts.

Definition:

The context of a book is both the *world* the book creates in the reader's mind (contexts of reading), and the *world* it came out from (contexts of writing).

How to use this Study Guide Edition

This study guide is deliberately interactive; it is full of questions, tasks and links to other sources of information. You will learn about Lewis Carroll's *Alice* novels much more effectively if you have a go at the questions and tasks set, rather than just copying out notes.

Contexts

Understanding Contexts

To appreciate a text fully, you need to appreciate the contexts in which it was written – known as its contexts of writing – and the contexts in which you read the book, or the contexts of reading.

This is potentially a huge area to explore because 'contexts' means the 'worlds' from which the book has arisen. For the best books, these are many and various. The most obvious starting point is the writer's own life: it is worth thinking about how and why the events in a writer's life might have influenced his or her fiction. However, you do have to be careful not to assume too much. For example, while it is true that Lewis Carroll modelled Alice on his 'child-friend' Alice Liddell, you must remember that the Alice of the books is a character in her own right in the novel – a vital cog in the narrative wheel, a literary construct and not a real person!

Thus, it is particularly fruitful to explore other contexts of writing. We can look at the broader world from which Lewis Carroll arose (Victorian culture), and consider carefully how, in his writing, he both adopted and rejected the morals of his time. Other contexts might be the influence of the literary & intellectual world that Lewis Carroll inhabited (what other authors were writing at the time), how religion, science and mathematics shaped his views, and so on.

Just as important as the contexts of *writing* are the contexts of *reading*: how we read the novel today. Central to this novel is the idea that the world fundamentally does not make sense, that we inhabit a nonsensical, farcical world which has all the logic of an incredible dream – some would say nightmare! This idea, which was radical during Lewis Carroll's time, is now commonly accepted amongst many scientists, artists, philosophers and writers. In this sense, the Alice novels have grown in relevance as time has passed. This said, the upper class Victorian world it represents of strange rules, roles, games and professions such as talking about "hatters", playing "croquet", dancing quadrilles may be quite foreign to many readers, although these pursuits still exist.

Questions

What do we mean by context? Why do you need to understand the idea of context to write well about Lewis Carroll's *Alice* novels?

Useful link

This BBC Bitesize website is good at explaining more about what we mean about context when analysing literature:
http://www.bbc.co.uk/education/guides/z8kyg82/revision

Contexts of Writing: Lewis Carroll's life

Lewis Carroll was the pseudonym (false name) of Charles Lutwidge Dodgson who was born in Cheshire in 1832. His father, also called Charles, was a Reverend, who lived with his large family in an old, small parsonage at Daresbury from 1827-1843 after which he become Rector of Croft in north Yorkshire, when the family moved to the large rectory in Croft-on-Tees. Charles Dodgson junior was the eldest son in a large family: he had seven sisters and three brothers. This was very important because the children had to make their own amusements. Charles Dodgson proved good at this from an early age when he began inventing games for his siblings to play. When they moved to Croft, Charles put together magazines which the whole family were supposed to contribute to; some of these still survive with Charles mostly writing them. They had titles such as *Useful and Instructive Poetry* (1845), *Mischmasch* (1853) and *The Rectory Umbrella* (1853). Some of this material found its way into the Alice books, so it was not entirely "childish", although it is "child-like" in spirit, a spirit which Dodgson never really lost.

He was sent away the boarding school Rugby when he was fourteen. Although he did well there academically, he disliked the school, where he was bullied. Conditions for boarding students were harsh. He left Rugby in 1849 and then became an undergraduate at his father's old college, Christ's Church, Oxford. Although he was lazy at times and periodically did not enjoy Oxford, he again did well, achieved a First-Class degree in Mathematics in 1854: the top grade. He won the Christ Church Mathematical Lectureship in 1855, which he held for the next 26 years: to assume this post, he had to become part of the Church of England. As a result, he was ordained as a Deacon in 1861. This shows the grip that the church had on English life at the time: you had to become a religious man to teach at university.

Dodgson suffered from ill health throughout his life, enduring a severe attack of whooping cough when he was 17. He also had a stammer, which he referred to as his "hesitation". Although much has been made of his stammer by both the people he knew and subsequent critics, there is no strong evidence that it ruined his life: he was sociable, singing in company and being noted for his comic talent at copying people's ways of talking. He also mingled in artistic circles, being friends with some of the most famous writers and artists of the day such as John Ruskin and Dante Gabriel Rossetti, who he was very close to. He was not a radical politically, being committed to the old-fashioned ways of the church and was conservative in his views about social reform. He certainly was not someone who called for revolution on the streets at a time when there was chronic poverty in many of the major cities. This would not have been a world that Dodgson saw often because Oxford was, by and large, a wealthy town, and he mingled mostly with rich people. This said, his friend John Ruskin was much more radical and there is no question they would have argued politically about things.

From the outset, Dodgson enjoyed writing but he first came to fame in 1856 when he published a romantic poem "Solitude" under the name Lewis Carroll. In the same year, Henry Liddell became Dean of Dodgson's college (the head) and Dodgson forged a strong friendship with the whole family, including Liddell's daughters, Loreina, Edith and Alice. Many critics believe that Dodgson based the Alice of the novels on Alice Liddell; the acrostic poem at the end of *Through the Looking Glass* spells her name out in full. But Dodgson said repeatedly that his protagonist was not based on a specific child.

Dodgson would take the children on rowing trips along the river Cherwell in Oxford. It was on one of these expeditions on 4th July 1862 that Dodgson told Alice Liddell his first version of *Alice in Wonderland*, who, after he told more of the story during some rainy days when they were indoors, begged him to write the story down. In November 1864, he gave her a handwritten, illustrated manuscript called *Alice's Adventures Under Ground*. It was published the followed year as *Alice in Wonderland* under his Lewis Carroll pen-name with the now famous illustrations by John Tenniel. Although it initially sold relatively few copies, over the years the story became a massive hit, with readers from all over the world sending Dodgson fan mail, which he did not appreciate being a shy person. Even Queen Victoria loved the book and demanded a sequel. In 1871, Dodgson published *Through the Looking-Glass and What Alice Found There*, which is darker in tone than the first book.

His father had died in 1868, and this clearly made Dodgson quite depressed. In 1876, he published his great nonsense poem "The Hunting of the Snark", which is about a crew and a beaver setting off to find a "snark". In 1895, thirty years after the publication of the first Alice book, he produced Sylvie and Bruno, a book which mocks English society and specially university life. Although considered not as good as the Alice novels, it has been popular for over a hundred years.

Dodgson was a very keen photographer, taking thousands of photographs at a time when you had to be very skilled to take photographs and process them properly. Although not considered as outrageous at the time, his pictures of young naked children are now considered as pornographic by some critics. There is no evidence that Dodgson was a "paedophile", but instead had intense relationships with young children, most particularly girls, before they reached puberty. Mostly, he would stop the friendships after they grew up. He stopped photographing very abruptly in 1880, by which time he had created 3,000 images.

He was also an inventor of a case that could hold stamps, and a writing tablet that could be used in the dark. He also came up with an early version of the word game Scrabble. He parodies his own inventions and his way of behaving in *Through the Looking Glass* when he describes the eccentric white knight with all of his inventions and his constant falling-off his horse; this said, the White Knight is also heroic, rescuing Alice at a vital time in the story. The knight's goodbye to Alice is the most moving moment in both novels and has a special poignancy because Dodgson wrote the book well after his friendship with Alice had ended: she was grown up when the novel was written.

He published many books about mathematics, specializing Algebra, Geometry and Logic. In recent years, there has been renewed interest in his maths work, with some mathematicians praising his approach to mathematical logic.

As if his story-writing, prolific mathematical research, inventions and photography were not enough, he was always writing letters, penning nearly 100,000 by the time of his death.

Although he became very famous later in life because of the *Alice* novels, his life-style did not change. He continued to teach at Christ Church until 1881, and thereafter lived there until he died of pneumonia in 1898, two weeks away from his 66th birthday.

Questions

Why do you think the books might be called *Alice in Wonderland* and *Alice through the Looking-Glass*?

What events, people and ideas in Dodgson's life and the wider society may have influenced the writing of the story?

Useful links

For more on Dodgson's life look here:
https://www.britannica.com/biography/Lewis-Carroll
https://en.wikipedia.org/wiki/Lewis_Carroll
The British Library has a very attractive website which explores the influences of *Alice in Wonderland*:
https://www.bl.uk/alice-in-wonderland/articles/influences-on-alice-in-wonderland

Selected Reading on Lewis Carroll's Life

Cohen, Morton (1996). Lewis Carroll: A Biography. Vintage Books. London.

Woolf, Jenny, The Mystery of Lewis Carroll. (2010). New York: St Martin's Press.

Contexts of Reading

In recent years, controversy has dogged Charles Dodgson and, by association, the Alice novels because of his relationship with young children. He appears to have formed very intense relationships with young children, almost falling in love with them. This is particularly true of Alice Liddell, who he was very close to, writing for her and paying her close attention until she was 12 years old, at which point he 'dropped' her. Modern critics have tried to read into his relationships with young children an attempt to find a substitute for married life, which he never chose. This though is a 'modern' interpretation. For a man of his position and class, it was perfectly acceptable for him to form close friendships with young children in a way that it is not today: there simply was not the 'taboo' around men being friendly with young children, and indeed, it was actively encouraged for unmarried men. There is no suggestion or evidence that Dodgson ever 'abused' children. So, while you may question his motives – as some critics have done – his relationships with young children need to be understood in context.

More troubling is his photography of young children, some of which would be considered possibly illegal today because it depicts naked young children in what some people consider to be sexually provocative poses. Again though, these photographs have been to be considered in context; they were not controversial at the time. The fact is that times have changed and people are much warier about 'child protection' issues than they were in Dodgson's day when the issue was never really considered. You have to bear in mind that it was only in 1864 that it was made illegal for anyone under 21 years of age to sweep a chimney.

The Alice novels also are controversial because they appear to refer at times to what are now illegal drugs such as opium (heroin) when depicting the Caterpillar who is smoking a hookah, or Alice when she eats a mushroom and changes body shape. Jefferson Airplane's classic song (covered brilliantly by Patti Smith) *White Rabbit* exploits the 'druggy' qualities of the books, reading the stories as sort of 'hippy' parables of self-discovery. Dodgson himself appears to have been against drug-taking, but quite happy to use it as a motif in his stories. Remember just because an author presents something in a story doesn't mean that he/she actually agrees with it.

Perhaps the most modern aspect of the Alice books is the exploration of identity: Alice is constantly changing identity both in how she is physically (she changes size), and the different roles that the situations in Wonderland and the Mirror World of the second book create for her: she is the 'lost girl', the questioner, the accused, the accuser, the game-player, the riddle-solver, the sympathizer, the condemner to name just a few. Every situation brings out a different side to her personality. She is never actually the same person. This is a very modern problem which all of us, in our confusing modern world, are dealing with, never quite certain of who we are or what we are doing.

There have been numerous film adaptations of the novel, with the Disney Cartoon and Tim Burton's two films being the most famous. This is because the book is so visually appealing and narratively intriguing. It is a pacey, fantastical story which puts Harry Potter to shame for sheer inventiveness. See the link below for more about the different film adaptations.

It has influenced countless artists, writers, musicians, actors, dancers, mathematicians and scientists, inspiring them to produce work that pays homage to the story in way or other.

Useful links

This BBC report covers the basics about Carroll's attitude towards children and drugs in the books:

http://www.bbc.co.uk/news/magazine-19254839

You can read about Jefferson Airplane's White Rabbit here:

https://en.wikipedia.org/wiki/White_Rabbit_(Jefferson_Airplane_song)

There is a brief discussion of the role of opium in the novels here:

http://www.victorianweb.org/victorian/authors/carroll/aiwl5.html

You can find a long list of films and television programmes influenced by Alice in Wonderland here:

https://en.wikipedia.org/wiki/Films_and_television_programmes_based_on_Alice_in_Wonderland

You can find about works influenced by Alice in Wonderland here:

https://en.wikipedia.org/wiki/Works_based_on_Alice_in_Wonderland

This review of an academic book about the Alice novels is very informative and clearly written:

https://www.timeshighereducation.com/books/review-alice-in-space-the-sideways-victorian-world-of-lewis-carroll-gillian-beer-university-of-chicago-press?utm_source=the_editorial_newsletter&utm_medium=email&utm_content=books&utm_campaign=the_editorial_newsletter

Questions

It is worth doing some work on contexts before starting the actual book. I would suggest you write an *Alice* **learning journal** that records all your thoughts and feelings about the book. Try to tell the truth!

There are two major questions to consider when thinking about contexts: where is the book coming from and where am I coming from?

The first question is best answered while reading the book; what sorts of values and ideas are enshrined in this book? What is its historical context? What is its literary context? What is its philosophical context? How does the book relate to the life of the author?

It is worth you trying to analyse where you are coming from. Everyone holds a set of assumptions and ideas that profoundly affects how he or she sees the world. Try and answer these questions:

What are your attitudes towards adult-child relationships?

What are your attitudes towards fantastical stories and dreams?

What children's stories do you like and why? What role have the Alice books played in your life, if any?

Now onto the text

What are the vital ingredients of a story? Why is it that we can believe that a "whole load of words" contain a new world?

Now jot down your expectations about the *Alice* books. What kind of book do you expect it to be?

Write out what you think the story will be. Write about how you think it will be structured. What will be the main events of the story? Who will be the main characters?

While reading the novel, look back over the notes you have made for this section and constantly ask yourself; how does my context affect the way I read the novel and feel/think about the characters/situations/themes? I have already suggested that you write a learning journal as you read it through, jotting down these thoughts as you go along. Then once you have finished reading, think about the novels' overall effects and how it speaks to you personally.

Why do you think the Alice novels are so popular today? Why have so many films/plays/operas etc. been made of it? Consider these questions before you read the books, during your reading and after you have finished reading them.

Structure and Theme

While the Alice novels appear, on first reading, to be structured in a crazy, haphazard way, if you look at them closely, they have a clear narrative structure. The structure of a story is the vital building blocks of it, without which it would not be a story. The structure of a story is closely tied to its themes or central ideas. There are many themes in the novels, as we will see, but for many critics the central idea of the books is that of "identity": Alice is always searching for who she is. Is she tall, small, mad, sane, a pawn or a queen, is she "real" or the figment of the Red King's dream? The novels represent her quest to find out who she is. She is prompted to ask these questions by entering the mad cap worlds of the Wonderland and the

Looking-Glass world, which do not obey the rules of "reality".

So, we could boil down both books to this quest in this way:

Beginnings: Alice enters another world and becomes someone/something else.

Middles: Alice tries to find out who she is, attempting to recover her 'old' identity of being a little girl and get 'home' or find 'reality'.

Ends: After a confrontation with the Queens (in both books), Alice finds a new, more powerful identity.

I have written out a more detailed outline for both narratives below, but it is the above point, you need to consider when thinking about both books. For all their apparent 'rule-breaking', they are very carefully structured stories.

Alice in Wonderland Structure

Opening

Alice follows a white rabbit and falls down the rabbit hole, shrinks after drinking from a bottle labelled 'DRINK ME' and grows after eating cake labelled 'EAT ME', and then cries because she is so big.

Complications

Alice shrinks again and swims in her own tears, meets a mouse and other animals who have been swept up in the river of her tears. She frightens the animals by talking about her cat. There is a Caucus-Race where is everyone is a winner. Being ordered by the White Rabbit to get the Duchess's glove and fan, Alice goes into a house where she grows again. Everyone throws cakes at her. She eats one and shrinks again.

Crisis

She meets a Caterpillar who tells her to eat a mushroom to solve her identity crisis, which she does. After some effort, she returns to a normal size. She is given a baby by the Duchess which turns into a pig, and a Cheshire Cat appears in a tree, and shows her the way to the March Hare's House. The cat disappears but his grin remains. Alice joins the Mad Hatter's Tea Party with the Mad Hatter, March Hare and Dormouse, but leaves, disillusioned with it. Alice meets the King and Queen and plays croquet with them using live flamingos as mallets. The Duchess is brought before the Queen from prison, and the Mock Turtle tells his sad story and then he and the Gryphon dance to the Lobster Quadrille.

Climax

Alice attends a trial in which the Knave of Hearts is accused to stealing the Queen's Tarts. During the trial, Alice grows larger again, much to the Dormouse's annoyance. The Hatter displeases the King with his indirect answers. Alice is called as a witness, knocking over the jury box with all the animals inside because she is so big. The King and Queen order her to be gone, but she refuses and the Queen shouts her catchphrase "Off with her head!"

Resolution

Alice calls the King and Queen a pack of cards just as they swarm over her. She wakes up and finds leaves not cards brushing over her on the river bank.

Alice Through the Looking Glass structure

Opening

Alice is playing with her kitten when she wonders what the world is like inside the mirror above the mantelpiece. She climbs onto the mantelpiece and steps into the mirror, where she finds an alternative world. In this reflected vision of her own house, she finds some looking-glass poetry, "Jabberwocky", written in reversed print, which she can only read by holding up to the mirror. She sees that her chess pieces have come to life, although they remain small.

Complications

She leaves her house and enters the garden where the flowers can speak. She meets the Red Queen, who is human-size now, and sees that the Queen can move, like the chess piece, at extraordinary speed across the "chessboard" of the Looking-Glass world. The Red Queen says that Alice herself can become a Queen, if like a pawn on a chessboard, she moves to the end of the board. Alice is now judged as one of the White Queen's pawns, and jumps two spaces on the board by taking the train which literally jumps over the third row and onto the fourth, like a pawn setting out can move an extra square. She meets Tweedledum and Tweedledee who recite the long poem "The Walrus and the Carpenter". She then meets the White Queen and they advance across the fifth square by crossing a stream together, after which the Queen transforms into a sheep in a small shop.

Crisis

After crossing the sixth rank by another brook, Alice meets Humpty Dumpty who gives her a strange translation of "Jabberwocky" before falling off his wall. 'All the king's men and horses' come to repair Humpty Dumpty accompanied by the White King, the Lion and the Unicorn. Alice leaves the Lion and the Unicorn fighting and crosses the seventh square of the chess board and enters the territory of the Red Knight, who wants to capture her because she is a white pawn, but she is saved by the White Knight who protects her. Taking her through the forest to the final brook crossing, the White Knight recites a long poem called "Haddocks' Eyes" and keeps falling off his horse.

Climax

Saying goodbye to the White Knight, Alice crosses the last brook and becomes a White Queen and soon finds herself with the White and Red Queen, who both try to trip her up with their logical talk and invite themselves to a party which they inform Alice she herself has called for, even though she has no knowledge of this. Alice arrives at her own party, which quickly becomes very chaotic, and grabs the Red Queen, who she blames for much of the bedlam. By capturing the Red Queen, Alice has unwittingly check-mated the Red King who has not moved for the whole of the game and then wakes up.

Resolution

Alice wakes in the armchair, shaking the black kitten who she figures out to have been the Red Queen all along, with the white kitten being the White Queen. She remembers the Tweedledum brothers saying that the whole story might have been a dream of the Red King and that Alice may be a figment of his imagination. The book ends with a poem saying that life is a dream.

Useful links to help you get to know the novels better

The following websites are useful because they can give you a strong overview of the novel, but you do need to think for yourself regarding your opinions of the novel.

Alice in Wonderland web summaries and quizzes

https://en.wikipedia.org/wiki/Alice%27s_Adventures_in_Wonderland

http://www.gradesaver.com/alice-in-wonderland/study-guide/summary

http://www.sparknotes.com/lit/alice/summary.html

https://www.cliffsnotes.com/literature/a/alices-adventures-in-wonderland/book-summary

http://www.shmoop.com/alice-in-wonderland-looking-glass/summary.html

These webpages contain quizzes which will test your knowledge:

http://www.gradesaver.com/alice-in-wonderland/study-guide/quiz1

http://www.gradesaver.com/alice-in-wonderland/study-guide/quiz1

https://www.cliffsnotes.com/literature/a/alices-adventures-in-wonderland/study-help/quiz

http://www.shmoop.com/alice-in-wonderland-looking-glass/quizzes.html

Alice Through the Looking-Glass web summaries and quizzes

http://www.gradesaver.com/through-the-looking-glass/study-guide/summary

http://www.sparknotes.com/lit/through-the-looking-glass/summary.html

https://en.wikipedia.org/wiki/Through_the_Looking-Glass

These webpages contain quizzes which will test your knowledge:

http://www.gradesaver.com/through-the-looking-glass/study-guide/quiz1

Questions/tasks

Once you have read each book, ask yourself these questions: to what extent is the novel a successful story? What are its exciting moments and why? Are there moments when the story feels less successful? Give reasons for your answers.

Compare one or two filmed versions with the novels; what events/characters/ideas do the film-makers use and what do they leave out, and why?

The Influence of Genre

Both Alice books are classified as children's prose fiction, in other words seen as made-up stories written for children. They were also important in establishing the whole genre (type) of children's fiction, which was not highly regarded until Lewis Carroll published his books.

They also fantasy books, containing as they do lots of characters and situations that are entirely 'unrealistic'. In this sense, they are deliberate reaction against the more realistic books of the day written by famous realist writers like Mrs. Gaskill. The fantasy elements in the books are tremendously important because, unlike much fantasy writing before and since, they do not contain a moral message. Until Carroll, most fantasy writing was religious in quality, carrying with it a strong moral message. So, for example, *The Water Babies*, published by the Reverend Charles Kingsley, just a few years before *Alice in Wonderland* in 1862 told the tale of a poor chimney sweep who falls into a stream and learns to be good and pure in an underwater fantasy land of speaking animals and spirits. It is like the Alice books in that it is about a child who travels from the 'real' world to a fantasy world which does not obey the normal rules of 'reality'. However, it has a strong Christian message and the character learns an important moral lesson about being good and subscribing to the fundamental tenets of Christianity. This is in common with many children's fantasy stories which are largely what might be called 'fables', fantasy stories with moral messages. Even modern fantasy books like *Harry Potter* are heavily informed by strong moral messages: Harry learns to become a better person by battling with the evil Voldemort. His education at Hogwarts, while fantastical, has a 'moral logic': Harry learns to be a true friend and a wise pupil.

The Alice books appear to be deliberately anarchic (breaking the rules) in that they do not provide an obvious moral message: Alice does not learn to become better at all. She searches for a new identity in both books and finds a more powerful one by the end, but there is no obvious moral. She has not learned to be more Christian, nicer or a cleverer person. Indeed, she actually appears to be a destructive force, destroying both worlds at the end of both books: Wonderland becomes a pack of cards, and she checkmates the Red King in the Looking-Glass world.

Another important element to the books is the way they 'mix-up' genres: both books contain a large amount of poetry, which is nearly all unrelated to the actual plot, but maintain the comic tone of the books. They also contain sections of philosophical dialogue, discussing the nature of identity, of language and of logic. They pose riddles such as the Cheshire Cat disappearing but only leaving only his grin. And they also use games such as card playing, croquet and chess. Indeed, the whole of the second book is a disguised chess game (see the Structure and Theme section for more on this). In this sense, the books break genre conventions in that they adhere to the rules of games rather than fiction or stories.

Finally, as has been alluded to, the books are primarily comedic nonsense books. They are meant to be funny and deliberately without any deep-rooted meanings. They poke fun at certain attitudes in the world such as the dictatorial arrogance of the Red Queen, the looniness of the Mad Hatter, and the ridiculous charade of the Trial. At certain points, as we will see when we read the book, they satirize certain viewpoints, poems and poets, and institutions such as the church, the law courts and politicians.

Here we can see Carroll appealing to an adult audience: while children may find much of the humour funny, adults have the pleasure in recognizing certain 'real' people, poems and institutions being mocked or 'satirized' amidst the nonsense.

Questions for Genre

To what extent are the Alice novels fantasy novels?
To what extent are the books comedy novels?
To what extent are they 'nonsense'?

Useful links

The British Library website contains a fascinating exploration of the diverse literature which influenced the Alice books:
https://www.bl.uk/alice-in-wonderland/articles/influences-on-alice-in-wonderland
This article on the Victorian web looks at Alice as a fantasy novel:
http://www.victorianweb.org/authors/carroll/carter.html

Critical Perspectives

Are the Alice novels really 'children's' books?

There is a huge wealth of scholarship about the Alice novels, but critics repeatedly return to the question: to what extent are the novels actually children's books? The more critics study the books, the more they begin to see their complexities and artistry.

There is no doubt that Carroll intended them to be children's books, having written the first one for his child-friend, Alice Liddell. They are written in a simple fashion with language that a literate seven-year-old even today could understand. The situations are immediately funny for children too, who can readily laugh at the fact that Alice turns into different sizes, meets talking animals, takes part in crazy games and must fight for her life, arguing with characters who are bizarrely unreasonable and sometimes murderous. Even children who are not from the social class or time of Alice Liddell can appreciate that the book is on the side of the children: it is the mad adult world which is clearly criticized in the book. The Queens in both books are psychotic, the Kings not much better, and other adult figures are clearly recognizable: the worrying White Rabbit with his watch, the dopey Caterpillar with his hookah, the pompous Humpty Dumpty with his portentous, absurd explanations, the long-winded White Knight and so on.

This said, both books contain satire which only educated adults could possibly grasp such as re-written versions of poems (see the notes to the poems in the text for more on this) and philosophical dialogue about the nature of language and logic. *Through the Looking-Glass* has a fiendishly clever underlying structure, using the template of a chess game, which might primarily appeal to adults, although there is no doubt an intelligent child could notice it as well.

The debate about whether the novels are really for children will rage on because it is unresolvable. The books are simultaneously children and adult's books, with enough in them to satisfy both young children and the cleverest university professors. This explains their enduring appeal.

Weblinks on the *Alice* novels

This Guardian article contains 10 things people don't know about *Alice in Wonderland*:

https://www.theguardian.com/childrens-books-site/2015/apr/17/10-things-you-didnt-know-about-alice-in-wonderland-lewis-carroll

This British Library article looks at the anthropomorphism (making people animals) in the books:

https://www.bl.uk/romantics-and-victorians/articles/anthropomorphism-in-alices-adventures-in-wonderland

Questions

To what extent do you think the Alice books are written for children? What elements of the stories make them 'children's' stories? To what extent are they written for adults? What elements of the books make them 'adult's' books?

Part 2: Complete text & tasks

How to read and study the novel

What follows is the complete text of both *Alice* novels interspersed with commentaries and questions on the text. The text is broken up with analysis and points for discussion. I have used Martin Gardner's superb *The Annotated Alice* (1990) extensively in the commentaries because this version is the most scholarly edition; I have referenced all the times when I have used Gardner's brilliant notes as a source: it is worth looking at the book if you are interested in the points because Gardner's notes are mostly much more detailed than mine. My aim was to keep the notes brief so that students would remain engaged. I have deliberately provided a variety of different question types at the ends of chapters; I have started with "simple" comprehension questions and then moved onto more analytical and creative questions, which not only require you to understand the plot but also arrive at your own personal responses, using evidence from the text to back up your points. The more complex questions that follow the comprehension ones are more difficult and don't usually have "right and wrong" answers. For this reason, the only answers I provide at the end of the book are the ones with "right" or "wrong" answers, the other answers could be peer-assessed or marked by teachers.

I would also suggest that you devise visual organisers to represent ideas/characters/plot-lines in the novels as you read through it; this means doing a spider-diagram/chart/flow diagram etc. depending upon what you feel is most relevant. To find out more (sometimes known as graphic organisers) look here:

https://www.teachingenglish.org.uk/article/graphic-organisers

Remember if you are uncertain about the plot, you can also refer to the websites listed in the section **'Useful links to help you get to know the story better'**. These websites are good at helping you understand the plot but they won't help you get the higher marks because you need to think for yourself if you are going to get the top grades.

As I have suggested, you could, while reading the book, put all your answers, notes, creative responses together into an *Alice* file or Learning Journal which I have suggested you do at the end of each chapter. You could be creative with this file: draw scenes of the important incidents; include spider-diagrams/visual organisers of significant characters and situations; storyboards of the key scenes; copies of articles/literary criticism which you have annotated; creative pieces etc.

I have also included "Teaching Points" at the beginning of nearly all the chapters. These are primarily for teachers to use as they see fit if they are teaching the text in class; these points are not very detailed, but offer a sketch of how a lesson might be taught on each chapter. Teachers and/or students should flesh out the finer details of the lessons themselves if they want to pursue the activities suggested. All the lessons follow the three-part structure of having a starter, main activities and a plenary. The activities are meant to add to the questions which are posed at the end of every chapter.

Helpful vocabulary to learn before you start reading

Throughout the book, **you should keep a vocabulary list**, writing down the difficult words and learning their meanings/spellings, and possibly using the vocabulary in your own writing. The complex vocabulary and sentence structures in the story can be off-putting at first but I feel you should not be put off by the language; embrace it, love it! You will become much better educated when you learn the vocabulary. This is why reading pre-20th century writing is so useful: it makes you more intelligent because you widen your vocabulary and ability to understand difficult passages.

There are some words, I would strongly advise you looking up the meanings of and learning their spellings/meanings before reading; the websites listed below are helpful in this regard as is my **Glossary** at the end of the book, which contains some of the difficult vocabulary, though not all.

Weblinks to help you learn difficult vocabulary

Key words can be found here:

Alice in Wonderland
Chapters 1-3
https://www.vocabulary.com/lists/198870
Chapters 4-6
https://www.vocabulary.com/lists/198880
Chapters 7-9
https://www.vocabulary.com/lists/199659
Chapter 10-12

Through the Looking-Glass
https://www.vocabulary.com/lists/300895
http://www.verbalworkout.com/b/b1086.htm

This workbook is useful for a number of things, including learning more

about the story, the characters and the vocabulary:
  **http://www.macmillan.ru/upload/iblock/d39/exp_l6_looking
glass_teachers_notes_text.pdf**

Both books:
There is a general glossary of terms here:
  **http://aliceinwonderland.wikia.com/wiki/Glossary_of_Alice_
in_Wonderland_Terms**

Alice in Wonderland

By Lewis Carroll

Prefatory Verses

All in the golden afternoon
Full leisurely we glide;
For both our oars, with little skill,
By little arms are plied,
While little hands make vain pretence
Our wanderings to guide.

Ah, cruel Three! In such an hour,
Beneath such dreamy weather,
To beg a tale of breath too weak
To stir the tiniest feather!
Yet what can one poor voice avail
Against three tongues together?

*Imperious Prima **(the eldest sister Lorina Charlotte, 13 yrs)** flashes*
forth
Her edict "to begin it"—
*In gentler tones Secunda **(the second sister Alice Pleasance, 10 yrs)***
hopes
"There will be nonsense in it!"—
*While Tertia **(the youngest sister Edith, 8 yrs)** interrupts the tale*
Not more than once a minute.

Anon, to sudden silence won,
In fancy they pursue
The dream-child moving through a land
Of wonders wild and new,
In friendly chat with bird or beast—
And half believe it true.

And ever, as the story drained
The wells of fancy dry,
And faintly strove that weary one
To put the subject by,
"The rest next time—" "It is next time!"
The happy voices cry.

Thus grew the tale of Wonderland:
Thus slowly, one by one,

Its quaint events were hammered out—
And now the tale is done,
And home we steer, a merry crew,
Beneath the setting sun.

Alice! A childish story take,
And with a gentle hand,
Lay it where Childhood's dreams are twined
In Memory's mystic band,
Like pilgrim's withered wreath of flowers
Plucked in far-off land.

Simple explanation: The author describes in a rhyming poem rowing down a river and telling the story of Wonderland to three sisters, Lorina, Alice and Edith.

Analysis: Carroll remembers a "golden afternoon" in 1862 when he and his friend Reverend Robinson Duckworth took three Liddell sisters rowing on the Thames. The trip was 3 miles. Carroll later recalled in his diary seven months later: "On which occasion I told them the fairy-tale of Alice's adventures underground..." Notice how from the outset, Alice is a "dream-girl", not a real girl at all. The emphasis here is upon the ways in which stories can help you enter a dream world, and take you into your "unconscious".

Discussion point: Why did Carroll write these opening verses for the story do you think? Who is his audience? What points is he making?

1 Down the Rabbit-Hole

Teaching points

Learning objective: to learn what makes an effective opening to a story.

Task one: what are your favourite openings to stories? What makes them appealing?

Task two: what are you expecting from this book? Devise a detailed concept map or brainstorm in which you note down what you think might happen in the book and why, what you would like to happen and why etc.

Task three: read Chapter 1, noting down your reactions in the form of a visual organizer, which possibly draws some of the key images, in your *Alice* learning journal. Students should explore and consider the points raised in the commentaries/discussion points as well as answering the questions at the end of the chapter as best they can.

The text

Alice was beginning to get very tired of sitting by her sister on the bank, and of having nothing to do: once or twice she had peeped into the book her sister was reading, but it had no pictures or conversations in it, "and what is the use of a book," thought Alice, "without pictures or conversations?"

So she was considering in her own mind (as well as she could, for the hot day made her feel very sleepy and stupid,) whether the pleasure of making a daisy-chain would be worth the trouble of getting up and picking the daisies, when suddenly a white rabbit with pink eyes ran close by her.

There was nothing so very remarkable in that; nor did Alice think it so very much out of the way to hear the Rabbit say to itself, "Oh dear! Oh dear! I shall be too late" (when she thought it over afterwards, it occurred to her that she ought to have wondered at this, but at the time it all seemed quite natural); but when the Rabbit actually took a watch out of its waistcoat-pocket, and looked at it, and then hurried on, Alice started to her feet, for it flashed across her mind that she had never before seen a rabbit with either a waistcoat-pocket or a watch to take out of it, and, burning with curiosity, she ran across the field after it, and was just in time to see it pop down a large rabbit-hole under the hedge.

In another moment down went Alice after it, never once considering how in the world she was to get out again.

The rabbit-hole went straight on like a tunnel for some way, and then dipped suddenly down, so suddenly that Alice had not a moment to think about stopping herself before she found herself falling down what seemed to be a very deep well.

Either the well was very deep, or she fell very slowly, for she had plenty of time as she went down to look about her, and to wonder what was going to happen next. First, she tried to look down and make out what she was coming to, but it was too dark to see anything: then she looked at the sides of the well, and noticed that they were filled with cupboards and bookshelves: here and there she saw maps and pictures hung upon pegs. She took down a jar from one of the shelves as she passed; it was labeled, "Orange Marmalade," but to her great disappointment it was empty: she did not like to drop the jar for fear of killing somebody underneath, so managed to put it into one of the cupboards as she fell past it.

> **Commentary:** Alice, feeling bored by a river bank, follows a White Rabbit with a watch down a rabbit hole and falls. We are taken here from the "real" world of a bored child, not wanting to read a book without pictures or conversations, into a fantasy world where normal laws of logic and science are not obeyed. We see this in her "free fall" when she can take a jar of marmalade from a shelf even though she is falling fast.

> **Discussion point:** how does Carroll conjure up such an unreal world so quickly? How does he make us believe this world is as real as the so-called 'real' world?

"Well!" thought Alice to herself, "after such a fall as this, I shall think nothing of tumbling down stairs! How brave they'll all think me at home! Why, I wouldn't say anything about it, even if I fell off the top of the house" (Which was very likely true.)

> **Commentary:** William Empson points out this is the first death joke in the Alice books. There are many others (Carroll L., Gardner M., 1990, p. 13).

> **Discussion point:** why are jokes about death funny?

Down, down, down. Would the fall never come to an end? "I wonder how many miles I've fallen by this time?" she said aloud. "I must be getting somewhere near the centre of the earth. Let me see: that would be four thousand miles down, I think - " (for, you see, Alice had learnt several things of this sort in her lessons in the schoolroom, and though this was not a very good opportunity for showing off her knowledge, as there was no one to listen to her, still it was good practice to say it over) " - yes, that's about the right distance - but then I wonder what Latitude or Longitude I've got to?" (Alice had not the slightest idea what Latitude was, or Longitude either, but she thought they were nice grand words to say.)

Presently she began again. "I wonder if I shall fall right through the earth!

> **Commentary:** In Carroll's time, people thought it might be possible to find a hole that dropped right down to the centre of the earth (Carroll L., Gardner M., 1990, p. 13).

> **Discussion point:** why are people obsessed with the centre of the earth?

How funny it'll seem to come out among the people that walk with their heads downwards! The Antipathies, I think - " (she was rather glad there was no one listening, this time, as it didn't sound at all the right word) " - but I shall have to ask them what the name of the country is, you know. Please, Ma'am, is this New Zealand or Australia?" (and she tried to curtsey as she spoke - fancy curtseying as you're falling through the air! Do you think you could manage it?) "And what an ignorant little girl she'll think me for asking! No, it'll never do to ask: perhaps I shall see it written up somewhere."

Down, down, down. There was nothing else to do, so Alice soon began talking again. "Dinah'll miss me very much to-night, I should think!" (Dinah was the cat.)

> **Commentary:** the Liddell sisters liked the family's tabby cats, Dinah and Villikens. (Carroll L., Gardner M., 1990, p. 14)

Discussion point (after you've read both books): what is the role of cats in the books?

"I hope they'll remember her saucer of milk at tea-time. Dinah, my dear! I wish you were down here with me! There are no mice in the air, I'm afraid, but you might catch a bat, and that's very like a mouse, you know. But do cats eat bats, I wonder?" And here Alice began to get rather sleepy, and went on saying to herself, in a dreamy sort of way, "Do cats eat bats? Do cats eat bats?" and sometimes, "Do bats eat cats?" for, you see, a she couldn't answer either question, it didn't much matter which way she put it. She felt that she was dozing off, and had just begun to dream that she was walking hand in hand with Dinah, and was saying to her very earnestly, "Now, Dinah, tell me the truth: did you ever eat a bat?" when suddenly, thump! thump! down she came upon a heap of sticks and dry leaves, and the fall was over.

Alice was not a bit hurt, and she jumped up on to her feet in a moment: she looked up, but it was all dark overhead; before her was another long passage, and the White Rabbit was still in sight, hurrying down it. There was not a moment to be lost: away went Alice like the wind, and was just in time to hear it say, as it turned a corner, "Oh my ears and whiskers, how late it's getting!" She was close behind it when she turned the corner, but the Rabbit was no longer to be seen: she found herself in a long, low hall, which was lit up by a row of lamps hanging from the roof.

There were doors all around the hall, but they were all locked, and when Alice had been all the way down one side and up the other, trying every door, she walked sadly down the middle, wondering how she was ever to get out again.

Suddenly she came upon a little three-legged table, all made of solid glass; there was nothing on it but a tiny golden key, and Alice's first idea was that this might belong to one of the doors of the hall; but alas! either the locks were too large, or the key was too small, but at any rate it would not open any of them. However, on the second time round, she came upon a low curtain she had not noticed before, and behind it was a little door about fifteen inches high; she tried the little golden key in the lock, and to her great delight it fitted!

> **Commentary:** Victorian fantasy stories often included gold keys which unlocked mysterious doors (Carroll L., Gardner M., 1990, p. 15).

> **Discussion point:** why are mysterious keys unlocking strange doors so appealing?

Alice opened the door and found that it led into a small passage, not much larger than a rathole: she knelt down and looked along the passage into the loveliest garden you ever saw. How she longed to get out of the dark hall, and wander about among those beds of bright flowers and those cool fountains, but she could not even get her head through the doorway; "and even if my head would go through," thought poor Alice, "it would be of very little use without my shoulders. Oh, how I wish I could shut up like a telescope! I think I could, if I only knew how to begin." For, you see, so many out-of-the-way things had happened lately that Alice had begun to think that very few things indeed were really impossible.

There seemed to be no use in waiting by the little door, so she went back to the table, half hoping she might find another key on it, or at any rate a book of rules for shutting people up like telescopes: this time she found a little bottle on it, ("which certainly was not here before," said Alice,) and tied round the neck of the bottle was a paper label with the words "Drink Me" beautifully printed on it in large letters.

> **Commentary:** Victorian medicine bottles had corks with paper labels on the side. (Carroll L., Gardner M., 1990, p. 16)

It was all very well to say "Drink me," but the wise little Alice was not going to do that in a hurry: "no, I'll look first," she said "and see whether it's marked 'poison' or not": for she had read several nice little stories about children who had got burnt, and eaten up by wild beasts, and other unpleasant things, all because they would not remember the simple rules their friends had taught them, such as, that a red-hot poker will burn you if you hold it too long; and that if you cut your finger very deeply with a knife, it usually bleeds; and she had never forgotten that, if you drink much from a bottle marked "poison," it is almost certain to disagree with you, sooner or later.

> **Commentary:** These stories are obviously not very nice at all, but contained 'moral messages'. Do, if you can, some further research into the gruesome Victorian children's stories, full of warnings for naughty children: **http://mentalfloss.com/article/33492/6-cautionary-tales-terrified-kids-yesteryear**

> **Discussion point:** why do you think the Alice books have no moral messages in them? What is the effect of the lack of any moral message?

However, this bottle was not marked "poison," so Alice ventured to taste it, and finding it very nice, (it had, in fact, a sort of mixed flavour of cherry-tart, custard, pine-apple, roast turkey, toffy, and hot buttered toast,) she very soon finished it off.

"What a curious feeling!" said Alice, "I must be shutting up like a telescope."

And so it was indeed: she was now only ten inches high, and her face brightened up at the thought that she was now the right size for going through the little door into that lovely garden. First, however, she waited for a few minutes to see if she was going to shrink any further: she felt a little nervous about this, "for it might end, you know," said Alice to herself, "in my going out altogether, like a candle. I wonder what I should be like then?" And she tried to fancy what the flame of a candle looks like after the candle is blown out, for she could not remember ever having seen such a thing.

After a while, finding that nothing more happened, she decided on going into the garden at once, but, alas for poor Alice! when she got to the door, she found she had forgotten the little golden key, and when she went back to the table for it, she found she could not possibly reach it: she could see it quite plainly through the glass, and she tried her best to climb up one of the legs of the table, but it was too slippery, and when she had tired herself out with trying, the poor little thing sat down and cried.

"Come, there's no use in crying like that!" said Alice to herself, rather sharply, "I advise you to leave off this minute!" She generally gave herself very good advice, (though she very seldom followed it,) and sometimes she scolded herself so severely as to bring tears into her eyes, and once she remembered trying to box her own ears for having cheated herself in a game of croquet she was playing against herself, for this curious child was very fond of pretending to be two people. "But it's no use now," thought poor Alice, "to pretend to be two people! Why, there's hardly enough of me left to make one respectable person!"

Soon her eye fell on a little glass box that was lying under the table: she opened it, and found in it a very small cake, on which the words "Eat Me" were beautifully marked in currants.

"Well, I'll eat it," said Alice, "and if it makes me grow larger, I can reach the key; and if it makes me grow smaller, I can creep under the door; so either way I'll get into the garden, and I don't care which happens!"

She ate a little bit, and said anxiously to herself "Which way? Which way?" holding her hand on the top of her head to feel which way it was growing, and she was quite surprised to find that she remained the same size: to be sure, this is what generally happens when one eats cake, but Alice had got so much into the way of expecting nothing but out-of-the-way things to happen, that it seemed quite dull and stupid for life to go on in the common way.

So she set to work, and very soon finished off the cake.

Questions/tasks

In your Learning Journal answer these questions and complete these activities:

Why is the White Rabbit worried?
Why does Alice fall down the rabbit hole?
What are the sides of the well covered in?
What is strange about the way Alice falls down the well and what does she do as she is falling?
What happens when Alice lands?
What does she discover behind a small curtain?
What happens when Alice drinks a bottle which says "DRINK ME"?
a problem when she shrinks?
Why is Alice disappointed when she eats the small cake?
Analytical response: what is so strange about the world down the rabbit hole?

Creative response: write Alice's diary for this chapter or write your own story in which a person enters a dream world. Plan it out carefully.

Textual re-casting: write a speech about the importance of giving children time to relax and enjoy themselves.

The phrase 'Down the Rabbit Hole' has entered the language now. What does it mean to you?

Where is the opening to this story set? How is this setting made interesting for the reader?

What do we learn about Alice in this chapter? Is she an interesting protagonist? Why/why not?

How is the opening chapter structured? Why is structure important?

What do you think of this as an opening to a story?

Did the opening to this story have any of the features which you thought of in your brainstorm earlier?

Did it have any features that you did not think of earlier?

Which of all these features do you think is the most important as regards creating an engaging opening to a story?

Devise a flow-chart of the major events of the chapter.

Write down in your responses to the characters and situations in the chapter, noting down your thoughts and feelings about the various things that happen. What do you think will happen next?

What reading strategies are you using to help you enjoy the book? How could you improve your reading?

See Answers to the questions at the back to mark your own work.

2 The Pool of Tears

Teaching points

Learning Objectives: To reflect upon and analyse the symbolic imagery of adolescence. To learn about the language of offence and the key elements of Chapter 2.

Key Words: Symbolism. Imagery. Adolescence, Openings.

Starter: Brainstorm feelings and thoughts associated with adolescence. Draw an image which you think could be an appropriate symbol for adolescence.

Task One: Read Chapter 2. Students should explore and consider the points raised in the commentaries/discussion points as well as answering the questions at the end of the chapter as best they can.

Task Two: What imagery in this chapter do you think is a symbol for adolescence? Find a quote copy down the quote and above the quote draw the image and explain why it is a suitable symbol for adolescence.

Task Three: In pairs, think of between three and ten stages (as abstract nouns) that the human animal progresses through, from birth to death (i.e. innocence – adolescence – rebellion...) Think of and draw a suitable symbolic image for each stage and so create a 'Life Of Man/Woman' storyboard of symbolic imagery. Explain each image.

Plenary: Feedback (presentations) from Task Three.

The text

'Curiouser and curiouser!" cried Alice (she was so much surprised, that for the moment she quite forgot how to speak good English); "now I'm opening out like the largest telescope that ever was! Good-bye, feet!" (for when she looked down at her feet, they seemed to be almost out of sight, they were getting so far off) "Oh, my poor little feet, I wonder who will put on your shoes and stockings for you now, dears? I'm sure I shan't be able! I shall be a great deal too far off to trouble myself about you: you must manage the best way you can - but I must be kind to them," thought Alice, "or perhaps they won't walk the way I want to go! Let me see: I'll give them a new pair of boots every Christmas."

And she went on planning to herself how she would manage it. "They must go by the carrier," she thought; "and how funny it'll seem, sending presents to one's own feet! And how odd the directions will look!

Alice's Right Foot, Esq., Hearthrug, near the Fender **(a low frame bordering a fireplace to prevent burning coals from falling out).** *(with Alice's love.)*

Oh dear, what nonsense I'm talking!"

Just at this moment her head struck against the roof of the hall: in fact she was now rather more than nine feet high, and she at once took up the little golden key and hurried off to the garden door.

Poor Alice! It was as much as she could do, lying down on one side, to look through into the garden with one eye; but to get through was more hopeless than ever: she sat down and began to cry again.

"You ought to be ashamed of yourself," said Alice, "a great girl like you," (she might well say this,) "to go on crying in this way! Stop this moment, I tell you!" But she went on all the same, shedding gallons of tears, until there was a large pool all round her, about four inches deep and reaching half down the hall.

After a time she heard a little pattering of feet in the distance, and she hastily dried her eyes to see what was coming. It was the White Rabbit returning, splendidly dressed, with a pair of white kid gloves in one hand and a large fan in the other: he came trotting along in a great hurry, muttering to himself as he came, "Oh! the Duchess, the Duchess! Oh! won't she be savage if I've kept her waiting!" Alice felt so desperate that she was ready to ask help of any one; so, when the Rabbit came near her, she began, in a low, timid voice, "If you please, sir - " The Rabbit started violently, dropped the white kid gloves and the fan, and scurried away into the darkness as hard as he could go.

Alice took up the fan and gloves, and, as the hall was very hot, she kept fanning herself all the time she went on talking: "Dear, dear! How queer everything is to-day! And yesterday things went on just as usual. I wonder if I've been changed in the night? Let me think: was I the same when I got up this morning? I almost think I can remember feeling a little different. But if I'm not the same, the next question is, Who in the world am I? Ah, that's the great puzzle!" And she began thinking over all the children she knew, that were of the same age as herself, to see if she could have been changed for any of them.

"I'm sure I'm not Ada," she said, "for her hair goes in such long ringlets, and mine doesn't go in ringlets at all; and I'm sure I can't be Mabel, for I know all sorts of things, and she, oh! she knows such a very little! Besides, she's she, and I'm I, and - oh dear, how puzzling it all is! I'll try if I know all the things I used to know. Let me see: four times five is twelve, and four times six is thirteen, and four times seven is - oh dear! I shall never get to twenty at that rate!

> **Commentary:** Alice probably does not get to 20 is because most schools stopped the times tables at 12.

> **Discussion point:** what do you feel about doing your times tables and multiplication and maths generally? Do you share Alice's confusion? Why? What do you think Carroll is saying here about learning in schools?

However, the Multiplication Table don't signify: let's try Geography. London is the capital of Paris, and Paris is the capital of Rome, and Rome - no, that's all wrong, I'm certain! I must have been changed for Mabel! I'll try and say 'How doth the little - '" and she crossed her hands on her lap, as if she were saying lessons, and began to repeat it, but her voice sounded hoarse and strange, and the words did not come the same as they used to do: -

> *"How doth the little crocodile*
> *Improve his shining tail,*
> *And pour the waters of the Nile*
> *On every golden scale!*
>
> *How cheerfully he seems to grin,*
> *How neatly spreads his claws,*
> *And welcomes little fishes in,*
> *With gently smiling jaws!"*

> **Commentary:** Nearly all the poems in the Alice books are parodies; they make fun of existing more serious poems (Carroll L., Gardner M., 1990, p. 23). This is a parody of a well-known poem by Isaac Watts, "Against Idleness and Mischief" from his Divine Songs for Children (1715):

> *How doth the little busy bee*
> *Improve each shining hour,*
> *And gather honey all the day*
> *From every opening flower!*
>
> *How skilfully she builds her cell!*

How neat she spreads the wax!
And labours hard to store it well
With the sweet food she makes.

In works of labour or of skill
I would be busy too:
For Satan finds some mischief still
For idle hands to do.

In books, or work, or healthful play
Let my first years be past,
That I may give for every day
Some good account at last.

Discussion point: how does Carroll's poem mock Watts's poem? What is the purpose of Carroll's parody?

"I'm sure those are not the right words," said poor Alice, and her eyes filled with tears again as she went on, "I must be Mabel after all, and I shall have to go and live in that poky little house, and have next to no toys to play with, and oh, ever so many lessons to learn! No, I've made up my mind about it: if I'm Mabel, I'll stay down here! It'll be no use their putting their heads down and saying, 'Come up again, dear!' I shall only look up and say, 'Who am I, then? Tell me that first, and then, if I like being that person, I'll come up: if not, I'll stay down here till I'm somebody else' - but, oh dear!" cried Alice, with a sudden burst of tears, "I do wish they would put their heads down! I am so very tired of being all alone here!"

Commentary: Alice asks a very familiar philosophical question here, discussed by philosophers, scientists and artists for thousands of years.

Discussion point: why is the question so important to Alice? Who do you think she is? Do some further research into how and why philosophers, artists and scientists etc. have explored the age-old question: "who am I?" There are some interesting responses here which you could use as a starting point: **https://philosophynow.org/issues/84/Who_Or_What_Am _I**

As she said this, she looked down at her hands, and was surprised to see that she had put on one of the Rabbit's little white kid gloves while she was talking. "How can I have done that?" she thought. "I must be growing small again." She got up and went to the table to measure herself by it, and found that, as nearly as she could guess, she was now about two feet high, and was going on shrinking rapidly: she soon found out that the cause of this was the fan she was holding, and she dropped it hastily, just in time to save herself from shrinking away altogether.

"That was a narrow escape!" said Alice, a good deal frightened at the sudden change, but very glad to find herself still in existence; "and now for the garden!" and she ran with all speed back to the little door: but alas! the little door was shut again, and the little golden key was lying on the glass table as before, "and things are worse than ever," thought the poor child, "for I never was so small as this before, never! And I declare it's too bad, that it is!"

As she said these words her foot slipped, and in another moment, splash! she was up to her chin in salt water. Her first idea was that she had somehow fallen into the sea, "and in that case I can go back by railway," she said to herself. (Alice had been to the seaside once in her life, and had come to the general conclusion, that wherever you go to on the English coast you find a number of bathing machines in the sea, some children digging in the sand with wooden spades, then a row of lodging houses, and behind them a railway station).

> **Commentary:** Bathing-machines were small locker rooms on wheels that were situated by the sea so that people could change inside them into their swimming costumes. (Carroll L., Gardner M., 1990, p. 25)

> **Discussion point:** why are changing rooms funny places?

However she soon made out that she was in the pool of tears which she had wept when she was nine feet high.

"I wish I hadn't cried so much!" said Alice, as she swam about, trying to find her way out. "I shall be punished for it now, I suppose, by being drowned in my own tears! That will be a queer thing, to be sure! However, everything is queer to-day."

Just then she heard something splashing about in the pool a little way off, and she swam nearer to make out what it was: at first she thought it must be a walrus or hippopotamus, but then she remembered how small she was now, and she soon made out that it was only a mouse, that had slipped in like herself.

"Would it be of any use, now," thought Alice, "to speak to this mouse? Everything is so out-of-the-way down here, that I should think very likely it can talk: at any rate there's no harm in trying." So she began: "O Mouse, do you know the way out of this pool? I am very tired of swimming about here, O Mouse!" (Alice thought this must be the right way of speaking to a mouse: she had never done such a thing before, but she remembered having seen in her brother's Latin Grammar, "A mouse - of a mouse - to a mouse - a mouse - O mouse!") The mouse looked at her rather inquisitively, and seemed to her to wink with one of its little eyes, but it said nothing.

"Perhaps it doesn't understand English," thought Alice. "I daresay it's a French mouse, come over with William the Conqueror." (For, with all her knowledge of history, Alice had no very clear notion how long ago anything had happened.) So she began again: "Ou est machatte?" which was the first sentence in her French lesson-book. The Mouse gave a sudden leap out of the water, and seemed to quiver all over with fright. "Oh, I beg your pardon!" cried Alice hastily, afraid that she had hurt the poor animal's feelings. "I quite forgot you didn't like cats."

"Not like cats!" cried the Mouse, in a shrill, passionate voice. "Would you like cats if you were me?"

"Well, perhaps not," said Alice in a soothing tone: "don't be angry about it. And yet I wish I could show you our cat Dinah: I think you'd take a fancy to cats if you could only see her. She is such a dear quiet thing," Alice went on, half to herself, as she swam lazily about in the pool, "and she sits purring so nicely by the fire, licking her paws and washing her face - and she is such a nice soft thing to nurse - and she's such a capital one for catching mice - oh, I beg your pardon!" cried Alice again, for this time the Mouse was bristling all over, and she felt certain it must be really offended. "We won't talk about her any more if you'd rather not."

"We, indeed!" cried the Mouse, who was trembling down to the end of his tail. "As if I would talk on such a subject! Our family always hated cats: nasty, low, vulgar things! Don't let me hear the name again!"

"I won't indeed!" said Alice, in a great hurry to change the subject of conversation. "Are you - are you fond - of - of dogs?" The Mouse did not answer, so Alice went on eagerly: "There is such a nice little dog near our house I should like to show you! A little bright-eyed terrier, you know, with oh! such long curly brown hair! And it'll fetch things when you throw them, and it'll sit up and beg for its dinner, and all sorts of things - I can't remember half of them - and it belongs to a farmer, you know, and he says it's so useful, it's worth a hundred pounds! He says it kills all the rats and - oh dear!" cried Alice in a sorrowful tone. "I'm afraid I've offended it again!" For the Mouse was swimming away from her as hard as it could go, and making quite a commotion in the pool as it went.

So she called softly after it, "Mouse dear! Do come back again, and we won't talk about cats or dogs either, if you don't like them?" When the Mouse heard this, it turned round and swam slowly back to her: its face was quite pale (with passion, Alice thought), and it said in a low, trembling voice, "Let us get to the shore, and then I'll tell you my history, and you'll understand why it is I hate cats and dogs."

It was high time to go, for the pool was getting quite crowded with the birds and animals that had fallen into it: there was a Duck and a Dodo, a Lory and an Eaglet, and several other curious creatures. Alice led the way, and the whole party swam to the shore.

> **Commentary:** A Dodo was a large extinct flightless bird with a stout body, stumpy wings, a large head, and a heavy hooked bill. It was found on Mauritius until the end of the 17th century. A Lory was a small Australasian and SE Asian parrot with a brush-tipped tongue for feeding on nectar and pollen, having mainly green plumage with patches of bright colour. An eaglet was a young eagle. (Carroll L., Gardner M., 1990, p. 27)

Questions/tasks

In your Learning Journal answer these questions and complete these activities:

What happens to Alice after eating the cake which says "EAT ME" after some time?

What does she do when she grows so tall?

What does the White Rabbit mutter to himself?

Why does Alice think she may not be the person that she once was and who does she think she maybe and why?

What does the fanning motion cause to happen?

What happens when she shrinks?

Who does she ask for help and why does she offend it?

How does Alice manage to get the Mouse to come back?

Who else does Alice meet in the pool of tears?

Analytical response: what questions about identity does Alice raise in this chapter?

Creative response: write Alice's diary or a story in which a person keeps changing size.

Textual re-casting: write some advice aimed at Alice and children generally, helping them deal with the changes that will happen to their bodies during childhood and adolescence.

Devise a flow-chart of the major events of the chapter.

Write down in your responses to the characters and situations in the chapter, noting down your thoughts and feelings about the various things that happen. What do you think will happen next?

What reading strategies are you using to help you enjoy the book? How could you improve your reading?

See Answers to the questions at the back to mark your own work.

3 A Caucus Race and a Long Tale

Teaching points

Learning Objectives: To explore and analyse the language of competition; to learn how to write persuasively.

Starter activity: hold a crazy competition such as the person who pulls on their earlobes in alternating fashion, whilst holding a pencil between their top lip and nose, whilst saying the alphabet backwards from 'I' is the winner. They win a great prize (a sock) to be awarded with considerable pomp, circumstance and po-faced solemnity at the end of the lesson.

Task One: Read Chapter 3. Students should explore and consider the points raised in the commentaries/discussion points as well as answering the questions at the end of the chapter as best they can.

Task Two: Writing to persuade: write a speech to the PE department saying that all competitions in school should be disposed of, including football matches.

Plenary: Students read out their work so far. Identify persuasive techniques.

The text

They were indeed a queer-looking party that assembled on the bank-the birds with draggled feathers, the animals with their fur clinging close to them, and all dripping wet, cross, and uncomfortable.

The first question of course was, how to get dry again: they had a consultation about this, and after a few minutes it seemed quite natural to Alice to find herself talking familiarly with them, as if she had known them all her life. Indeed, she had quite a long argument with the Lory, who at last turned sulky, and would only say, 'I am older than you, and must know better'; and this Alice would not allow without knowing how old it was, and, as the Lory positively refused to tell its age, there was no more to be said.

At last the Mouse, who seemed to be a person of authority among them, called out, 'Sit down, all of you, and listen to me! I'LL soon make you dry enough!' They all sat down at once, in a large ring, with the Mouse in the middle. Alice kept her eyes anxiously fixed on it, for she felt sure she would catch a bad cold if she did not get dry very soon.

'Ahem!' said the Mouse with an important air, 'are you all ready? This is the driest thing I know. Silence all round, if you please! "William the Conqueror, whose cause was favoured by the pope, was soon submitted to by the English, who wanted leaders, and had been of late much accustomed to usurpation and conquest. Edwin and Morcar, the earls of Mercia and Northumbria-"'

'Ugh!' said the Lory, with a shiver.

'I beg your pardon!' said the Mouse, frowning, but very politely: 'Did you speak?'

'Not I!' said the Lory hastily.

'I thought you did,' said the Mouse. '-I proceed. "Edwin and Morcar, the earls of Mercia and Northumbria, declared for him: and even Stigand, the patriotic archbishop of Canterbury, found it advisable-"'

'Found WHAT?' said the Duck.

'Found IT,' the Mouse replied rather crossly: 'of course you know what "it" means.'

'I know what "it" means well enough, when I find a thing,' said the Duck: 'it's generally a frog or a worm. The question is, what did the archbishop find?'

The Mouse did not notice this question, but hurriedly went on, '"-found it advisable to go with Edgar Atheling to meet William and offer him the crown. William's conduct at first was moderate. But the insolence of his

Normans-" How are you getting on now, my dear?' it continued, turning to Alice as it spoke.

'As wet as ever,' said Alice in a melancholy tone: 'it doesn't seem to dry me at all.'

'In that case,' said the Dodo solemnly, rising to its feet, 'I move that the meeting adjourn, for the immediate adoption of more energetic remedies-'

'Speak English!' said the Eaglet. 'I don't know the meaning of half those long words, and, what's more, I don't believe you do either!' And the Eaglet bent down its head to hide a smile: some of the other birds tittered audibly.

'What I was going to say,' said the Dodo in an offended tone, 'was, that the best thing to get us dry would be a Caucus-race.'

> **Commentary:** A Caucus is (in North America and New Zealand) a meeting of the members of a legislative body who are members of a particular political party, to select candidates or decide policy or a group of people with shared concerns within a political party or larger organization. (Carroll L., Gardner M., 1990, p. 31)

> **Discussion point:** why does the Dodo talk about a Caucus race do you think, bearing in mind what a Caucus means?

'What IS a Caucus-race?' said Alice; not that she wanted much to know, but the Dodo had paused as if it thought that SOMEBODY ought to speak, and no one else seemed inclined to say anything.

'Why,' said the Dodo, 'the best way to explain it is to do it.' (And, as you might like to try the thing yourself, some winter day, I will tell you how the Dodo managed it.)

First it marked out a race-course, in a sort of circle, ('the exact shape doesn't matter,' it said,) and then all the party were placed along the course, here and there. There was no 'One, two, three, and away,' but they began running when they liked, and left off when they liked, so that it was not easy to know when the race was over. However, when they had been running half an hour or so, and were quite dry again, the Dodo suddenly called out 'The race is over!' and they all crowded round it, panting, and asking, 'But who has won?'

This question the Dodo could not answer without a great deal of thought, and it sat for a long time with one finger pressed upon its forehead (the position in which you usually see Shakespeare, in the pictures of him), while the rest waited in silence. At last the Dodo said, 'EVERYBODY has won, and all must have prizes.'

'But who is to give the prizes?' quite a chorus of voices asked.

'Why, SHE, of course,' said the Dodo, pointing to Alice with one finger; and the whole party at once crowded round her, calling out in a confused way, 'Prizes! Prizes!'

Alice had no idea what to do, and in despair she put her hand in her pocket, and pulled out a box of comfits **(a sweet consisting of a nut, seed, or other centre coated in sugar)**, (luckily the salt water had not got into it), and handed them round as prizes. There was exactly one a-piece all round.

'But she must have a prize herself, you know,' said the Mouse.

'Of course,' the Dodo replied very gravely. 'What else have you got in your pocket?' he went on, turning to Alice.

'Only a thimble,' said Alice sadly.

'Hand it over here,' said the Dodo.

Then they all crowded round her once more, while the Dodo solemnly presented the thimble, saying 'We beg your acceptance of this elegant thimble'; and, when it had finished this short speech, they all cheered.

Alice thought the whole thing very absurd, but they all looked so grave that she did not dare to laugh; and, as she could not think of anything to say, she simply bowed, and took the thimble, looking as solemn as she could.

The next thing was to eat the comfits: this caused some noise and confusion, as the large birds complained that they could not taste theirs, and the small ones choked and had to be patted on the back. However, it was over at last, and they sat down again in a ring, and begged the Mouse to tell them something more.

'You promised to tell me your history, you know,' said Alice, 'and why it is you hate-C and D,' she added in a whisper, half afraid that it would be offended again.

'Mine is a long and a sad tale!' said the Mouse, turning to Alice, and sighing.

'It IS a long tail, certainly,' said Alice, looking down with wonder at the Mouse's tail; 'but why do you call it sad?' And she kept on puzzling about it while the Mouse was speaking, so that her idea of the tale was something like this:-

'Fury said to a
mouse, That he
met in the
house,
"Let us
both go to
law: I will
prosecute
YOU.-Come,
I'll take no
denial; We
must have a
trial: For
really this
morning I've
nothing
to do."
Said the
mouse to the

cur, "Such
a trial,
dear Sir,
With
no jury
or judge,
would be
wasting
our
breath."
"I'll be
judge, I'll
be jury,"
Said
cunning
old Fury:
"I'll
try the
whole
cause,
and
condemn
you
to
death."'

Commentary: The mouse's tale is a very famous example of emblematic or figured verse: poems printed to look similar to their subject matter (Carroll L., Gardner M., 1990, p. 34).

Discussion point: why does Carroll use emblematic verse here?

Creative response: write your own emblematic poem, writing about something you really like or hate.

'You are not attending!' said the Mouse to Alice severely. 'What are you thinking of?'

'I beg your pardon,' said Alice very humbly: 'you had got to the fifth bend, I think?'

'I had NOT!' cried the Mouse, sharply and very angrily.

'A knot!' said Alice, always ready to make herself useful, and looking anxiously about her. 'Oh, do let me help to undo it!'

'I shall do nothing of the sort,' said the Mouse, getting up and walking away. 'You insult me by talking such nonsense!'

'I didn't mean it!' pleaded poor Alice. 'But you're so easily offended, you know!'

The Mouse only growled in reply.

'Please come back and finish your story!' Alice called after it; and the others all joined in chorus, 'Yes, please do!' but the Mouse only shook its head impatiently, and walked a little quicker.

'What a pity it wouldn't stay!' sighed the Lory, as soon as it was quite out of sight; and an old Crab took the opportunity of saying to her daughter 'Ah, my dear! Let this be a lesson to you never to lose YOUR temper!' 'Hold your tongue, Ma!' said the young Crab, a little snappishly. 'You're enough to try the patience of an oyster!'

'I wish I had our Dinah here, I know I do!' said Alice aloud, addressing nobody in particular. 'She'd soon fetch it back!'

'And who is Dinah, if I might venture to ask the question?' said the Lory.

Alice replied eagerly, for she was always ready to talk about her pet: 'Dinah's our cat. And she's such a capital one for catching mice you can't think! And oh, I wish you could see her after the birds! Why, she'll eat a little bird as soon as look at it!'

This speech caused a remarkable sensation among the party. Some of the birds hurried off at once: one old Magpie began wrapping itself up very carefully, remarking, 'I really must be getting home; the night-air doesn't suit my throat!' and a Canary called out in a trembling voice to its children, 'Come away, my dears! It's high time you were all in bed!' On various pretexts they all moved off, and Alice was soon left alone.

'I wish I hadn't mentioned Dinah!' she said to herself in a melancholy tone. 'Nobody seems to like her, down here, and I'm sure she's the best cat in the world! Oh, my dear Dinah! I wonder if I shall ever see you any more!' And here poor Alice began to cry again, for she felt very lonely and low-spirited. In a little while, however, she again heard a little pattering of footsteps in the distance, and she looked up eagerly, half hoping that the Mouse had changed his mind, and was coming back to finish his story.

Questions/tasks

In your Learning Journal answer these questions and complete these activities:

What history lesson does the Mouse tell the animals and Alice and why? What does the Dodo suggest and why?

What is strange about the Caucus race?

What job does the Dodo give Alice and what does she have to do as a result?

What is strange about the Mouse's tale?

Why does the Mouse tell off Alice?

How does Alice frighten off all the animals?

What does Alice do when they run off?

Analytical question: how does Carroll generate sympathy for Alice in this chapter and also comedy as well?

Creative response: write Alice's diary for this chapter, or write the

Mouse's diary. You decide.

Textual re-casting: write a match report of the Caucus Race.

Devise a flow-chart/spider diagram/storyboard of the major events of the chapter.

Write down in your responses to the characters and situations in the chapter, noting down your thoughts and feelings about the various things that happen. What do you think will happen next?

What reading strategies are you using to help you enjoy the book? How could you improve your reading?

Extension questions

This chapter is a very famous piece of satire. Some people today think that the Dodo's "everyone wins" philosophy now exists in schools and homes and that this philosophy is making children very 'soft' – unable to deal with losing: see this article for more **http://www.huffingtonpost.com/michael-sigman/when-everyone-gets-a-trop_b_1431319.html**

What do you think about this? Is competition a good thing, or would you rather that there was no competition? Do you think everyone should have a prize for doing some work in school? What you think of prize giving at school? Explain your answer with reasons.

Think of one or two competitions you have been in (sport's days, board games, football in the park.). Is there a ridiculous side to these competitions?

What do you think is Carroll's attitude towards competition? Find two or three quotes from the chapter which show or suggest Carroll's attitude, and explain how these quotes suggest his attitude.

See Answers to the questions at the back to mark your own work.

4 The Rabbit Sends in a Little Bill

Teaching points

Learning Objective: To explore the idea of perspective and relativism; for pupils to appreciate the way in which your own perspective affects your perceptions of the world.

Starter activity: Three or four pupils put their heads on the floor underneath their desks and chairs. Tucked away from danger. Then pupils walk into their vision and sit down on the desks. The student should feel worried and anxious. Link also to relativism.

Show students Escher's perspective pictures to emphasize point – link to key words: **http://www.mcescher.com/gallery/most-popular/**

Students write down definitions of both key words (point of view/ how opinions and ideas are determined by your point of view) and then brainstorm their feelings upon being introduced to unusual perspectives.

Task One: Read Chapter 4. Students should explore and consider the points raised in the commentaries/discussion points as well as answering the questions at the end of the chapter as best they can.

Task Two: Complete questions/tasks at the end of the chapter.

Extension: Re-write a day at school as a pupil who is one inch high. Try to show how changes of perspective can create confusion and disorientation.

Plenary: Feedback from above

The text

It was the White Rabbit, trotting slowly back again, and looking anxiously about as it went, as if it had lost something; and she heard it muttering to itself, "The Duchess! The Duchess! Oh my dear paws! Oh my fur and whiskers! She'll get me executed, as sure as ferrets **(small furry brown animal, often a pet, from the weasel family)** are ferrets! Where can I have dropped them, I wonder!" Alice guessed in a moment that it was looking for the fan and the pair of white kid gloves, and she very goodnaturedly began hunting about for them, but they were nowhere to be seen - everything seemed to have changed since her swim in the pool, and the great hall, with the glass table and the little door, had vanished completely.

Very soon the Rabbit noticed Alice, as she went hunting about, and called out to her in an angry tone, "Why, Mary Ann, what are you doing out here? Run home this moment, and fetch me a pair of gloves and a fan! Quick, now!" And Alice was so much frightened that she ran off at once in the direction it pointed to, without trying to explain the mistake that it had made.

> **Commentary:** Mary Ann may have been a euphemism (polite phrase) for a servant girl. The White Rabbit, who is normally quite frightened and timid, likes to order around his 'inferiors', those lower than him, i.e. servants (Carroll L., Gardner M., 1990, p. 39).

> **Discussion point:** what do we learn about the White Rabbit here? What do you think the book says about the hierarchies in English society at the time?

"He took me for his housemaid," she said to herself as she ran. "How surprised he'll be when he finds out who I am! But I'd better take him his fan and gloves - that is, if I can find them." As she said this, she came upon a neat little house, on the door of which was a bright brass plate with the name "W. Rabbit," engraved upon it. She went in without knocking, and hurried upstairs, in great fear lest she should meet the real Mary Ann, and be turned out of the house before she had found the fan and gloves.

"How queer it seems," Alice said to herself, "to be going messages for a rabbit! I suppose Dinah'll be sending me on messages next!" And she began fancying the sort of thing that would happen: "'Miss Alice! Come here directly, and get ready for your walk!' 'Coming in a minute, nurse! But I've got to watch this mousehole till Dinah comes back, and see that the mouse doesn't get out.' Only I don't think," Alice went on, "that they'd let Dinah stop in the house if it began ordering people about like that!"

By this time she had found her way into a tidy little room with a table in the window, and on it (as she had hoped) a fan and two or three pairs of tiny white kid gloves: she took up the fan and a pair of the gloves, and was just going to leave the room, when her eye fell upon a little bottle that stood near the looking-glass. There was no label this time with the words "Drink Me," but nevertheless she uncorked it and put it to her lips. "I know something interesting is sure to happen," she said to herself, "whenever I eat or drink anything; so I'll just see what this bottle does. I do hope it'll make me grow large again, for really I'm quite tired of being such a tiny little thing!"

It did so indeed, and much sooner than she had expected: before she had drunk half the bottle, she found her head pressing against the ceiling, and had to stoop to save her neck from being broken. She hastily put down the bottle, saying to herself, "That's quite enough - I hope I shan't grow any more - As it is, I can't get out at the door - I do wish I hadn't drunk quite so much!"

Alas! It was too late to wish that! She went on growing and growing, and very soon had to kneel down on the floor: in another minute there was not even room for this, and she tried the effect of lying down, with one elbow against the door, and the other arm curled round her head. Still she went on growing, and, as a last resource, she put one arm out of the window, and one foot up the chimney, and said to herself, "Now I can do no more, whatever happens. What will become of me?"

Luckily for Alice, the little magic bottle had now had its full effect, and she grew no larger: still it was very uncomfortable, and, as there seemed to be no sort of chance of her ever getting out of the room again, no wonder she felt unhappy.

"It was much pleasanter at home," thought poor Alice, "when one wasn't always growing larger and smaller, and being ordered about by mice and rabbits. I almost wish I hadn't gone down that rabbit-hole - and yet - and yet it's rather curious, you know, this sort of life! I do wonder what can have happened to me! When I used to read fairy tales, I fancied that kind of thing never happened, and now here I am in the middle of one! There ought to be a book written about me, that there ought! And when I grow up, I'll write one-but I'm grown up now," she added in a sorrowful tone, "at least there's no room to grow up any more here."

"But then," thought Alice, "shall I never get any older than I am now? That'll be a comfort, one way - never to be an old woman - but then - always to have lessons to learn! Oh, I shouldn't like that!"

"Oh, you foolish Alice!" she answered herself. "How can you learn lessons in here? Why, there's hardly room for you, and no room at all for any lesson-books!"

And so she went on, taking first one side and then the other, and making quite a conversation of it altogether, but after a few minutes she heard a voice outside, and stopped to listen.

"Mary Ann! Mary Ann!" said the voice. "Fetch me my gloves this moment!"

> **Commentary:** this is the second time the White Rabbit has called for his gloves. The White Rabbit may be Carroll mocking himself; Carroll was known to wear gloves a great deal of the time (Carroll L., Gardner M., 1990, p. 40).

> **Discussion point:** why might Carroll mock himself in the book?

Then came a little pattering of feet on the stairs. Alice knew it was the Rabbit coming to look for her, and she trembled till she shook the house, quite forgetting that she was now about a thousand times as large as the Rabbit, and had no reason to be afraid of it.

Presently the Rabbit came up to the door, and tried to open it, but as the door opened inwards, and Alice's elbow was pressed hard against it, that attempt proved a failure. Alice heard it say to itself, "Then I'll go round and get in at the window."

"That you won't!" thought Alice, and, after waiting till she fancied she heard the Rabbit just under the window, she suddenly spread out her hand, and made a snatch in the air. She did not get hold of anything, but she heard a little shriek and a fall, and a crash of broken glass, from which she concluded that it was just possible it had fallen into a cucumber-frame **(a heated frame for growing cucumbers)**, or something of the sort.

Next came an angry voice - the Rabbit's - "Pat! Pat! Where are you?" And then a voice she had never heard before, "Sure then I'm here! Digging for apples, yer honour!"

"Digging for apples, indeed!" said the Rabbit angrily. "Here! Come and help me out of this!" (Sounds of more broken glass.)

"Now tell me, Pat, what's that in the window?"

"Sure, it's an arm, yer honour!" (He pronounced it "arrum.")

"An arm, you goose! Who ever saw one that size? Why, it fills the whole window!"

"Sure, it does, yer honour: but it's an arm for all that."

"Well, it's got no business there, at any rate: go and take it away!"

There was a long silence after this, and Alice could only hear whispers now and then, such as "Sure, I don't like it, yer honour, at all at all!" "Do as I tell you, you coward!" and at last she spread out her hand again and made another snatch in the air. This time there were two little shrieks, and more sounds of broken glass. "What a number of cucumber-frames there must be!" thought Alice. "I wonder what they'll do next! As for pulling me out of the window, I only wish they could! I'm sure I don't want to stay in here any longer!"

She waited for some time without hearing anything more: at last came a rumbling of little cart-wheels, and the sound of a good many voices all talking together: she made out the words, "Where's the other ladder? - Why, I hadn't to bring but one. Bill's got the other - Bill! Fetch it here, lad! -

Here, put 'em up at this corner - No, tie 'em together first - they don't reach half high enough yet - Oh, they'll do well enough. Don't be particular - Here, Bill! Catch hold of this rope - Will the roof bear? - Mind that loose slate - Oh, it's coming down! Heads below!" (a loud crash) - "Now, who did that? - It was Bill, I fancy - Who's to go down the chimney? - Nay, I shan't! You do it! - That I won't, then! - Bill's got to go down - Here, Bill! the master says you've got to go down the chimney!"

"Oh, so Bill's got to come down the chimney, has he?" said Alice to herself. "Why, they seem to put everything upon Bill! I wouldn't be in Bill's place for a good deal: this fireplace is narrow, to be sure, but I think I can kick a little!"

She drew her foot as far down the chimney as she could, and waited till she heard little animal (she couldn't guess of what sort it was) scratching and scrambling about in the chimney close above her: then, saying to herself "This is Bill," she gave one sharp kick, and waited to see what would happen next.

The first thing she heard was a general chorus of "There goes Bill!" then the Rabbit's voice alone - "Catch him, you by the hedge!" then silence, and then another confusion of voices - "Hold up his head - Brandy now - Don't choke him - How was it, old fellow? What happened to you? Tell us all about it!"

Last came a little feeble squeaking voice. ("That's Bill," thought Alice,) "Well, I hardly know - No more, thank'ye, I'm better now - but I'm a deal too flustered to tell you - all I know is, something comes at me like a Jack-in-the-box, and up I goes like a sky-rocket!"

"So you did, old fellow!" said the others.

"We must burn the house down!" said the Rabbit's voice, and Alice called out as loud as she could, "If you do, I'll set Dinah at you!"

There was a dead silence instantly, and Alice thought to herself, "I wonder what they will do next! If they had any sense, they'd take the roof off." After a minute or two they began moving about again, and Alice heard the Rabbit say, "A barrowful will do, to begin with."

"A barrowful of what?" thought Alice. But she had not long to doubt, for the next moment a shower of little pebbles came rattling in at the window, and some of them hit her in the face. "I'll put a stop to this," she said to herself and shouted out, "You'd better not do that again!" which produced another dead silence.

Alice noticed with some surprise that the pebbles were all turning into little cakes as they lay on the floor, and a bright idea came into her head. "If I eat one of these cakes," she thought, "it's sure to make some change in my size: and as it can't possibly make me larger, it must make me smaller, I suppose."

So she swallowed one of the cakes, and was delighted to find that she began shrinking directly. As soon as she was small enough to get through the door, she ran out of the house, and found quite a crowd of little animals and birds waiting outside. The poor little Lizard, Bill, was in the middle, being held up by two guineapigs, who were giving it something out of a bottle. They all made a rush at Alice the moment she appeared, but she ran off as hard as she could, and soon found herself safe in a thick wood.

"The first thing I've got to do," said Alice to herself, as she wandered about in the wood, "is to grow to my right size again; and the second thing is to find my way into that lovely garden. I think that will be the best plan."

It sounded an excellent plan, no doubt, and very neatly and simply arranged; the only difficulty was, that she had not the smallest idea how to set about it; and while she was peering about anxiously among the trees, a little sharp bark just over her head made her look up in a great hurry.

An enormous puppy was looking down at her with large round eyes, and feebly stretching out one paw, trying to touch her.

> **Commentary:** many critics feel the puppy is out of place in Wonderland. It is the only important creature in Wonderland who does not speak to Alice. (Carroll L., Gardner M., 1990, p. 45)

> **Discussion point:** what role do pets play in the stories? Why do they have such an important place in the novels?

"Poor little thing!" said Alice, in a coaxing tone, and she tried hard to whistle to it, but she was terribly frightened all the time at the thought that it might be hungry, in which case it would be very likely to eat her up in spite of all her coaxing.

Hardly knowing what she did, she picked up a little bit of stick, and held it out to the puppy; whereupon the puppy jumped into the air off all its feet at once, with a yelp of delight, and rushed at the stick, and made believe to worry it; then Alice dodged behind a great thistle, to keep herself from being run over, and, the moment she appeared on the other side, the puppy made another rush at the stick, and tumbled head over heels in its hurry to get hold of it; then Alice, thinking it was very like having a game of play with a cart-horse, and expecting every moment to be trampled under its feet, ran round the thistle again; then the puppy began a series of short charges at the stick, running a very little way forwards each time and a long way back, and barking hoarsely all the while, till at last it sat down a good way off, panting, with its tongue hanging out of its mouth, and its great eyes half shut.

This seemed to Alice a good opportunity for making her escape, so she set off at once, and ran till she was quite tired and out of breath, and till the puppy's bark sounded quite faint in the distance.

"And yet what a dear little puppy it was!" said Alice, as she leant against a buttercup to rest herself, and fanned herself with one of the leaves; "I should have liked teaching it tricks very much, if - if I'd only been the right size to do it! Oh dear! I'd nearly forgotten that I've got to grow up again! Let me see - how is it to be managed? I suppose I ought to eat or drink something or other; but the great question is, what?"

The great question certainly was, what? Alice looked all round her at the flowers and the blades of grass, but she could not see anything that looked like the right thing to eat or drink under the circumstances. There was a large mushroom growing near her, about the same height as herself, and when she had looked under it, and on both sides of it, and behind it, it occurred to her that she might as well look and see what was on the top of it.

She stretched herself up on tiptoe, and peeped over the edge of the mushroom, and her eyes immediately met those of a large blue caterpillar, that was sitting on the top with its arms folded, quietly smoking a long hookah, and taking not the smallest notice of her or of anything else.

Questions/tasks

In your Learning Journal answer these questions and complete these activities:

What is the White Rabbit looking for?

Who does the White Rabbit mistake Alice for and what does he ask her to do?

What does Alice do and think?

What does she find in the house?

What happens when Alice drinks the bottle?

What does Alice think when she is tall?

What do the animals threaten to do to Alice?

What happens to the pebbles and what does Alice do?

How and why does Alice run?

What two animals does she next encounter?

Analytical question: how does Carroll build suspense in this chapter?

Creative response: write Alice's diary for this chapter, noting her responses to growing taller, and the angry animals. Or write your own story/poem called 'The Angry Animals'.

Textual re-casting: write a set of instructions for what to drink and eat in Wonderland, and what not to drink and eat.

Devise a flow-chart/spider diagram/storyboard of the major events of the chapter.

Write down in your responses to the characters and situations in the chapter, noting down your thoughts and feelings about the various things that happen. What do you think will happen next?

What reading strategies are you using to help you enjoy the book? How could you improve your reading?

See Answers to the questions at the back to mark your own work.

5 Advice from a Caterpillar

Teaching points

Learning objectives: To learn about parody and how to create your own parodies.

Key words: Parody. Imagery.

Starter: Brainstorm your attitudes towards old people. Think of all the old people you know: what are their typical attitudes and behaviours? What do you judge to be old? Do you think old people are wiser? Do you know any silly old people? How do you behave towards old people?

Task One: Read Chapter 5 up to and including the "Father William" poem. Read Robert Southey's "The Old Man's Comforts and How He Gained" which is printed here:

> You are old, Father William, the young man cried,
> The few locks which are left you are grey;
> You are hale, Father William, a hearty old man,
> Now tell me the reason I pray.
>
> In the days of my youth, Father William replied,
> I remember'd that youth would fly fast,
> And abused not my health and my vigour at first
> That I never might need them at last.
>
> You are old, Father William, the young man cried,
> And pleasures with youth pass away,
> And yet you lament not the days that are gone,
> Now tell me the reason I pray.
>
> In the days of my youth, Father William replied,
> I remember'd that youth could not last;
> I thought of the future whatever I did,
> That I never might grieve for the past.
>
> You are old, Father William, the young man cried,
> And life must be hastening away;
> You are cheerful, and love to converse upon death!
> Now tell me the reason I pray.
>
> I am cheerful, young man, Father William replied,
> Let the cause thy attention engage;
> In the days of my youth I remember'd my God!
> And He hath not forgotten my age.

Task Two: Students must explain what both poems are about, and how they are similar and different. They could devise a chart to do this if they wish, and/or a visual organiser, e.g. spider diagram.

Key teaching point: Father William mocks the moralising of the previous poem by using absurd and surreal imagery, characterising the old man as an incredibly stupid and fat creature who does back-somersaults. Crucially the poem uses a similar structure and rhyming scheme, key proper nouns, adjectives and verbs are the same, but the tone is very different. One poem seeks to advise and instruct, the other poem seeks to entertain and mock the earnestness of the previous poem.

Task Three: Students collaboratively draw up a set of rules that a parody must follow to be a parody. This PDF is helpful: **http://www.evergladeshs.org/ourpages/auto/2016/1/12/505252 46/2015%20How-to-Write-Parody-and-Satire.pdf**

Task Four: Now students write their own parodies. Firstly, they will need to look back over their brainstorms about what being old is. Begin parodies in class. Write the first verse minimum.

Task Five: Feedback from Task Three. Students assess per the rules drawn up in Task Two.

Task Five: Finish reading the chapter. Students should explore and consider the points raised in the commentaries/discussion points as well as answering the questions at the end of the chapter as best they can.

Independent study: Finish writing final drafts of parodies.

The text

The Caterpillar and Alice looked at each other for some time in silence: at last the Caterpillar took the hookah out of its mouth, and addressed her in a languid, sleepy voice.

`Who are *YOU*?' said the Caterpillar.

This was not an encouraging opening for a conversation. Alice replied, rather shyly, `I--I hardly know, sir, just at present-- at least I know who I *WAS* when I got up this morning, but I think I must have been changed several times since then.'

`What do you mean by that?' said the Caterpillar sternly. `**Explain yourself!'**

`I can't explain *MYSELF*, I'm afraid, sir' said Alice, `because I'm not myself, you see.'

`I don't see,' said the Caterpillar.

`I'm afraid I can't put it more clearly,' Alice replied very politely, `for I can't understand it myself to begin with; and being so many different sizes in a day is very confusing.'

`It isn't,' said the Caterpillar.

`Well, perhaps you haven't found it so yet,' said Alice; `but when you have to turn into a chrysalis--you will some day, you know--and then after that into a butterfly, I should think you'll feel it a little queer, won't you?'

`Not a bit,' said the Caterpillar.

`Well, perhaps your feelings may be different,' said Alice; `all I know is, it would feel very queer to *ME*.'

`You!' said the Caterpillar contemptuously. `Who are **YOU**?'

Which brought them back again to the beginning of the conversation. Alice felt a little irritated at the Caterpillar's making such *VERY* short remarks, and she drew herself up and said, very gravely, `I think, you out to tell me who *YOU* are, first.'

`Why?' said the Caterpillar.

Here was another puzzling question; and as Alice could not think of any good reason, and as the Caterpillar seemed to be in a *VERY* unpleasant state of mind, she turned away.

`Come back!' the Caterpillar called after her. `I've something important to say!'

This sounded promising, certainly: Alice turned and came back again.

`Keep your temper,' said the Caterpillar.

`Is that all?' said Alice, swallowing down her anger as well as she could.

`No,' said the Caterpillar.

Alice thought she might as well wait, as she had nothing else to do, and perhaps after all it might tell her something worth hearing. For some minutes it puffed away without speaking, but at last it unfolded its arms, took the hookah out of its mouth again, and said, `So you think you're changed, do you?'

`I'm afraid I am, sir,' said Alice; `I can't remember things as I used--and I don't keep the same size for ten minutes together!'

`Can't remember *WHAT* things?' said the Caterpillar.

`Well, I've tried to say *"HOW DOTH THE LITTLE BUSY BEE,"* but it all came different!' Alice replied in a very melancholy voice.

`Repeat, *"YOU ARE OLD, FATHER WILLIAM,"'* said the Caterpillar.

Alice folded her hands, and began:--

> `You are old, Father William,' the young man said,
>   `And your hair has become very white;
> And yet you incessantly stand on your head--
>   Do you think, at your age, it is right?'

> `In my youth,' Father William replied to his son,
>   `I feared it might injure the brain;
> But, now that I'm perfectly sure I have none,
>   Why, I do it again and again.'

> `You are old,' said the youth, `as I mentioned before,
>   And have grown most uncommonly fat;
> Yet you turned a back-somersault in at the door--
>   Pray, what is the reason of that?'

> `In my youth,' said the sage, as he shook his grey locks,
>   `I kept all my limbs very supple
> By the use of this ointment--one shilling the box--
>   Allow me to sell you a couple?'

> `You are old,' said the youth, `and your jaws are too weak
>   For anything tougher than suet;
> Yet you finished the goose, with the bones and the beak--
>   Pray how did you manage to do it?'

> `In my youth,' said his father, `I took to the law,
>   And argued each case with my wife;

And the muscular strength, which it gave to my jaw,
  Has lasted the rest of my life.'

`You are old,' said the youth, `one would hardly suppose
  That your eye was as steady as ever;
Yet you balanced an eel on the end of your nose--
  What made you so awfully clever?'

`I have answered three questions, and that is enough,'
  Said his father; `don't give yourself airs!
Do you think I can listen all day to such stuff?
  Be off, or I'll kick you down stairs!'

`That is not said right,' said the Caterpillar.

`Not *QUITE* right, I'm afraid,' said Alice, timidly; some of the words have got altered.'

`It is wrong from beginning to end,' said the Caterpillar decidedly, and there was silence for some minutes.

The Caterpillar was the first to speak.

`What size do you want to be?' it asked.

`Oh, I'm not particular as to size,' Alice hastily replied; `only one doesn't like changing so often, you know.'

`I *DON'T* know,' said the Caterpillar.

Alice said nothing: she had never been so much contradicted in her life before, and she felt that she was losing her temper.

`Are you content now?' said the Caterpillar.

`Well, I should like to be a *LITTLE* larger, sir, if you wouldn't mind,' said Alice: `three inches is such a wretched height to be.'

`It is a very good height indeed!' said the Caterpillar angrily, rearing itself upright as it spoke (it was exactly three inches high).

`But I'm not used to it!' pleaded poor Alice in a piteous tone. And she thought of herself, `I wish the creatures wouldn't be so easily offended!'

`You'll get used to it in time,' said the Caterpillar; and it put the hookah into its mouth and began smoking again.

This time Alice waited patiently until it chose to speak again. In a minute or two the Caterpillar took the hookah out of its mouth and yawned once or twice, and shook itself. Then it got down off the mushroom, and crawled away in the grass, merely remarking as it went, `One side will make you grow taller, and the other side will make you grow shorter.'

`One side of *WHAT*? The other side of *WHAT*?' thought Alice to herself.

`Of the mushroom,' said the Caterpillar, just as if she had asked it aloud; and in another moment it was out of sight.

> **Commentary:** the Caterpillar has read Alice's mind. Carroll did not believe in the spirit world, but he did believe people could mind-read (ESP) and move objects with their minds (psychokinesis).

Discussion point: do you believe people can read other people's minds? If so, what are the consequences of this?

Alice remained looking thoughtfully at the mushroom for a minute, trying to make out which were the two sides of it; and as it was perfectly round, she found this a very difficult question. However, at last she stretched her arms round it as far as they would go, and broke off a bit of the edge with each hand.

`And now which is which?' she said to herself, and nibbled a little of the right-hand bit to try the effect: the next moment she felt a violent blow underneath her chin: it had struck her foot!

She was a good deal frightened by this very sudden change, but she felt that there was no time to be lost, as she was shrinking rapidly; so she set to work at once to eat some of the other bit. Her chin was pressed so closely against her foot, that there was hardly room to open her mouth; but she did it at last, and managed to swallow a morsel of the lefthand bit.

* * * * * * *

* * * * * *

* * * * * * *

`Come, my head's free at last!' said Alice in a tone of delight, which changed into alarm in another moment, when she found that her shoulders were nowhere to be found: all she could see, when she looked down, was an immense length of neck, which seemed to rise like a stalk out of a sea of green leaves that lay far below her.

`What *CAN* all that green stuff be?' said Alice. `And where **HAVE** my shoulders got to? And oh, my poor hands, how is it I can't see you?' She was moving them about as she spoke, but no result seemed to follow, except a little shaking among the distant green leaves.

As there seemed to be no chance of getting her hands up to her head, she tried to get her head down to them, and was delighted to find that her neck would bend about easily in any direction, like a serpent. She had just succeeded in curving it down into a graceful zigzag, and was going to dive in among the leaves, which she found to be nothing but the tops of the trees under which she had been wandering, when a sharp hiss made her draw back in a hurry: a large pigeon had flown into her face, and was beating her violently with its wings.

`Serpent!' screamed the Pigeon.

`I'm *NOT* a serpent!' said Alice indignantly. `Let me alone!'

`Serpent, I say again!' repeated the Pigeon, but in a more subdued tone, and added with a kind of sob, `I've tried every way, and nothing seems to suit them!'

`I haven't the least idea what you're talking about,' said Alice.

`I've tried the roots of trees, and I've tried banks, and I've tried hedges,' the Pigeon went on, without attending to her; `but those serpents! There's no pleasing them!'

Alice was more and more puzzled, but she thought there was no use in saying anything more till the Pigeon had finished.

`As if it wasn't trouble enough hatching the eggs,' said the Pigeon; `but I must be on the look-out for serpents night and day! Why, I haven't had a wink of sleep these three weeks!'

`I'm very sorry you've been annoyed,' said Alice, who was beginning to see its meaning.

`And just as I'd taken the highest tree in the wood,' continued the Pigeon, raising its voice to a shriek, `and just as I was thinking I should be free of them at last, they must needs come wriggling down from the sky! Ugh, Serpent!'

`But I'm *NOT* a serpent, I tell you!' said Alice. `I'm a--I'm a--'

`Well! **WHAT** are you?' said the Pigeon. `I can see you're trying to invent something!'

`I--I'm a little girl,' said Alice, rather doubtfully, as she remembered the number of changes she had gone through that day.

`A likely story indeed!' said the Pigeon in a tone of the deepest contempt. `I've seen a good many little girls in my time, but never *ONE* with such a neck as that! No, no! You're a serpent; and there's no use denying it. I suppose you'll be telling me next that you never tasted an egg!'

`I *HAVE* tasted eggs, certainly,' said Alice, who was a very truthful child; `but little girls eat eggs quite as much as serpents do, you know.'

`I don't believe it,' said the Pigeon; `but if they do, why then they're a kind of serpent, that's all I can say.'

This was such a new idea to Alice, that she was quite silent for a minute or two, which gave the Pigeon the opportunity of adding, `You're looking for eggs, I know *THAT* well enough; and what does it matter to me whether you're a little girl or a serpent?'

`It matters a good deal to *ME*,' said Alice hastily; `but I'm not looking for eggs, as it happens; and if I was, I shouldn't want *YOURS*: I don't like them raw.'

`Well, be off, then!' said the Pigeon in a sulky tone, as it settled down again into its nest. Alice crouched down among the trees as well as she could, for her neck kept getting entangled among the branches, and every now and then she had to stop and untwist it. After a while she remembered that she still held the pieces of mushroom in her hands, and she set to work very carefully, nibbling first at one and then at the other, and growing sometimes taller and sometimes shorter, until she had succeeded in bringing herself down to her usual height.

It was so long since she had been anything near the right size, that it felt quite strange at first; but she got used to it in a few minutes, and began talking to herself, as usual. `Come, there's half my plan done now! How puzzling all these changes are! I'm never sure what I'm going to be, from one minute to another! However, I've got back to my right size: the next thing is, to get into that beautiful garden--how *IS* that to be done, I wonder?' As she said this, she came suddenly upon an open place, with a little house in it about four feet high. `Whoever lives there,' thought Alice, `it'll never do to come upon them *THIS* size: why, I should frighten them out of their wits!' So she began nibbling at the righthand bit again, and did not venture to go near the house till she had brought herself down to nine inches high.

Questions/tasks

In your Learning Journal answer these questions and complete these activities:

What question does the Caterpillar ask Alice and why does she become depressed?

What does the Caterpillar ask Alice to do when she tries to leave?

Why is the Caterpillar offended by Alice's answer to his question about what size she would like to be?

What does the Caterpillar say as he goes off in a huff?

What problems does Alice encounter as she eats the mushroom?

Why does the Pigeon attack her?

What does Alice look for when she grows back to a normal size?

Why does Alice eat all the mushroom?

Analytical question: how does Carroll make the Caterpillar such an intriguing and horrible character?

Creative response: write either Alice or the Caterpillar's diary for this and the previous chapter, noting their responses to the questions asked.

Textual re-casting: Write the Caterpillar's Facebook page, or his blog.

Devise a flow-chart/spider diagram/storyboard of the major events of the chapter.

Write down in your responses to the characters and situations in the chapter, noting down your thoughts and feelings about the various things that happen. What do you think will happen next?

What reading strategies are you using to help you enjoy the book? How could you improve your reading?

See Answers to the questions at the back to mark your own work.

6 Pig and Pepper

Teaching points

Learning Objectives: To analyse how Carroll uses language devices to convey character and a moral meaning.

Key words: Symbolism. Simile. Metaphor. Homophones. Rhetorical Questions. Verbs.

Students define and write down examples of each of the key words above.

Task One: Read Chapter 6. Students should explore and consider the points raised in the commentaries/discussion points as well as answering the questions at the end of the chapter as best they can.

Task Two: Students, in pairs, find and copy down a relevant quote culled from the chapter for each key word and explain how it conveys either character or a moral meaning. Write in full sentences.

Task Three: One student is nominated to be a scribe who writes the following comments of other students on the board. Pick a student to start off a class revision of "what-how-why" paragraphs: these are paragraphs which explain "what" happens in a passage, "how" the writer uses literary techniques to make "what" happens interesting, and "why" the writer might have written he/she did, i.e. the purposes of the writing. One student asks the "what" question and nominates a student to answer it. The next student asks the next ("how") question and nominates a student to answer it. And then someone is picked to answer the "why" question. The scribe puts relevant notes on the board. Using the stimulus of what other students have said, everyone writes their own individual "what-how-why" paragraphs.

Task Four: Students swap books and assess each other's work by writing two comments: "What I Learnt" (WIL), "What I Want To Learn More About" (WIWT-LMA)

Plenary: Students feedback is listened to by the teacher, who suggests improvements where necessary.

The text

For a minute or two she stood looking at the house, and wondering what to do next, when suddenly a footman in livery came running out of the wood - (she considered him to be a footman because he was in livery: otherwise, judging by his face only, she would have called him a fish) - and rapped loudly at the door with his knuckles. It was opened by another footman in livery, with a round face and large eyes like a frog; and both footmen, Alice noticed, had powdered hair that curled all over their heads. She felt very curious to know what it was all about, and crept a little way out of the wood to listen.

The Fish-Footman began by producing from under his arm a great letter, nearly as large as himself, and this he handed over to the other, saying in a solemn tone, "For the Duchess. An invitation from the Queen to play croquet." The Frog-Footman repeated, in the same solemn tone, only changing the order of the words a little, "From the Queen. An invitation for the Duchess to play croquet."

Then they both bowed low, and their curls got entangled together.

Alice laughed so much at this that she had to run back into the wood for fear of their hearing her, and when she next peeped out the Fish-Footman was gone, ane the other was sitting on the ground near the door, staring stupidly up into the sky.

Alice went timidly up to the door, and knocked.

"There's no sort of use in knocking," said the Footman, "and that for two reasons. First, because I'm on the same side of the door as you are; secondly, because they're making such a noise inside, no one could possibly hear you." And certainly there was a most extraordinary noise going on within - a constant howling and sneezing, and every now and then a great crash, as if a dish or kettle had been broken to pieces.

"Please, then," said Alice, "how am I to get in?"

"There might be some sense in your knocking," the Footman went on without attending to her, "if we had the door between us. For instance, if you were inside, you might knock, and I could let you out, you know." He was looking up into the sky all the time he was speaking, and this Alice thought decidedly uncivil. "But perhaps he can't help it," she said to herself; "his eyes are so very nearly at the top of his head. But at any rate he might answer questions - How am I to get in?" she repeated, aloud.

"I shall sit here," the Footman remarked, "till to-morrow - "

At this moment the door of the house opened, and a large plate came skimming out, straight at the Footman's head: it just grazed his nose, and broke to pieces against one of the trees behind him.

" - or next day, maybe," the Footman continued in the same tone, exactly as if nothing had happened.

"How am I to get in?" Alice asked again in a louder tone.

"Are you to get in at all?" said the Footman. "That's the first question, you know."

It was, no doubt: only Alice did not like to be told so. "It's really dreadful," she muttered to herself, "the way all the creatures argue. It's enough to drive one crazy!"

The Footman seemed to think this a good opportunity for repeating his remark, with variations. "I shall sit here," he said, "on and off, for days and days."

"But what am I to do?" said Alice.

"Anything you like," said the Footman, and began whistling.

"Oh, there's no use in talking to him," said Alice desperately: "he's perfectly idiotic!" And she opened the door and went in.

The door led right into a large kitchen, which was full of smoke from one end to the other: the Duchess was sitting on a three-legged stool in the middle, nursing a baby; the cook was leaning over the fire, stirring a large cauldron which seemed to be full of soup.

> **Commentary:** we are told for the first time here that the Duchess is very ugly. (Carroll L., Gardner M., 1990, p. 60).

> **Discussion points:** do you think Alice is "lookist"? What are our attitudes towards "ugly" people now? How are they similar and different to people's attitudes when this book was written? Consider

the presentation of people in the media, perhaps looking at TV shows like "The Undateables" etc.

"There's certainly too much pepper in that soup!" Alice said to herself, as well as she could for sneezing.

There was certainly too much of it in the air. Even the Duchess sneezed occasionally; and as for the baby, it was sneezing and howling alternately without a moment's pause. The only two creatures in the kitchen that did not sneeze, were the cook, and a large cat which was sitting on the hearth and grinning from ear to ear.

"Please, would you tell me," said Alice, a little timidly, for she was not quite sure whether it was good manners for her to speak first, "why your cat grins like that?"

"It's a Cheshire cat," said the Duchess, "and that's why. Pig!"

Commentary: "Grin like a Cheshire cat" was a common phrase in Carroll's time, although it is less common now, it is sometimes used (Carroll L., Gardner M., 1990, p. 61).

Discussion point: what other well-known phrases do people use to describe smiling, happiness and smugness? E.g. the sun has got his hat on etc.

She said the last word with such sudden violence that Alice quite jumped; but she saw in another moment that it was addressed to the baby, and not to her, so she took courage, and went on again: -

"I didn't know that Cheshire cats always grinned; in fact, I didn't know that cats could grin."

"They all can," said the Duchess; "and most of 'em do."

"I don't know of any that do," Alice said very politely, feeling quite pleased to have got into a conversation.

"You don't know much," said the Duchess; "and that's a fact."

Alice did not at all like the tone of this remark, and thought it would be as well to introduce some other subject of conversation. While she was trying to fix on one, the cook took the cauldron of soup off the fire, and at once set to work throwing everything within her reach at the Duchess and the baby - the fire-irons came first; then followed a shower of saucepans, plates, and dishes. The Duchess took no notice of them, even when they hit her; and the baby was howling so much already, that it was quite impossible to say whether the blows hurt it or not.

"Oh, please mind what you're doing!" cried Alice, jumping up and down in an agony of terror. "Oh, there goes his precious nose!" as an unusually large saucepan flew close by it, and very nearly carried it off.

"If everybody minded their own business," said the Duchess in a hoarse growl, "the world would go round a deal faster than it does."

"Which would not be an advantage," said Alice, who felt very glad to get an opportunity of showing off a little of her knowledge. "Just think what work it would make with the day and night! You see the earth takes twenty-four hours to turn round on its axis - "

"Talking of axes," said the Duchess, "chop off her head!"

Alice glanced rather anxiously at the cook, to see if she meant to take the hint; but the cook was busily stirring the soup, and seemed not to be listening, so she went on again: "Twenty-four hours, I think; or is it twelve? I - "

"Oh, don't bother me," said the Duchess, "I never could abide figures." And with that she began nursing her child again, singing a sort of lullaby to it as she did so, and giving it a violent shake at the end of every line: -

"Speak roughly to your little boy,
And beat him when he sneezes;
He only does it to annoy,
Because he knows it teases."
Chorus (in which the cook and the baby joined): -
"Wow! wow! wow!"

While the Duchess sang the second verse of the song, she kept tossing the baby violently up and down, and the poor little thing howled so, that Alice could hardly hear the words: -

"I speak severely to my boy,
I beat him when he sneezes;
For he can thoroughly enjoy
The pepper when he pleases!"
Chorus
"Wow! wow! wow!"

> **Commentary:** this poem is a parody of G.W. Langford's poem "Speak gently..." (Carroll L., Gardner M., 1990, p. 62).

> *Speak gently! It is better far*
> *To rule by love than fear;*
> *Speak gently; let no harsh words mar*
> *The good we might do here!*
>
> *Speak gently! Love doth whisper low*
> *The vows that true hearts bind;*
> *And gently Friendship's accents flow;*
> *Affection's voice is kind.*
>
> *Speak gently to the little child!*
> *Its love be sure to gain;*
> *Teach it in accents soft and mild;*
> *It may not long remain.*
>
> *Speak gently to the young, for they*
> *Will have enough to bear;*
> *Pass through this life as best they may,*
> *'Tis full of anxious care!*
>
> *Speak gently to the aged one,*
> *Grieve not the care-worn heart;*
> *Whose sands of life are nearly run,*
> *Let such in peace depart!*

Speak gently, kindly, to the poor;
Let no harsh tone be heard;
They have enough they must endure,
Without an unkind word!

Speak gently to the erring; know
They may have toiled in vain;
Perchance unkindness made them so;
Oh, win them back again!

Speak gently! He who gave his life
To bend man's stubborn will,
When elements were in fierce strife,
Said to them, "Peace, be still."

Speak gently! 'tis a little thing
Dropped in the heart's deep well;
The good, the joy, that it may bring,
Eternity shall tell.

Discussion point: how and why has Carroll parodied this poem?

"Here! you may nurse it a bit, if you like!" said the Duchess to Alice, flinging the baby at her as she spoke. "I must go and get ready to play croquet with the Queen," and she hurried out of the room. The cook threw a fryingpan after her as she went, but it just missed her.

Alice caught the baby with some difficulty, as it was a queer-shaped little creature, and held out its arms and legs in all directions, "just like a starfish," thought Alice. The poor little thing was snorting like a steam-engine when she caught it, and kept doubling itself up and straightening itself out again, so that altogether, for the first minute or two, it was as much as she could do to hold it.

As soon as she had made out the proper way of nursing it (which was to twist it up into a sort of knot, and then keep tight hold of its right ear and left foot, so as to prevent its undoing itself,) she carried it out into the open air. "If I don't take this child away with me," thought Alice, "they're sure to kill it in a day or two: wouldn't it be murder to leave it behind?" She said the last words out loud, and the little thing grunted in reply (it had left off sneezing by this time). "Don't grunt," said Alice: "that's not at all a proper way of expressing yourself."

The baby grunted again, and Alice looked very anxiously into its face to see what was the matter with it. There could be no doubt that it had a very turn-up nose, much more like a snout than a real nose; also its eyes were getting extremely small, for a baby: altogether Alice did not like the look of the thing at all, " - but perhaps it was only sobbing," she thought, and looked into its eyes again, to see if there were any tears.

No, there were no tears. "If you're going to turn into a pig, my dear," said Alice, seriously, "I'll have nothing more to do with you. Mind now!" the poor little thing sobbed again, (or grunted, it was impossible to say which,) and they went on for some while in silence.

Alice was just beginning to think to herself, "Now, what am I to do with this creature when I get it home?" when it grunted again, so violently, that she looked down into its face in some alarm. This time there could be no mistake about it: it was neither more nor less than a pig, and she felt that it would be quite absurd for her to carry it any further.

> **Commentary:** Carroll did not like little boys, but liked little girls very much. Perhaps this explains why the little boy is turned into a pig? (Carroll L., Gardner M., 1990, p. 64)

> **Discussion point:** What is your attitude towards young children? Do you think gender categories of girl and boy are fair? Do you think children should be "gender neutral"?

So she set the little creature down, and felt quite relieved to see it trot away quietly into the wood. "If it had grown up," she said to herself, "it would have been a dreadfully ugly child: but it makes rather a handsome pig, I think." And she began thinking over other children she knew, who might do very well as pigs, and was just saying to herself, "if one only knew the right way to change them - " when she was a little startled by seeing the Cheshire Cat sitting on a bough of a tree a few yards off.

The Cat only grinned when it saw Alice. It looked goodnatured, she thought: still it had very long claws and a great many teeth, so she felt it ought to be treated with respect.

"Cheshire Puss," she began, rather timidly, as she did not at all know whether it would like the name: however, it only grinned a little wider. "Come, it's pleased so far," thought Alice, and she went on, "Would you tell me, please which way I ought to walk from here?"

"That depends a good deal on where you want to get to," said the Cat.

"I don't much care where - " said Alice.

"Then it doesn't matter which way you walk," said the Cat.

> **Commentary:** this phrase from the Cat is one of the most famous phrases in the books.

> **Discussion point:** why has this phrase become so famous?

" - so long as I get somewhere," Alice added as an explanation.

"Oh, you're sure to do that," said the Cat, "if you only walk long enough."

Alice felt that this could not be denied, so she tried another question. "What sort of people live about here?"

"In that direction," the Cat said, waving its right paw round, "lives a Hatter: and in that direction," waving the other paw, "lives a March Hare. Visit either you like: they're both mad."

> **Commentary:** the phrase "mad as a hatter" was commonly known in Carroll's time. Carroll wrote in his diary in 1856:

'Query: when we are dreaming and, as often happens, have a dim consciousness of the fact and try to wake, do we not say and do things which in waking life would be insane ? May we not then sometimes define insanity as an inability to distinguish which is the waking and which the sleeping life'—a remark which suggests the Cheshire Cat's 'We're all mad here'. (Carroll L., Gardner M., 1990, p. 67)

Discussion point: do some research into phrases that describe madness, including "mad as a hatter". What do they reveal about attitudes towards madness? This Wikipedia page is a good starting point: **https://en.wikipedia.org/wiki/Mad_as_a_hatter**

"But I don't want to go among mad people," Alice remarked.

"Oh, you can't help that," said the Cat: "we're all mad here. I'm mad. You're mad."

"How do you know I'm mad?" said Alice.

"You must be," said the Cat, "or you wouldn't have come here."

Alice didn't think that proved it at all; however, she went on: "and how do you know that you're mad?"

"To begin with," said the Cat, "a dog's not mad. You grant that?"

"I suppose so," said Alice.

"Well then," the Cat went on, "you see a dog growls when it's angry, and wags its tail when it's pleased. Now I growl when I'm pleased, and wag my tail when I'm angry. Therefore I'm mad."

"I call it purring, not growling," said Alice.

"Call it what you like," said the Cat. "Do you play croquet with the Queen to-day?"

"I should like it very much," said Alice, "but I haven't been invited yet."

"You'll see me there," said the Cat, and vanished.

Alice was not much surprised at this, she was getting so well used to queer things happening. While she was still looking at the place where it had been, it suddenly appeared again.

"By-the-bye, what became of the baby?" said the Cat. "I'd nearly forgotten to ask."

"It turned into pig," Alice answered very quietly, just as if the Cat had come back in a natural way.

"I thought it would," said the Cat, and vanished again.

Alice waited a little, half expecting to see it again, but it did not appear, and after a minute or two she walked on in the direction in which the March Hare was said to live. "I've seen hatters before," she said to herself: "the March Hare will be much the most interesting, and perhaps as this is May it won't be raving mad - at least not so mad as it was in March." As she said this, she looked up, and there was the Cat again, sitting on a branch of a tree.

"Did you say pig, or fig?" said the Cat.

"I said pig," replied Alice; "and I wish you wouldn't keep appearing and vanishing so suddenly: you make one quite giddy."

"All right," said the Cat; and this time it vanished quite slowly, beginning with the end of the tail, and ending with the grin, which remained some time after the rest of it had gone.

"Well! I've often seen a cat without a grin," thought Alice; "but a grin without a cat! It's the most curious thing I ever saw in all my life!"

She had not gone much farther before she came in sight of the house of the March Hare: she thought it must be the right house, because the chimneys were shaped like cars and the roof was thatched with fur. It was so large a house, that she did not like to go nearer till she had nibbled some more of the left-hand bit of mushroom, and raised herself to about two feet high: even then she walked up towards it rather timidly, saying to herself, "Suppose it should be raving mad after all! I almost wish I'd gone to see the Hatter instead!"

Questions/tasks

In your Learning Journal answer these questions and complete these activities:

How are the fish and frog dressed? What does the letter delivered by the Fish Footman say? What does the Frog Footman say about people answering the door? What does Alice think of the Frog Footman and why?

What and who does Alice encounter when she enters the kitchen?

How does the Duchess insult Alice?

What does the Cook throw and at whom?

Why does the Duchess say "chop off her head"?

Why does the Duchess fling the baby at Alice?

What is the baby really?

What does the Cheshire Cat reply when Alice asks him where she might go next?

Why does the Cheshire Cat think Alice must be mad?

Where does the Cheshire Cat say he will see Alice again?

What happens to the Cheshire Cat? Why does Alice eat more of the Caterpillar's mushroom?

Analytical question: how does Carroll suggest the madness of Wonderland in this chapter?

Creative response: write Alice's diary for this scene, or the Cheshire Cat's, outlining their thoughts and feelings about the characters evoked.

Textual re-casting: write a social worker's report about the treatment of the baby pig.

Devise a flow-chart/spider diagram/storyboard of the major events of the chapter.

Write down in your responses to the characters and situations in the chapter, noting down your thoughts and feelings about the various things that happen. What do you think will happen next?

What reading strategies are you using to help you enjoy the book? How could you improve your reading?

See Answers to the questions at the back to mark your own work.

7 A Mad Tea Party

Teaching points

Learning Objectives: To analyse how Carroll manipulates language to suggest madness.

Key words: Semantics. Logic. False logic. Homonyms. Personification. Synonyms. Connotations.

Starter: Define and generate examples of key words. For example: semantics – how the meanings of words change depending upon their order in a sentence and their overall context; e.g. "I say what I mean / I mean what I say".

Then, discuss the meaning of "madness": students should brainstorm synonyms and adjectives associated with madness. Are connotations of these words positive or negative?

Activity One: Read Chapter seven. Students should explore and consider the points raised in the commentaries/discussion points as well as answering the questions at the end of the chapter as best they can.

Activity Two: In pairs, find three instances in the chapter where Alice becomes confused. Individually, write an explanation for each incident to outline the reasons why Alice was confused. If possible, use the key words provided above.

Activity Three: In pairs, write a dialogue between two people who have just met, with a traveler asking directions and the other person, a local person, deliberately misunderstanding everything the traveler says. If possible, use examples of false logic, homonyms, synonyms in order to confuse the traveler, e.g. the traveler asks where he might get a haircut and the local person says that you might be able to get a "hare" cut at a butcher.

Listen to the dialogues.

Plenary: students to assess each other's work using the "What I Learnt" (WIL) and "What I Want To Learn More About" (WIWT- LMA) in order to respond to the points.

The text

There was a table set out under a tree in front of the house, and the March Hare and the Hatter were having tea at it: a Dormouse was sitting between them, fast asleep, and the other two were using it as a cushion, resting their elbows on it, and talking over its head. "Very uncomfortable for the Dormouse," thought Alice; "only, as it's asleep, I suppose it doesn't mind."

> **Commentary:** this chapter was added in after Carroll had written his first version of the story for Alice Liddell. The Hatter is said to be like Theophilus Carter, a furniture dealer near Oxford, or possibly William Gladstone, the Prime Minister of the time. Carter was known as the Mad Hatter because he wore a top hat and had strange ideas. He invented the "alarm clock bed" which threw the sleeper out of

bed, which may explain why the Hatter is so concerned to wake up the Dormouse. Furniture is also important in the scene. The Dormouse is a rat which lives in a tree and looks more like squirrel; the Dormouse hibernates in the winter and is nocturnal, sleeping in the day. (Carroll L., Gardner M., 1990, p. 69-70).

Discussion point: What makes the Hatter so mad? How does Carroll generate comedy in this chapter generally?

The table was a large one, but the three were all crowded together at one corner of it: "No room! No room!" they cried out when they saw Alice coming. "There's plenty of room!" said Alice indignantly, and she sat down in a large arm-chair at one end of the table.

"Have some wine," the March Hare said in an encouraging tone.

Alice looked all round the table, but there was nothing on it but tea. "I don't see any wine," she remarked.

"There isn't any," said the March Hare.

"Then it wasn't very civil of you to offer it," said Alice angrily.

"It wasn't very civil of you to sit down without being invited," said the March Hare.

"I didn't know it was your table," said Alice; "it's laid for a great many more than three."

"Your hair wants cutting," said the Hatter. He had been looking at Alice for some time with great curiosity, and this was his first speech.

"You should learn not to make personal remarks," Alice said with some severity: "It's very rude."

The Hatter opened his eyes very wide on hearing this; but all he said was, "Why is a raven like a writing-desk?"

Commentary: This famous riddle has been given many explanations, but no one has answered it satisfactorily.

Discussion point: what do you think the answer is? What do you think of riddles generally? Are they funny, annoying, intriguing, or do they leave you cold? Why are so many people fascinated by them? Can you think of other riddles? Do some research into famous riddles. You could start here:
https://www.riddleministry.com/famous-riddles/

"Come, we shall have some fun now!" thought Alice. "I'm glad they've begun asking riddles - I believe I can guess that," she added aloud.

"Do you mean that you think you can find out the answer to it?" said the March Hare.

"Exactly so," said Alice.

"Then you should say what you mean," the March Hare went on.

"I do," Alice hastily replied; "at least - at least I mean what I say - that's the same thing, you know."

"Not the same thing a bit!" said the Hatter. "Why, you might just as well say that 'I see what I eat' is the same thing as 'I eat what I see'!"

"You might just as well say," added the March Hare, "that 'I like what I get' is the same thing as 'I get what I like'!"

"You might just as well say," added the Dormouse, who seemed to be talking in his sleep, "that 'I breathe when I sleep' is the same thing as 'I sleep when I breathe'!"

"It is the same thing with you," said the Hatter, and here the conversation dropped, and the party sat silent for a minute, while Alice thought over all she could remember about ravens and writing-desks, which wasn't much.

The Hatter was the first to break the silence. "What day of the month is it?" he said, turning to Alice: he had taken his watch out of his pocket, and was looking at it uneasily, shaking it every now and then, and holding it to his ear.

Alice considered a little, and said, "The fourth."

> **Commentary:** we now know that the date is the 4th of May, being told the month in the previous chapter. May 4th, 1854 was Alice Liddell's birthday. Her age in the story is probably 7, although she was 10 years old when Carroll told her the story.
>
> **Discussion point:** What age do you think Alice is? Why is her age important to consider? What ages would like this book the best and why?

"Two days wrong!" sighed the Hatter. "I told you butter wouldn't suit the works!" he added, looking angrily at the March Hare.

"It was the best butter," the March Hare meekly replied.

"Yes, but some crumbs must have got in as well," the Hatter grumbled: "you shouldn't have put it in with the bread-knife."

The March Hare took the watch and looked at it gloomily: then he dipped it into his cup of tea, and looked at it again: but he could think of nothing better to say than his first remark, "It was the best butter, you know."

Alice had been looking over his shoulder with some curiosity. "What a funny watch!" she remarked. "It tells the day of the month, and doesn't tell what o'clock it is!"

"Why should it?" muttered the Hatter. "Does your watch tell you what year it is?"

"Of course not," Alice replied very readily: "but that's because it stays the same year for such a long time together."

"Which is just the case with mine," said the Hatter.

Alice felt dreadfully puzzled. The Hatter's remark seemed to her to have no sort of meaning in it, and yet it was certainly English. "I don't quite understand you," she said, as politely as she could.

"The Dormouse is asleep again," said the Hatter, and he poured a little hot tea on to its nose.

The Dormouse shook its head impatiently, and said, without opening its eyes, "Of course, of course: just what I was going to remark myself."

"Have you guessed the riddle yet?" the Hatter said, turning to Alice again.

"No, I give it up," Alice replied: "what's the answer?"

"I haven't the slightest idea," said the Hatter.

"Nor I," said the March Hare.

Alice sighed wearily. "I think you might do something better with the time," she said, "than wasting it in asking riddles that have no answers."

"If you knew Time as well as I do," said the Hatter, "you wouldn't talk about wasting it. It's him."

"I don't know what you mean," said Alice.

"Of course you don't!" the Hatter said, tossing his head contemptuously. "I dare say you never even spoke to Time!"

"Perhaps not," Alice cautiously replied: "but I know I have to beat time when I learn music."

"Ah! That accounts for it," said the Hatter. "He won't stand beating. Now, if you only kept on good terms with him, he'd do almost anything you liked with the clock.

"For instance, suppose it were nine o'clock in the morning, just time to begin lessons: you'd only have to whisper a hint to Time, and round goes the clock in a twinkling! Half-past one, time for dinner!"

("I only wish it was," the March Hare said to itself in a whisper.)

"That would be grand, certainly," said Alice thoughtfully: "but then - I shouldn't be hungry for it, you know."

"Not at first, perhaps," said the Hatter: "but you could keep it to half-past one as long as you liked."

"Is that the way you manage?" Alice asked.

The Hatter shook his head mournfully. "Not I!" he replied. "We quarreled last March - just before he went mad, you know - " (pointing with his teaspoon at the March Hare,) " - it was at the great concert given by the Queen of Hearts, and I had to sing

'Twinkle, twinkle, little bat!
How I wonder what you're at!'

You know the song, perhaps?"

"I've heard something like it," said Alice.

"It goes on, you know," the Hatter continued, "in this way: -

'Up above the world you fly,
Like a teatray in the sky.
Twinkle, twinkle - '"

> **Commentary:** This was an 'inside' joke because Carroll's good friend, Bartholomew Price, a brilliant Maths professor at Oxford, was known as the "The Bat" probably because his lectures soared above his listerners. This is a parody of the famous poem Jane Taylor's "The Star" (Carroll L., Gardner M., 1990, p. 74):
>
> *Twinkle, twinkle, little star,*
> *How I wonder what you are!*
> *Up above the world so high,*
> *Like a diamond in the sky.*
>
> *When the blazing sun is gone,*
> *When he nothing shines upon,*
> *Then you show your little light,*
> *Twinkle, twinkle, all the night.*

Then the traveler in the dark
Thanks you for your tiny spark,
How could he see where to go,
If you did not twinkle so?

In the dark blue sky you keep,
Often through my curtains peep
For you never shut your eye,
Till the sun is in the sky.

As your bright and tiny spark
Lights the traveler in the dark,
Though I know not what you are,
Twinkle, twinkle, little star.

Discussion point: how and why does Carroll make fun of this poem?

Here the Dormouse shook itself, and began singing in its sleep "Twinkle, twinkle, twinkle, twinkle - " and went on so long that they had to pinch it to make it stop.

"Well, I'd hardly finished the first verse," said the Hatter, "when the Queen bawled out 'He's murdering the time! Off with his head!'"

Commentary: in other words, he "murdering" the rhythm (or metre) of the original poem.

"How dreadfully savage!" exclaimed Alice.

"And ever since that," the Hatter went on in a mournful tone, "he won't do a thing I ask! It's always six o'clock now."

A bright idea came into Alice's head. "Is that the reason so many tea-things are put out here?" she asked.

"Yes, that's it," said the Hatter with a sigh: "it's always tea-time, and we've no time to wash the things between whiles."

"Then you keep moving round, I suppose?" said Alice.

"Exactly so," said the Hatter: "as the things get used up."

"But when you come to the beginning again?" Alice ventured to ask.

"Suppose we change the subject," the March Hare interrupted, yawning. "I'm getting tired of this. I vote the young lady tells us a story."

"I'm afraid I don't know one," said Alice, rather alarmed at the proposal.

"Then the Dormouse shall!" they both cried. "Wake up, Dormouse!" And they pinched it on both sides at once.

The Dormouse slowly opened his eyes. "I wasn't asleep," he said in a hoarse, feeble voice: "I heard every word you fellows were saying."

"Tell us a story!" said the March Hare.

"Yes, please do!" pleaded Alice.

"And be quick about it," added the Hatter, "or you'll be asleep again before it's done."

"Once upon a time there were three little sisters," the Dormouse began in a great hurry; "and their names were Elsie, Lacie, and Tillie; and they lived at the bottom of a well - "

> **Commentary:** these are the three Liddell sisters: Elsie is L.C. (Lorina Charlotte), Tillis refers to Edith's family nickname of Matilda and Lacie is an anagram of Alice.

> **Discussion point:** why do people like anagrams so much? Do some research into anagrams and have a go at making some of your own names and of the people in your class/family etc. You could start here with this anagram maker with your research: **http://wordsmith.org/anagram/**

"What did they live on?" said Alice, who always took a great interest in questions of eating and drinking.

"They lived on treacle," said the Dormouse, after thinking a minute or two.

"They couldn't have done that, you know," Alice gently remarked. "They'd have been ill."

"So they were," said the Dormouse; "very ill."

Alice tried a little to fancy to herself what such an extraordinary way of living would be like, but it puzzled her too much, so she went on: "But why did they live at the bottom of a well?"

"Take some more tea," the March Hare said to Alice, very earnestly.

"I've had nothing yet," Alice replied in an offended tone, "so I can't take more."

"You mean you can't take less," said the Hatter: "it's very easy to take more than nothing."

"Nobody asked your opinion," said Alice.

"Who's making personal remarks now?" the Hatter asked triumphantly.

Alice did not quite know what to say to this: so she help ed herself to some tea and bread-and-butter, and then turned to the Dormouse, and repeated her question. "Why did they live at the bottom of a well?"

The Dormouse again took a minute or two to think about it, and then said, "It was a treacle-well."

"There's no such thing!" Alice was beginning very angrily, but the Hatter and the March Hare went "Sh! sh!" and the Dormouse sulkily remarked, "If you can't be civil, you'd better finish the story for yourself."

"No, please go on!" Alice said very humbly. "I won't interrupt you again. I dare say there may be one."

"One, indeed!" said the Dormouse indignantly. However, he consented to go on. "And so these three little sisters - they were learning to draw, you know - "

"What did they draw?" said Alice, quite forgetting her promise.

"Treacle," said the Dormouse, without considering at all this time.

"I want a clean cup," interrupted the Hatter: "let's all move one place on."

He moved on as he spoke, and the Dormouse followed him: the March Hare moved into the Dormouse's place, and Alice rather unwillingly took the place of the March Hare. The Hatter was the only one who got any advantage from the change: and Alice was a good deal worse off than before, as the March Hare had just upset the milk-jug into his plate.

Alice did not wish to offend the Dormouse again, so she began very cautiously: "But I don't understand. Where did they draw the treacle from?"

"You can draw water out of a water-well," said the Hatter; "so I should think you could draw treacle out of a treacle - well - eh, stupid?"

"But they were in the well," Alice said to the Dormouse, not choosing to notice this last remark.

"Of course they were," said the Dormouse, - "well in."

This answer so confused poor Alice, that she let the Dormouse go on for some time without interrupting it.

"They were learning to draw," the Dormouse went on, yawning and rubbing its eyes, for it was getting very sleepy; "and they drew all manner of things - everything that begins with an M - "

"Why with an M?" said Alice.

"Why not?" said the March Hare.

Alice was silent.

The Dormouse had closed its eyes by this time, and was going off into a doze, but, on being pinched by the Hatter, it woke up again with a little shriek, and went on: " - that begins with an M, such as mousetraps, and the moon, and memory, and muchness - you know you say things are 'much of a muchness' - did you ever see such a thing as a drawing of a muchness?"

"Really, now you ask me," said Alice, very much confused, "I don't think - "

"Then you shouldn't talk," said the Hatter.

This piece of rudeness was more than Alice could bear: she got up in great disgust, and walked off: the Dormouse fell asleep instantly, and neither of the others took the least notice of her going, though she looked back once or twice, half hoping that they would call after her: the last time she saw them, they were trying to put the Dormouse into the teapot.

"At any rate I'll never go there again!" said Alice as she picked her way through the wood. "It's the stupidest tea-party I ever was at in all my life!"

Just as she said this, she noticed that one of the trees had a door leading right into it. "That's very curious!" she thought. "But everything's curious to-day. I think I may as well go in at once." And in she went.

Once more she found herself in the long hall, and close to the little glass table. "Now, I'll manage better this time," she said to herself, and began by taking the little golden key, and unlocking the door that led into the garden. Then she set to work nibbling at the mushroom (she had kept a piece of it in her pocket) till she was about a foot high: then she walked down the little passage: and then - she found herself at last in the beautiful garden, among the bright flowerbeds and the cool fountains.

Questions/tasks

In your Learning Journal answer these questions and complete these activities:

How do the March Hare and Mad Hatter treat the Dormouse?

What do the March Hare and the Mad Hatter say to Alice?

What does the March Hare offer Alice and why is this odd?

What does the Mad Hatter think of Alice's hair?

What riddle does the Mad Hatter pose? Why is a raven like a writing desk?

Why does the Mad Hatter become angry?

How does the March Hare treat the watch? Why does Alice become angry with the Mad Hatter?

Why is Time upset according to the Mad Hatter?

What has happened to Time as a result?

What story does the Dormouse tell?

Why does Alice walk off?

What does she find in the wood?

What happens when she finally open the door?

Analytical question: how does Carroll convey both the logic and the madness of the Mad Hatter?

Creative Response: Write your own story called the 'The Mad Party'. Or you could write Alice or the Mad Hatter's diary for this chapter.

Textual re-casting: Write an article for a science magazine about the nature of time in Wonderland.

Devise a flow-chart/spider diagram/storyboard of the major events of the chapter.

Write down in your responses to the characters and situations in the chapter, noting down your thoughts and feelings about the various things that happen. What do you think will happen next?

What reading strategies are you using to help you enjoy the book? How could you improve your reading?

Why is the Tea Party so stupid?

See Answers to the questions at the back to mark your own work.

8 The Queen's Croquet Ground

Teaching points

Learning Objectives: To explore the roles of character types as well as the arbitrariness of punishment: to script and dramatise a scenario involving character types and arbitrary punishment.

Key Words: Character Types. Arbitrariness. Chance. Random events.

Activity One: Read Chapter 8. Students should explore and consider the points raised in the commentaries/discussion points as well as answering the questions at the end of the chapter as best they can.

Activity Two: Students make a list of characters in the novel so far who qualify as the following character types: punisher; victim; onlooker; troublemaker. Students make a list of characteristics (gender, class, language; appearance, size, personality) shared by each character group.

Activity Three: Speaking and Listening Assessment. Devise a punishment scenario involving all of the above character types. Script the scenario, being careful to ascribe to each character the decided character traits.

Activity Four: Formulate Speaking and Listening assessment objectives of your own, e.g. AO1: to speak persuasively, AO2: to listen responsively and respond sensitively, AO3: to use standard English and formal vocabulary where appropriate etc. Practice acting out the scenario.

Activity Five: Act out the scenarios (first versions of) Class feedback for each group as regards Assessment Objectives met and **not** met.

Activity Six: Students use class feedback (above) to finalise their scenarios. (to be performed at the beginning of the next lesson)

Plenary: Is there consensus in the class as to what character traits constitute each of the given character types? E.g. should the "punisher" always be stern and strict and never laugh? Should the "victim" always be a "weak person"?

The text

A large rose-tree stood near the entrance of the garden: the roses growing on it were white, but there were three gardeners at it, busily painting them red. Alice thought this a very curious thing, and she went nearer to watch them, and just as she came up to them she heard one of them say, "Look out now, Five! Don't go splashing paint over me like that!"

"I couldn't help it," said Five in a sulky tone; "Seven jogged my elbow."

On which Seven looked up and said, "That's right, Five! Always lay the blame on others!"

"You'd better not talk!" said Five. "I heard the Queen say only yesterday you deserved to be beheaded."

"What for?" said the one who had spoken first.

"That's none of your business, Two!" said Seven.

"Yes, it is his business!" said Five. "And I'll tell him - it was for bringing the cook tulip-roots instead of onions."

Seven flung down his brush, and had just begun, "Well, of all the unjust things - " when his eye chanced to fall upon Alice, as she stood watching them, and he checked himself suddenly: the others looked round also, and all of them bowed low.

"Would you tell me, please," said Alice, a little timidly, "why you are painting those roses?"

Five and Seven said nothing, but looked at Two. Two began, in a low voice, "Why, the fact is, you see, Miss, this here ought to have been a red rose-tree, and we put a white one in by mistake, and if the Queen was to find it out, we should all have our heads cut off, you know. So you see, Miss, we're doing our best, afore she comes, to - " At this moment, Five, who had been anxiously looking across the garden, called out "The Queen! The Queen!" and the three gardeners instantly threw themselves flat upon their faces. There was a sound of many footsteps, and Alice looked around, eager to see the Queen.

First came ten soldiers carrying clubs; these were all shaped like the three gardeners, oblong and flat, with their hands and feet at the corners: next the ten courtiers; these were ornamented all over with diamonds, and walked two and two, as the soldiers did. After these came the royal children; there were ten of them, and the little dears came jumping merrily along hand in hand, in couples: they were all ornamented with hearts.

> **Commentary:** among the spot cards, the spades are the gardeners, the clubs are soldiers, diamonds are courtiers, and hearts are the ten royal children. The court cards are members of the court (Carroll L., Gardner M., 1990, p. 81).

> **Discussion point:** how does Carroll link the behaviour of the characters in the chapter with the actual playing cards? What do you think of playing cards generally? Do you like playing cards? Why do you think card playing is so popular and addictive? Do some research into the different kinds of card games. You could start with your research here: **https://www.pagat.com/**

Next came the guests, mostly Kings and Queens, and among them Alice recognized the White Rabbit: it was talking in a hurried nervous manner, smiling at everything that was said, and went by without noticing her. Then followed the Knave of Hearts, carrying the King's crown on a crimson velvet cushion; and, last of all this grand procession, came The King And Queen Of Hearts.

Alice was rather doubtful whether she ought not to lie down on her face like the three gardeners, but she could not remember ever having heard of such a rule at processions; "and besides, what would be the use of a procession," she thought, "if people had all to lie down on their faces, so that they couldn't see it?" So she stood where she was, and waited.

When the procession came opposite to Alice, they all stopped and looked at her, and the Queen said severely, "Who is this?" She said it to the Knave of Hearts, who only bowed and smiled in reply.

"Idiot!" said the Queen, tossing her head impatiently; and, turning to Alice, she went on, "What's your name, child?"

"My name is Alice, so please your Majesty," said Alice very politely; but she added, to herself, "Why, they're only a pack of cards, after all. I needn't be afraid of them!"

"And who are these?" said the Queen, pointing to the three gardeners who were lying round the rose-tree; for you see, as they were lying on their faces, and the pattern on their backs was the same as the rest of the pack, she could not tell whether they were gardeners, or soldiers, or courtiers, or three of her own children.

"How should I know?" said Alice, surprised at her own courage. "It's no business of mine."

The Queen turned crimson with fury, and, after glaring at her for a moment like a wild beast, began screaming, "Off with her head! Off - "

> **Commentary:** Carroll wrote: "I pictured to myself the Queen of Hearts...as a sort of embodiment of ungovernable passion – a blind and aimless Fury."

> **Discussion point:** why are the Alice books so violent? What is the effect of this violence upon you and possibly other children?

"Nonsense!" said Alice, very loudly and decidedly, and the Queen was silent.

The King laid his hand upon her arm, and timidly said, "Consider, my dear: she is only a child!"

The Queen turned angrily away from him, and said to the Knave, "Turn them over!"

The Knave did so, very carefully, with one foot.

"Get up!" said the Queen in a shrill, loud voice, and the three gardeners instantly jumped up, and began bowing to the King, the Queen, the royal children, and everybody else.

"Leave off that!" screamed the Queen. "You make me giddy." And then, turning to the rose-tree, she went on, "What have you been doing here?"

"May it please your Majesty," said Two, in a very humble tone, going down on one knee as he spoke, "we were trying - "

"I see!" said the Queen, who had meanwhile been examining the roses. "Off with their heads!" and the procession moved on, three of the soldiers remaining behind to execute the unfortunate gardeners, who ran to Alice for protection.

"You shan't be beheaded!" said Alice, and she put them into a large flower-pot that stood near. The three soldiers wandered about for a minute or two, looking for them, and then quietly marched off after the others.

"Are their heads off?" shouted the Queen.

"Their heads are gone, if it please your Majesty!" the soldiers shouted in reply.

"That's right!" shouted the Queen. "Can you play croquet?"

The soldiers were silent, and looked at Alice, as the question was evidently meant for her.

"Yes!" shouted Alice.

"Come on, then!" roared the Queen, and Alice joined the procession, wondering very much what would happen next.

"It's - it's a very fine day!" said a timid voice at her side. She was walking by the White Rabbit, who was peeping anxiously into her face.

"Very," said Alice: - "Where's the Duchess?"

"Hush! Hush!" said the Rabbit in a low, hurried tone. He looked anxiously over his shoulder as he spoke, and then raised himself upon tiptoe, put his mouth close to her ear, and whispered, "She's under sentence of execution."

"What for?" said Alice.

"Did you say 'What a pity!'?" the Rabbit asked.

"No, I didn't," said Alice: "I don't think it's at all a pity. I said 'What for?'"

"She boxed the Queen's ears - " the Rabbit began. Alice gave a little scream of laughter. "Oh, hush!" the Rabbit whispered in a frightened tone. "The Queen will hear you! You see she came rather late, and the Queen said - "

"Get to your places!" shouted the Queen in a voice of thunder, and people began running about in all directions, tumbling up against each other: however, they got settled down in a minute or two, and the game began.

Alice thought she had never seen such a curious croquet-ground in her life: it was all ridges and furrows; the croquet-balls were live hedgehogs, and the mallets live flamingoes, and the soldiers had to double themselves up and stand on their hands and feet, to make the arches.

> **Commentary:** Carroll spent much time inventing strange ways of playing familiar games.

> **Discussion point:** why are games so important in the Alice books? What is their role? How are they represented? Can you think of strange ways of playing familiar games such as hide and seek, snakes and ladders etc?

The chief difficulty Alice found at first was in managing her flamingo: she succeeded in getting its body tucked away, comfortably enough, under her arm, with its legs hanging down, but generally, just as she had got its neck nicely straightened out, and was going to give the hedgehog a blow with its head, it would twist itself round and look up into her face, with such a puzzled expression that she could not help bursting out laughing: and when she had got its head down, and was going to begin again, it was very provoking to find that the hedgehog had unrolled itself, and was in the act of crawling away: besides all this, there was generally a ridge or a furrow in the way wherever she wanted to send the hedgehog to, and, as the doubled-up soldiers were always getting up and walking off to other parts of the ground, Alice soon came to the conclusion that it was a very difficult game indeed.

The players all played at once without waiting for turns, quarrelling all the while, and fighting for the hedgehogs; and in a very short time the

Queen was in a furious passion, and went stamping about, and shouting, "Off with his head!" or "Off with her head!" about once in a minute.

Alice began to feel very uneasy: to be sure, she had not as yet had any dispute with the Queen, but she knew that it might happen any minute, "and then," thought she, "what would become of me? They're dreadfully fond of beheading people here: the great wonder is, that there's any one left alive!"

She was looking about for some way of escape, and wondering whether she could get away without being seen, when she noticed a curious appearance in the air: it puzzled her very much at first, but after watching it a minute or two she made it out to be a grin, and she said to herself, "It's the Cheshire Cat: now I shall have somebody to talk to."

"How are you getting on?" said the Cat, as soon as there was mouth enough for it to speak with.

Alice waited till the eyes appeared, and then nodded. "It's no use speaking to it," she thought, "till its ears have come, or at least one of them." In another minute the whole head appeared, and then Alice put down her flamingo, and began an account of the game, feeling very glad she had some one to listen to her. The Cat seemed to think that there was enough of it now in sight, and no more of it appeared.

"I don't think they play at all fairly," Alice began, in rather a complaining tone, "and they all quarrel so dreadfully one can't hear one's - self speak - and they don't seem to have any rules in particular; at least, if there are, nobody attends to them - and you've no idea how confusing it is all the things being alive; for instance, there's the arch I've got to go through next walking about at the other end of the ground - and I should have croqueted the Queen's hedgehog just now, only it ran away when it saw mine coming!"

"How do you like the Queen?" said the Cat in a low voice.

"Not at all," said Alice: "she's so extremely - " Just then she noticed that the Queen was close behind her, listening: so she went on " - likely to win, that it's hardly worth while finishing the game."

The Queen smiled and passed on.

"Who are you talking to?" said the King, coming up to Alice, and looking at the Cat's head with great curiosity.

"It's a friend of mine - a Cheshire Cat," said Alice: "allow me to introduce it."

"I don't like the look of it at all," said the King: "however, it may kiss my hand if it likes."

"I'd rather not," the Cat remarked.

"Don't be impertinent," said the King, "and don't look at me like that!" He got behind Alice as he spoke.

"A cat may look at a king," said Alice. "I've read that in some book, but I don't remember where."

"Well, it must be removed," said the King very decidedly, and he called to the Queen, who was passing at the moment, "My dear! I wish you would have this cat removed!"

The Queen had only one way of settling all difficulties, great or small. "Off with his head!" she said without even looking round.

"I'll fetch the executioner myself," said the King eagerly, and he hurried off.

Alice thought she might as well go back and see how the game was going on, as she heard the Queen's voice in the distance, screaming with passion. She had already heard her sentence three of the players to be executed for having missed their turns, and she did not like the look of things at all, as the game was in such confusion that she never knew whether it was her turn or not. So she went off in search of her hedgehog.

The hedgehog was engaged in a fight with another hedgehog, which seemed to Alice an excellent opportunity for croqueting one of them with the other: the only difficulty was, that her flamingo was gone across to the other side of the garden, where Alice could see it trying in a help less sort of way to fly up into a tree.

By the time she had caught the flamingo and brought it back, the fight was over, and both the hedgehogs were out of sight: "but it doesn't matter much," thought Alice, "as all the arches are gone from this side of the ground." So she tucked it away under her arm, that it might not escape again, and went back to have a little more conversation with her friend.

When she got back to the Cheshire Cat, she was surprised to find quite a large crowd collected round it: there was a dispute going on between the executioner, the King, and the Queen, who were all talking at once, while all the rest were quite silent, and looked very uncomfortable.

The moment Alice appeared, she was appealed to by all three to settle the question, and they repeated their arguments to her, though, as they all spoke at once, she found it very hard to make out exactly what they said.

The executioner's argument was, that you couldn't cut off a head unless there was a body to cut it off from: that he had never had to do such a thing before, and he wasn't going to begin at his time of life.

The King's argument was, that anything that had a head could be beheaded, and that you weren't to talk nonsense.

The Queen's argument was, that if something wasn't done about it in less than no time, she'd have everybody executed, all round. (It was this last remark that had made the whole party look so grave and anxious.)

Alice could think of nothing else to say but "It belongs to the Duchess: you'd better ask her about it."

"She's in prison," the Queen said to the executioner: "fetch her here." And the executioner went off like an arrow.

The Cat's head began fading away the moment he was gone, and, by the time he had come back with the Duchess, it had entirely disappeared: so the King and executioner ran wildly up and down looking for it, while the rest of the party went back to the game.

Questions/tasks

In your Learning Journal answer these questions and complete these activities:

What is strange about the gardeners?
What are the gardeners doing and why?
Why does the Queen ask for Alice's head to be chopped off?
How does Alice save the gardeners from beheading?
What does Alice find out from the White Rabbit?
What is odd about the croquet match?
Who does Alice see when she tries to get away and what does this creature say?
Why does the Queen want the Cheshire Cat beheaded?
What do the executioner and the King have a problem with?
What advice does Alice give and why?
Analytical question: how does Carroll explore the theme of justice in this chapter?
Creative response: write a story about someone who is told he/she will be executed. Or write the Cheshire Cat's diary entry for this chapter.
Textual re-casting: write a newspaper article about the events at the croquet match.
Devise a flow-chart/spider diagram/storyboard of the major events of the chapter.
Write down in your responses to the characters and situations in the chapter, noting down your thoughts and feelings about the various things that happen. What do you think will happen next?
What reading strategies are you using to help you enjoy the book? How could you improve your reading?

See Answers to the questions at the back to mark your own work.

9 The Mock Turtle's Story

Teaching points

Starter: Give students three innocuous, meaningless anecdotes and ask them to find the moral in each one, e.g. "I met a man who was cleaning windows. I asked him why and he said the sun was shining". Ask them to summarise the moral of each one with an aphorism.

Activity One: Read Chapter 9. Students should explore and consider the points raised in the commentaries/discussion points as well as answering the questions at the end of the chapter as best they can. Do some research into moral fables: **http://www.moralstories.org/fables/**

Activity Two: In groups, discuss: Are there any morals to be drawn from the Mock Turtle's fables? Are there any morals to be drawn from the novel so far? Should stories have morals? Why/Why not? Can you think of any stories or novels that you have read which do not have morals? Why do writers so often write stories with morals? What do you think Carroll is trying to say about the value of morals?

Activity Three: write your own moral fable, with a commentary about why you wrote it.

Plenary: Class Feedback/Discussion.

The text

'You can't think how glad I am to see you again, you dear old thing!' said the Duchess, as she tucked her arm affectionately into Alice's, and they walked off together.

Alice was very glad to find her in such a pleasant temper, and thought to herself that perhaps it was only the pepper that had made her so savage when they met in the kitchen.

'When *I'm* a Duchess,' she said to herself, (not in a very hopeful tone though), 'I won't have any pepper in my kitchen *at all*. Soup does very well without—Maybe it's always pepper that makes people hot-tempered,' she went on, very much pleased at having found out a new kind of rule, 'and vinegar that makes them sour—and camomile that makes them bitter—and—and barley-sugar and such things that make children sweet-tempered. I only wish people knew *that*: then they wouldn't be so stingy about it, you know—'

> **Commentary:** Camomile was a very bitter medicine used in Victorian England. Barley sugar was a transparent, brittle sweet, using sold like seaside 'rock'.

> **Discussion point:** what role do sweets and food generally play in the novel?

She had quite forgotten the Duchess by this time, and was a little startled when she heard her voice close to her ear. 'You're thinking about something, my dear, and that makes you forget to talk. I can't tell you just now what the moral of that is, but I shall remember it in a bit.'

'Perhaps it hasn't one,' Alice ventured to remark.

'Tut, tut, child!' said the Duchess. 'Everything's got a moral, if only you can find it.' And she squeezed herself up closer to Alice's side as she spoke.

> **Commentary:** one of the key elements to the books is that they do not have a moral: there is no sententious message conveyed in the text.

> **Discussion point:** think deeply about why do the books have no morals? What is the effect of this?

Alice did not much like keeping so close to her: first, because the Duchess was *very* ugly; and secondly, because she was exactly the right height to rest her chin upon Alice's shoulder, and it was an uncomfortably sharp chin. However, she did not like to be rude, so she bore it as well as she could.

'The game's going on rather better now,' she said, by way of keeping up the conversation a little.

''Tis so,' said the Duchess: 'and the moral of that is—"Oh, 'tis love, 'tis love, that makes the world go round!"'

'Somebody said,' Alice whispered, 'that it's done by everybody minding their own business!'

'Ah, well! It means much the same thing,' said the Duchess, digging her sharp little chin into Alice's shoulder as she added, 'and the moral of *that* is—"Take care of the sense, and the sounds will take care of themselves."'

'How fond she is of finding morals in things!' Alice thought to herself.

'I dare say you're wondering why I don't put my arm round your waist,' the Duchess said after a pause: 'the reason is, that I'm doubtful about the temper of your flamingo. Shall I try the experiment?'

'He might bite,' Alice cautiously replied, not feeling at all anxious to have the experiment tried.

'Very true,' said the Duchess: 'flamingoes and mustard both bite. And the moral of that is—"Birds of a feather flock together."'

'Only mustard isn't a bird,' Alice remarked.

'Right, as usual,' said the Duchess: 'what a clear way you have of putting things!'

'It's a mineral, I *think*,' said Alice.

'Of course it is,' said the Duchess, who seemed ready to agree to everything that Alice said; 'there's a large mustard-mine near here. And the moral of that is—"The more there is of mine, the less there is of yours."'

> **Commentary:** Carroll seems to have invented this proverb. It describes a "zero-sum game" where the winner gains just as much as the loser loses (Carroll L., Gardner M., 1990, p. 92).

> **Discussion point:** Is Alice in Wonderland the story of a zero-sum game? Do some research into zero-sum games and have a discussion about their purpose: **https://en.wikipedia.org/wiki/Zero-sum_game**

'Oh, I know!' exclaimed Alice, who had not attended to this last remark, 'it's a vegetable. It doesn't look like one, but it is.'

> **Commentary:** Alice has muddled up the familiar parlour game "animal, mineral, vegetable".

> **Discussion point:** why do children love playing games? How and why do they get confused with many games?

'I quite agree with you,' said the Duchess; 'and the moral of that is—"Be what you would seem to be"—or if you'd like it put more simply—"Never imagine yourself not to be otherwise than what it might appear to others that what you were or might have been was not otherwise than what you had been would have appeared to them to be otherwise."'

'I think I should understand that better,' Alice said very politely, 'if I had it written down: but I can't quite follow it as you say it.'

'That's nothing to what I could say if I chose,' the Duchess replied, in a pleased tone.

'Pray don't trouble yourself to say it any longer than that,' said Alice.

'Oh, don't talk about trouble!' said the Duchess. 'I make you a present of everything I've said as yet.'

'A cheap sort of present!' thought Alice. 'I'm glad they don't give birthday presents like that!' But she did not venture to say it out loud.

'Thinking again?' the Duchess asked, with another dig of her sharp little chin.

'I've a right to think,' said Alice sharply, for she was beginning to feel a little worried.

'Just about as much right,' said the Duchess, 'as pigs have to fly; and the m—'

But here, to Alice's great surprise, the Duchess's voice died away, even in the middle of her favourite word 'moral,' and the arm that was linked into hers began to tremble. Alice looked up, and there stood the Queen in front of them, with her arms folded, frowning like a thunderstorm.

'A fine day, your Majesty!' the Duchess began in a low, weak voice.

'Now, I give you fair warning,' shouted the Queen, stamping on the ground as she spoke; 'either you or your head must be off, and that in about half no time! Take your choice!'

The Duchess took her choice, and was gone in a moment.

'Let's go on with the game,' the Queen said to Alice; and Alice was too much frightened to say a word, but slowly followed her back to the croquet-ground.

The other guests had taken advantage of the Queen's absence, and were resting in the shade: however, the moment they saw her, they hurried back to the game, the Queen merely remarking that a moment's delay would cost them their lives.

All the time they were playing the Queen never left off quarrelling with the other players, and shouting 'Off with his head!' or 'Off with her head!' Those whom she sentenced were taken into custody by the soldiers, who of course had to leave off being arches to do this, so that by the end of half an hour or so there were no arches left, and all the players, except the King, the Queen, and Alice, were in custody and under sentence of execution.

Then the Queen left off, quite out of breath, and said to Alice, 'Have you seen the Mock Turtle yet?'

'No,' said Alice. 'I don't even know what a Mock Turtle is.'

'It's the thing Mock Turtle Soup is made from,' said the Queen.

> **Commentary:** mock turtle soup is copy of green turtle soup, usually made from veal (Carroll L., Gardner M., 1990, p. 94)

> **Discussion:** why is the idea of soup so appealing to writers? Do some research and find out when broths, soups, potions etc. are used in literature: research the potion used by the witches in Macbeth, Stone Soup, Chicken Soup for the Soul etc.

'I never saw one, or heard of one,' said Alice.

'Come on, then,' said the Queen, 'and he shall tell you his history,'

As they walked off together, Alice heard the King say in a low voice, to the company generally, 'You are all pardoned.' 'Come, *that's* a good thing!' she said to herself, for she had felt quite unhappy at the number of executions the Queen had ordered.

They very soon came upon a Gryphon, lying fast asleep in the sun. (If you don't know what a Gryphon is, look at the picture.) 'Up, lazy thing!' said the Queen, 'and take this young lady to see the Mock Turtle, and to hear his history. I must go back and see after some executions I have ordered'; and she walked off, leaving Alice alone with the Gryphon. Alice did not quite like the look of the creature, but on the whole she thought it would be quite as safe to stay with it as to go after that savage Queen: so she waited.

> **Commentary:** the gryphon, or griffin, is a fabulous monster with head and wings of an eagle and lower body of a lion.

> **Discussion point:** why do the books contain so many fabulous creatures?

The Gryphon sat up and rubbed its eyes: then it watched the Queen till she was out of sight: then it chuckled. 'What fun!' said the Gryphon, half to itself, half to Alice.

'What *is* the fun?' said Alice.

'Why, *she*,' said the Gryphon. 'It's all her fancy, that: they never executes nobody, you know. Come on!'

'Everybody says "come on!" here,' thought Alice, as she went slowly after it: 'I never was so ordered about in all my life, never!'

They had not gone far before they saw the Mock Turtle in the distance, sitting sad and lonely on a little ledge of rock, and, as they came nearer, Alice could hear him sighing as if his heart would break. She pitied him deeply. 'What is his sorrow?' she asked the Gryphon, and the Gryphon answered, very nearly in the same words as before, 'It's all his fancy, that: he hasn't got no sorrow, you know. Come on!'

So they went up to the Mock Turtle, who looked at them with large eyes full of tears, but said nothing.

'This here young lady,' said the Gryphon, 'she wants for to know your history, she do.'

'I'll tell it her,' said the Mock Turtle in a deep, hollow tone: 'sit down, both of you, and don't speak a word till I've finished.'

So they sat down, and nobody spoke for some minutes. Alice thought to herself, 'I don't see how he can *ever* finish, if he doesn't begin.' But she waited patiently.

'Once,' said the Mock Turtle at last, with a deep sigh, 'I was a real Turtle.'

These words were followed by a very long silence, broken only by an occasional exclamation of 'Hjckrrh!' from the Gryphon, and the constant heavy sobbing of the Mock Turtle. Alice was very nearly getting up and saying, 'Thank you, sir, for your interesting story,' but she could not help thinking there *must* be more to come, so she sat still and said nothing.

'When we were little,' the Mock Turtle went on at last, more calmly, though still sobbing a little now and then, 'we went to school in the sea. The master was an old Turtle—we used to call him Tortoise—'

'Why did you call him Tortoise, if he wasn't one?' Alice asked.

'We called him Tortoise because he taught us,' said the Mock Turtle angrily: 'really you are very dull!'

'You ought to be ashamed of yourself for asking such a simple question,' added the Gryphon; and then they both sat silent and looked at poor Alice, who felt ready to sink into the earth. At last the Gryphon said to the Mock Turtle, 'Drive on, old fellow! Don't be all day about it!' and he went on in these words:

'Yes, we went to school in the sea, though you mayn't believe it—'

'I never said I didn't!' interrupted Alice.

'You did,' said the Mock Turtle.

> **Commentary:** Alice falls into a verbal trap here, as she does with Humpty Dumpty in *Through the Looking Glass.*

> **Discussion point:** when does Alice get caught out in the way she talks? Why does she? What is her response? What do the books suggest about the dangers of conversation?

'Hold your tongue!' added the Gryphon, before Alice could speak again. The Mock Turtle went on.

'We had the best of educations—in fact, we went to school every day—'

'*I've* been to a day-school, too,' said Alice; 'you needn't be so proud as all that.'

'With extras?' asked the Mock Turtle a little anxiously.

'Yes,' said Alice, 'we learned French and music.'

'And washing?' said the Mock Turtle.

'Certainly not!' said Alice indignantly.

'Ah! then yours wasn't a really good school,' said the Mock Turtle in a tone of great relief. 'Now at *ours* they had at the end of the bill, "French, music, *and washing*—extra."'

'You couldn't have wanted it much,' said Alice; 'living at the bottom of the sea.'

'I couldn't afford to learn it.' said the Mock Turtle with a sigh. 'I only took the regular course.'

'What was that?' inquired Alice.

'Reeling and Writhing, of course, to begin with,' the Mock Turtle replied; 'and then the different branches of Arithmetic—Ambition, Distraction, Uglification, and Derision.'

'I never heard of "Uglification,"' Alice ventured to say. 'What is it?'

> **Commentary:** these are all puns decoded: reading, writing, addition, subtraction, multiplication, division, history, geography, drawing, sketching, painting in oils, Latin, Greek.

> **Discussion point:** when, where and why does Carroll use puns in this chapter? What is their effect? Why are puns so appealing? Do some research and have a discussion: **http://examples.yourdictionary.com/examples-of-puns.html**

The Gryphon lifted up both its paws in surprise. 'What! Never heard of uglifying!' it exclaimed. 'You know what to beautify is, I suppose?'

'Yes,' said Alice doubtfully: 'it means—to—make—anything—prettier.'

'Well, then,' the Gryphon went on, 'if you don't know what to uglify is, you *are* a simpleton.'

Alice did not feel encouraged to ask any more questions about it, so she turned to the Mock Turtle, and said 'What else had you to learn?'

'Well, there was Mystery,' the Mock Turtle replied, counting off the subjects on his flappers, '—Mystery, ancient and modern, with Seaography: then Drawling—the Drawling-master was an old conger-eel, that used to come once a week: *he* taught us Drawling, Stretching, and Fainting in Coils.'

'What was *that* like?' said Alice.

'Well, I can't show it you myself,' the Mock Turtle said: 'I'm too stiff. And the Gryphon never learnt it.'

'Hadn't time,' said the Gryphon: 'I went to the Classics master, though. He was an old crab, *he* was.'

'I never went to him,' the Mock Turtle said with a sigh: 'he taught Laughing and Grief, they used to say.'

'So he did, so he did,' said the Gryphon, sighing in his turn; and both creatures hid their faces in their paws.

'And how many hours a day did you do lessons?' said Alice, in a hurry to change the subject.

'Ten hours the first day,' said the Mock Turtle: 'nine the next, and so on.'

'What a curious plan!' exclaimed Alice.

'That's the reason they're called lessons,' the Gryphon remarked: 'because they lessen from day to day.'

This was quite a new idea to Alice, and she thought it over a little before she made her next remark. 'Then the eleventh day must have been a holiday?'

'Of course it was,' said the Mock Turtle.

'And how did you manage on the twelfth?' Alice went on eagerly.

> **Commentary:** Alice's question puzzles the Gryphon because it suggests negative numbers, a difficult concept in maths.

> **Discussion point:** how and why do the Alice books use maths? Do some research if necessary: **https://www.maa.org/external_archive/devlin/devlin_03_10.html**

'That's enough about lessons,' the Gryphon interrupted in a very decided tone: 'tell her something about the games now.'

Questions/tasks

In your Learning Journal answer these questions and complete these activities:

Why does Alice become uncomfortable in the Duchess's presence?

Why does Alice think the Duchess is being nice?

What does the Queen order?

Why do only the King, Alice and the Queen end up playing the croquet game?

Why does the Queen end the game?

What does the Gryphon tell Alice about the Queen?

Why is the Mock Turtle sad?

Why did the Mock Turtle's lesson become shorter?

Analytical question: how and why does Carroll use puns so much in this chapter and elsewhere in the books?

Creative Response: write Alice's diary for this chapter discussing her response to the croquet match and the Mock Turtle's story.

Textual re-casting: Write an "agony aunt/uncle's" response to the Mock Turtle's problems.

Devise a flow-chart/spider diagram/storyboard of the major events of the chapter.

Write down in your responses to the characters and situations in the chapter, noting down your thoughts and feelings about the various things that happen. What do you think will happen next?

What reading strategies are you using to help you enjoy the book? How could you improve your reading?

Why is the Tea Party so stupid?

See Answers to the questions at the back to mark your own work.

10 The Lobster Quadrille

Teaching points

Learning objectives: To write your own "dance" poetry using syllabic metre and rhyming couplets; to learn that poetry can be linked to dance, song and rhythm.

Key Words: Syllabic metre; rhyming couplets; rhythm; rhyme; quadrilles; nonsense poetry.

Starter: Working in pairs, devise some rhyming couplets to do with "liking things" with Person 1 coming up with the first line, then Person 2 finding a rhyme for that line. E.g. Person 1: I like ice cream, Person 2: But not with Plasticine. Try to make the rhymes funny or nonsensical to keep to the spirit of the Alice books.

Activity One: Read Chapter 10 in pairs or small groups. Students should explore and consider the points raised in the commentaries/discussion points as well as answering the questions at the end of the chapter as best they can. Take some time to analyse the ingredients of "The Lobster Quadrille" working out the patterns of repetition, the number of syllables in each line, the rhythm, the rhyme scheme.

Activity Two: Finish the unfinished poem "Tis the voice of the sluggard", keeping to a consistent syllabic metre and also a rhyming couplet.

Activity Three: In pairs, write your own animal dance poem using "The Lobster Quadrille" as a model.

Plenary: Recital of above and have a go at peer-assessment, using "What I Learnt" (WIL) and "What I Would Like To Learn More About" (WIWT-LMA).

The text

The Mock Turtle sighed deeply, and drew the back of one flapper across his eyes. He looked at Alice and tried to speak, but for a minute or two sobs choked his voice. "Same as if he had a bone in his throat," said the Gryphon, and it set to work shaking him and punching him in the back. At last the Mock Turtle recovered his voice, and, with tears running down his cheeks, he went on again: -

"You may not have lived much under the sea - " ("I haven't," said Alice) - "and perhaps you were never even introduced to a lobster - " (Alice began to say "I once tasted - " but checked herself hastily, and said, "No, never") - "so you can have no idea what a delightful thing a Lobster-Quadrille is!"

> **Commentary:** a quadrille is a square dance performed typically by four couples and containing five figures, each of which is a complete dance in itself. It was one of the most difficult ballroom dances of the time and was very fashionable.

> **Discussion:** what role does dancing and partying play in the Alice books? Do some research into dances. You can find more about quadrilles here: **https://en.wikipedia.org/wiki/Quadrille** and a video here: **https://www.youtube.com/watch?v=3JPrMGiGJdo**

"No, indeed," said Alice. "What sort of a dance is it?"

"Why," said the Gryphon, "you first form into a line along the seashore - "

"Two lines!" cried the Mock Turtle. "Seals, turtles, salmon, and so on: then, when you've cleared all the jelly-fish out of the way - "

"That generally takes some time," interrupted the Gryphon.

" - you advance twice - "

"Each with a lobster as a partner!" cried the Gryphon.

"Of course," the Mock Turtle said: "advance twice, set to partners - "

" - change lobsters, and retire in same order," continued the Gryphon.

"Then, you know," the Mock Turtle went on, "you throw the - "

"The lobsters!" shouted the Gryphon, with a bound into the air.

" - as far out to sea as you can - "

"Swim after them!" screamed the Gryphon.

"Turn a somersault in the sea!" cried the Mock Turtle, capering wildly about.

"Change lobsters again!" yelled the Gryphon at the top of its voice.

"Back to land again, and - that's all the first figure," said the Mock Turtle, suddenly dropping his voice, and the two creatures, who had been jumping about like mad things all this time, sat down again very sadly and quietly, and looked at Alice.

"It must be a very pretty dance," said Alice timidly.

"Would you like to see a little of it?" said the Mock Turtle.

"Very much indeed," said Alice.

"Come, let's try the first figure!" said the Mock Turtle to the Gryphon. "We can do it without lobsters, you know. Which shall sing?"

"Oh, you sing," said the Gryphon. "I've forgotten the words."

So they began solemnly dancing round and round Alice, every now and then treading on her toes when they passed too close, and waving their fore-paws to mark the time, while the Mock Turtle sang this, very slowly and sadly: -

"Will you walk a little faster?" said a whiting to a snail,
"There's a porpoise close behind us, and he's treading on my tail.
See how eagerly the lobsters and the turtles all advance!
They are waiting on the shingle - will you come and join the dance?
Will you, won't you, will you, won't you, will you join the dance? Will
you, won't you, will you, won't you, won't you join the dance?
"You can really have no notion how delightful it will be
When they take us up and throw us, with the lobsters, out to sea!"
But the snail replied "Too far, too far!" and gave a look askance –
Said he thanked the whiting kindly, but he would not join the dance.
Would not, could not, would not, could not, would not join the dance.
Would not, could not, would not, could not, could not join the dance.
"What matters it how far we go?" his scaly friend replied,
"There is another shore, you know, upon the other side.
The further off from England the nearer is to France –
Then turn not pale, beloved snail, but come and join the dance.
Will you, won't you, will you, won't you, will you join the dance?
Will you, won't you, will you, won't you, won't you join the dance?"

Commentary: The Mock Turtle is a parody of Mary Howitt's poem "The Spider and the Fly":

"Will you walk into my parlor?" said the spider to the fly;
"'Tis the prettiest little parlor that ever you may spy.
The way into my parlor is up a winding stair,
And I have many curious things to show when you are there."
"Oh no, no," said the little fly; "to ask me is in vain,
For who goes up your winding stair can ne'er come down again."

"I'm sure you must be weary, dear, with soaring up so high.
Well you rest upon my little bed?" said the spider to the fly.
"There are pretty curtains drawn around; the sheets are fine and thin,
And if you like to rest a while, I'll snugly tuck you in!"

"Oh no, no," said the little fly, "for I've often heard it said,

They never, never wake again who sleep upon your bed!"

Said the cunning spider to the fly: "Dear friend, what can I do
To prove the warm affection I've always felt for you?
I have within my pantry good store of all that's nice;
I'm sure you're very welcome - will you please to take a slice?"
"Oh no, no," said the little fly; "kind sir, that cannot be:
I've heard what's in your pantry, and I do not wish to see!"

"Sweet creature!" said the spider, "you're witty and you're wise;
How handsome are your gauzy wings; how brilliant are your eyes!
I have a little looking-glass upon my parlor shelf;
If you'd step in one moment, dear, you shall behold yourself."
"I thank you, gentle sir," she said, "for what you're pleased to say,
And, bidding you good morning now, I'll call another day."

The spider turned him round about, and went into his den,
For well he knew the silly fly would soon come back again:
So he wove a subtle web in a little corner sly,
And set his table ready to dine upon the fly;
Then came out to his door again and merrily did sing:
"Come hither, hither, pretty fly, with pearl and silver wing;
Your robes are green and purple; there's a crest upon your head;
Your eyes are like diamond bright, but mine are dull as lead!"

Alas, alas! how very soon this silly little fly,
Hearing his wily, flattering words, came slowly flitting by;
With buzzing wings she hung aloft, then near and nearer grew,

Thinking only of her brilliant eyes and green and purple hue,
Thinking only of her crested head. Poor, foolish thing! at last
Up jumped the cunning spider, and fiercely held her fast;
He dragged her up his winding stair, into the dismal den -
Within his little parlor - but she ne'er came out again!

And now, dear little children, who may this story read,
To idle, silly flattering words I pray you ne'er give heed;
Unto an evil counselor close heart and ear and eye,
And take a lesson from this tale of the spider and the fly.

Discussion point: how and why does Carroll mock the original?

"Thank you, it's a very interesting dance to watch," said Alice, feeling very glad that it was over at last; "and I do so like that curious song about the whiting!"

"Oh, as to the whiting," said the Mock Turtle, "they - you've seen them, of course?"

"Yes," said Alice, "I've often seen them at dinn - " she checked herself hastily.

"I don't know where Dinn may be," said the Mock Turtle, "but if you've seen them so often, of course you know what they're like?"

"I believe so," Alice replied thoughtfully. "They have their tails in their mouths; - and they're all over crumbs."

"You're wrong about the crumbs," said the Mock Turtle: "crumbs would all wash off in the sea. But they have their tails in their mouths; and the reason is - " here the Mock Turtle yawned and shut his eyes. - "Tell her about the reason and all that," he said to the Gryphon.

"The reason is," said the Gryphon, "that they would go with the lobsters to the dance. So they got thrown out to sea. So they had to fall a long way. So they got their tails fast in their mouths. So they couldn't get them out again. That's all."

"Thank you," said Alice, "it's very interesting. I never knew so much about a whiting before."

"I can tell you more than that, if you like," said the Gryphon. "Do you know why it's called a whiting?"

"I never thought about it," said Alice. "Why?"

"It does the boots and shoes," the Gryphon replied very solemnly.

Alice was thoroughly puzzled. "Does the boots and shoes!" she repeated in a wondering tone.

"Why, what are your shoes done with?" said the Gryphon. "I mean, what makes them so shiny?"

Alice looked down at them, and considered a little before she gave her answer. "They're done with blacking, I believe."

"Boots and shoes under the sea," the Gryphon went on in a deep voice, "arc done with whiting. Now you know."

"And what are they made of?" Alice asked in a tone of great curiosity.

"Soles and eels, of course," the Gryphon replied rather impatiently: "any shrimp could have told you that."

"If I'd been the whiting," said Alice, whose thoughts were still running on the song, "I'd have said to the porpoise, 'Keep back, please: we don't want you with us!'"

"They were obliged to have him with them," the Mock Turtle said: "no wise fish would go anywhere without a porpoise."

"Wouldn't it really?" said Alice in a tone of great surprise.

"Of course not," said the Mock Turtle: "why, if a fish came to me, and told me he was going a journey, I should say 'With what porpoise?'"

"Don't you mean 'purpose?'" said Alice.

"I mean what I say," the Mock Turtle replied in an offended tone. And the Gryphon added "Come, let's hear some of your adventures."

"I could tell you my adventures - beginning from this morning," said Alice a little timidly: "but it's no use going back to yesterday, because I was a different person then."

"Explain all that," said the Mock Turtle.

"No, no! The adventures first," said the Gryphon in an impatient tone: "explanations take such a dreadful time."

So Alice began telling them her adventures from the time when she first saw the White Rabbit. She was a little nervous about it just at first, the two creatures got so close to her, one on each side, and opened their eyes and mouths so very wide, but she gained courage as she went on. Her listeners were perfectly quiet till she got to the part about her repeating "You are old, Father William," to the Caterpillar, and the words all coming different, and then the Mock Turtle drew a long breath, and said, "That's very curious!"

"It's all about as curious as it can be," said the Gryphon.

"It all came different!" the Mock Turtle repeated thoughtfully. "I should like to hear her try and repeat something now. Tell her to begin." He looked at the Gryphon as if he thought it had some kind of authority over Alice.

"Stand up and repeat "Tis the voice of the sluggard,"" said the Gryphon.

"How the creatures order one about, and make one repeat lessons!" thought Alice, "I might just as well be at school at once." However, she got up, and began to repeat it, but her head was so full of the Lobster-Quadrille, that she hardly knew what she was saying, and the words came very queer indeed: -

'Tis the voice of the lobster; I heard him declare,
'You have baked me too brown, I must sugar my hair.'
As a duck with its eyelids, so he with his nose
Trims his belt and his buttons, and turns out his toes.
When the sands are all dry, he is gay as a lark,
And will talk in contemptuous tones of the Shark:
But, when the tide rises and sharks are around,
His voice has a timid and tremulous sound."

Commentary: the poem is a parody of Isaac Watt's "The Sluggard":

'Tis the voice of the sluggard; I heard him complain,
"You have waked me too soon, I must slumber again."
As the door on its hinges, so he on his bed,
Turns his sides and his shoulders and his heavy head.

"A little more sleep, and a little more slumber;"
Thus he wastes half his days, and his hours without number,
And when he gets up, he sits folding his hands,
Or walks about sauntering, or trifling he stands.

I pass'd by his garden, and saw the wild brier,
The thorn and the thistle grow broader and higher;
The clothes that hang on him are turning to rags;
And his money still wastes till he starves or he begs.

I made him a visit, still hoping to find
That he took better care for improving his mind:
He told me his dreams, talked of eating and drinking;
But scarce reads his Bible, and never loves thinking.

Said I then to my heart, "Here's a lesson for me,"
This man's but a picture of what I might be:
But thanks to my friends for their care in my breeding,
Who taught me betimes to love working and reading.

Discussion point: how and why does Carroll parody the poem?

"That's different from what I used to say when I was a child," said the Gryphon.

"Well, I never heard it before," said the Mock Turtle; "but it sounds uncommon nonsense."

Alice said nothing: she had sat down again with her face in her hands, wondering if anything would ever happen in a natural way again.

"I should like to have it explained," said the Mock Turtle.

"She can't explain it," said the Gryphon hastily. "Go on with the next verse."

"But about his toes?" the Mock Turtle persisted. "How could he turn them out with his nose, you know?"

"It's the first position in dancing," Alice said; but she was dreadfully puzzled by the whole thing, and longed to change the subject.

"Go on with the next verse," the Gryphon repeated impatiently: "it begins 'I passed by his garden.'" Alice did not dare to disobey, though she felt sure it would all come wrong, and she went on in a trembling voice: -

"I passed by his garden, and marked, with one eye, How the Owl and the Panther were sharing a pie: The Panther took pie-crust, and gravy, and meat, While the Owl had the dish as its share of the treat. When the pie was all finished, the Owl, as a boon, Was kindly permitted to pocket the spoon: While the Panther received knife and fork with a growl, And concluded the banquet by - "

"What is the use of repeating all that stuff," the Mock Turtle interrupted, "if you don't explain it as you go on? It's by far the most confusing thing I ever heard!"

"Yes, I think you'd better leave off," said the Gryphon, and Alice was only too glad to do so.

"Shall we try another figure of the Lobster-Quadrille?" the Gryphon went on. "Or would you like the Mock Turtle to sing you a song?"

"Oh, a song, please, if the Mock Turtle would be so kind," Alice replied, so eagerly that the Gryphon said, in a rather offended tone, "Hm! No accounting for tastes! Sing her 'Turtle Soup,' will you, old fellow?"

The Mock Turtle sighed deeply, and began, in a voice sometimes choked with sobs, to sing this: -

"Beautiful Soup, so rich and green,
Waiting in a hot tureen!
Who for such dainties would not stoop?
Soup of the evening, beautiful Soup!
Soup of the evening, beautiful Soup!
Beau-ootiful Soo-oop! Beau-ootiful Soo-oop!
Soo-oop of the e-e-evening,
Beautiful, beautiful Soup! "Beautiful Soup!
Who cares for fish, Game, or any other dish?
Who would not give all else for two
Pennyworth only of beautiful Soup?

Pennyworth only of beautiful Soup?
Beau-ootiful Soo-oop! Beau-ootiful Soo-oop!
Soo-oop of the e-e-evening, Beautiful, beauti-Ful Soup!"

Commentary: this is a parody of James M. Sayles song "Star of the Evening":

Beautiful star in Heaven so bright,
Softly falls thy silv'ry light,
As thou movest from earth afar,
Star of the evening, Beautiful star.
Star of the evening, Beautiful star.

CHORUS
Beautiful star, (Beautiful star,)
Beautiful star, (beautiful star,)
Star of the eve-ning
Beautiful, beautiful star.

In fancy eye's thou seem'st to say,
Come, come with me from earth away,
Upwards thy spirit's pinions try,
To realms of peace beyond the sky,
To realms of peace beyond the sky.

Shine on oh! star of love divine,
May our soul's affections twine A
Around thee, as thou mov'st afar,
Star of the twilight, Beautiful star,
Star of the twilight, Beautiful star.

Discussion point: how and why does Carroll parody this song?

"Chorus again!" cried the Gryphon, and the Mock Turtle had just begun to repeat it, when a cry of "The trial's beginning!" was heard in the distance.

"Come on!" cried the Gryphon, and, taking Alice by the hand, it hurried off, without waiting for the end of the song.

"What trial is it?" Alice panted as she ran, but the Gryphon only answered "Come on!" and ran the faster, while more and more faintly came, carried on the breeze that followed them, the melancholy words: -

"Soo-oop of the e-e-evening,
Beautiful, beautiful Soup!"

Questions/tasks

In your Learning Journal answer these questions and complete these activities:

What is the Lobster-Quadrille?
What do the Mock Turtle and the Gryphon do for Alice?

Why, according to the Mock Turtle, is a whiting called a whiting?

What is unwise to do according to the Mock Turtle?

Why do the Mock Turtle and the Gryphon interrupt Alice's story about her adventures?

Why does the Mock Turtle become confused?

What cry does the Gryphon hear?

Analytical question: how and why does Carroll represent misunderstandings in the book?

Creative Response: write the Mock Turtle's diary for this chapter.

Textual re-casting: write the Mock Turtle's Facebook page.

Devise a flow-chart/spider diagram/storyboard of the major events of the chapter.

Write down in your responses to the characters and situations in the chapter, noting down your thoughts and feelings about the various things that happen. What do you think will happen next?

What reading strategies are you using to help you enjoy the book? How could you improve your reading?

See Answers to the questions at the back to mark your own work.

11 Who Stole the Tarts?

Teaching points

Learning objectives: To learn how to write reports, using formal and informal language; to develop your independent reading and writing skills.

Key Words: The Zoom Effect. The Five Senses. Emotive Language. Formal and informal language.

Starter: Teacher holds up an object or picture at the front of the class. Student X stands at the back of the class and describes the object/picture. Student Y writes onto the board Student X's description. Student X moves forward to the middle of the room and the process is repeated. Student X moves as close to the picture/object as he/she can and the process is repeated again. The emphasis should be on the emergence of big and small details so, for example, the description of the object from a distance might just describe the basic colours and shapes, while the "close-up" description might describe the different shades of the colour, the cracks in the surface etc. This should illustrate the zoom effect (a good example of which can be found in a Roald Dahl short story called 'Only This')

Activity One: Model an example of emotive language by changing, with the help of Student's A – Z, one of the three passages of writing (above) so as to invest it with a suggested emotion. For example, an interactive whiteboard described from afar might have been described as "white", but it could be emotively described by placing the adjective "nasty" in front of it so that it is a "nasty white" colour. Emphasis should be on changing verbs, adjectives and punctuation (for pace).

Students choose to rewrite one of the three passages to invest it with an emotion of their choosing: with anger, disgust, joy, sadness, fear. More able students should try also to incorporate some or all the five senses.

Activity Two: Read Chapter 11. Students should explore and consider the points raised in the commentaries/discussion points as well as answering the questions at the end of the chapter as best they can.

Activity Three: Students write a description of the Trial Court from the perspective of a character of their choice or divide up the characters so that the class between them cover most of them. Use emotive language to capture the character's emotions at this point in the narrative. Incorporate the Zoom Effect and the Five Senses, and any other descriptive language devices you think might help.

Activity Four: Readings of descriptive writings and peer assessment using "What I Learnt" (WIL) and "What I Want To Learn More About" (WIWT-LMA).

Activity Five: Finish reading the chapter. Students should explore and consider the points raised in the commentaries/discussion points as well as answering the questions at the end of the chapter as best they can.

Extension work: Finish final versions of descriptive writing pieces to be compiled into a class newspaper or blog about the trial.

The text

The King and Queen of Hearts were seated on their throne when they arrived, with a great crowd assembled about them - all sorts of little birds and beasts, as well as the whole pack of cards: the Knave was standing before them, in chains, with a soldier on each side to guard him; and near the King was the White Rabbit, with a trumpet in one hand, and a scroll of parchment in the other. In the very middle of the court was a table, with a large dish of tarts upon it: they looked so good, that it made Alice quite hungry to look at them - "I wish they'd get the trial done," she thought, "and hand round the refreshments!" But there seemed to be no chance of this, so she began looking at everything about her to pass away the time.

Alice had never been in a court of justice before, but she had read about them in books, and she was quite pleased to find that she knew the name of nearly everything there. "That's the judge," she said to herself, "because of his great wig."

The judge, by the way, was the King, and as he wore his crown over the wig, (look at the frontispiece if you want to see how he did it,) he did not look at all comfortable, and it was certainly not becoming.

"And that's the jury-box," thought Alice, "and those twelve creatures," (she was obliged to say "creatures," you see, because some of them were animals, and some were birds,) "I suppose they are the jurors." She said this last word two or three times over to herself being rather proud of it: for she thought, and rightly too, that very few little girls of her age knew the meaning of it at all. However, "jurymen" would have done just as well.

The twelve jurors were all writing very busily on slates. "What are they doing?" Alice whispered to the Gryphon. "They can't have anything to put down yet, before the trial's begun."

"They're putting down their names," the Gryphon whispered in reply, "for fear they should forget them before the end of the trial."

"Stupid things!" Alice began in a loud indignant voice, but she stopped herself hastily, for the White Rabbit cried out, "Silence in the court!" and the King put on his spectacles and looked anxiously round, to make out who was talking.

Alice could see, as well as if she were looking over their shoulders, that all the jurors were writing down "Stupid things!" on their slates, and she could even make out that one of them didn't know how to spell "stupid," and that he had to ask his neighbour to tell him. "A nice muddle their slates'll be in before the trial's over!" thought Alice.

One of the jurors had a pencil that squeaked. This, of course, Alice could not stand, and she went round the court and got behind him, and very soon found an opportunity of taking it away. She did it so quickly that the poor little juror (it was Bill, the Lizard) could not make out at all what had become of it; so, after hunting all about for it, he was obliged to write with one finger for the rest of the day; and this was of very little use, as it left no mark on the slate.

"Herald, read the accusation!" said the King.

On this the White Rabbit blew three blasts on the trumpet, and then unrolled the parchment scroll, and read as follows: -

"The Queen of Hearts, she made some tarts,
All on a summer day:
The Knave of Hearts, he stole those tarts
And took them quite away!"

Commentary: this is the complete poem, not quoted in the story:

The Queen of Hearts

The queen of hearts
She made some tarts,
All on a summer's day
The knave of Hearts
He stole those tarts
And with them ran away:
The king of hearts
Call'd for those tarts,
And beat the knave full sore;
The knave of hearts
brought back those tarts
And said he'll ne'er steal more.

The King of Spades

The king of spades
He kiss'd the maids,
Which vexed the queen full sore;
The queen of spades
She beat those maids,
And turn'd them out of door:
The knave of spades
Griev'd for these jades
And did for them implore;
The queen so gent
She did relent,
And vow'd she ne're strike more.

The King of Clubs

The king of clubs
He often drubs
His loving queen and wife,
The queen of clubs
returns him snubs:
And all is noise and strife:
The knave of clubs
Gives winks and rubs,
And swears he'll take no parts;
For when our kings
Will do such things,
They should be made to smart

The Diamond King

The diamond king,
I fain would sing
And likewise his fair queen,
But that the knave,
A haughty slave,
Must needs step in between.
Good diamond king
With hempen string,
This haughty knave destroy,
Then may your queen,
With mind serene,
Your royal bed enjoy.

Discussion point: why does Carroll not quote the whole poem? What is the effect of using this poem at this point in the story?

"Consider your verdict," the King said to the jury.

"Not yet, not yet!" the Rabbit hastily interrupted. "There's a great deal to come before that!"

"Call the first witness," said the King; and the White Rabbit blew three blasts on the trumpet, and called out "First witness!"

The first witness was the Hatter. He came in with a teacup in one hand and a piece of bread-and-butter in the other. "I beg pardon, your Majesty," he began, "for bringing these in: but I hadn't quite finished my tea when I was sent for."

"You ought to have finished," said the King. "When did you begin?"

The Hatter looked at the March Hare, who had followed him into the court, arm-in-arm with the Dormouse. "Fourteenth of March, I think it was," he said.

"Fifteenth," said the March Hare.

"Sixteenth," added the Dormouse.

"Write that down," the King said to the jury, and the jury eagerly wrote down all three dates on their slates, and then added them up, and reduced the answer to shillings and pence.

"Take off your hat," the King said to the Hatter.

"It isn't mine," said the Hatter.

"Stolen!" the King exclaimed, turning to the jury, who instantly made a memorandum of the fact.

"I keep them to sell," the Hatter added as an explanation: "Ive none of my own. I'm a hatter."

Here the Queen put on her spectacles, and began staring hard at the Hatter, who turned pale and fidgeted.

"Give your evidence," said the King; "and don't be nervous, or I'll have you executed on the spot."

This did not seem to encourage the witness at all: he kept shifting from one foot to the other, looking uneasily at the Queen, and in his confusion he bit a large piece out of his teacup instead of the bread-and-butter.

Just at this moment Alice felt a very curious sensation, which puzzled her a good deal until she made out what it was: she was beginning to grow larger again, and she thought at first she would get up and leave the court; but on second thoughts she decided to remain where she was as long as there was room for her.

"I wish you wouldn't squeeze so," said the Dormouse, who was sitting next to her. "I can hardly breathe."

"I can't help it," said Alice very meekly: "I'm growing."

"You've no right to grow here," said the Dormouse.

"Don't talk nonsense," said Alice more boldly: "you know you're growing too."

"Yes, but I grow at a reasonable pace," said the Dormouse: "not in that ridiculous fashion." And he got up very sulkily and crossed over to the other side of the court.

All this time the Queen had never left off staring at the Hatter, and, just as the Dormouse crossed the court, she said to one of the officers of the court, "Bring me the list of the singers in the last concert!" on which the wretched Hatter trembled so, that he shook both his shoes off.

Commentary: the Queen is remembering when the Hatter sang "Twinkle, Twinkle Little Bat".

Discussion point: how and why is Wonderland a dangerous place?

"Give your evidence," the King repeated angrily, "or I'll have you executed, whether you are nervous or not."

"I'm a poor man, your Majesty," the Hatter began in a trembling voice, "and I hadn't but just begun my tea - not above a week or so - and what with the bread-and-butter getting so thin - and the twinkling of the tea - "

"The twinkling of what?" said the King.

"It began with the tea," the Hatter replied.

"Of course twinkling begins with a T!" said the King sharply. "Do you take me for a dunce? Go on!"

"I'm a poor man," the Hatter went on, "and most things twinkled after that - only the March Hare said - "

"I didn't!" the March Hare interrupted in a great hurry.

"You did!" said the Hatter.

"I deny it!" said the March Hare.

"He denies it," said the King: "leave out that part."

"Well, at any rate, the Dormouse said - " the Hatter went on, looking anxiously round to see if he would deny it too: but the Dormouse denied nothing, being fast asleep.

"After that," continued the Hatter, "I cut some more bread-and-butter - "

"But what did the Dormouse say?" one of the jury asked.

"That I can't remember," said the Hatter.

"You must remember," remarked the King, "or I'll have you executed."

The miserable Hatter dropped his teacup and bread-and-butter, and went down on one knee. "I'm a poor man, your Majesty," he began.

"You're a very poor speaker," said the King.

Here one of the guinea-pigs cheered, and was immediately suppressed by the officers of the court. (As that is rather a hard word, I will just explain to you how it was done. They had a large canvas bag, which tied up at the mouth with strings: into this they slipped the guinea-pig, head first, and then sat upon it.)

"I'm glad I've seen that done," thought Alice. "I've so often read in the newspapers, at the end of trials, 'There was some attempt at applause, which was immediately suppressed by the officers of the court,' and I never understood what it meant till now."

"If that's all you know about it, you may stand down," continued the King.

"I can't go no lower," said the Hatter: "I'm on the floor, as it is."

"Then you may sit down," the King replied.

Here the other guinea-pig cheered, and was suppressed.

"Come, that finishes the guinea-pigs!" thought Alice. "Now we shall get on better."

"I'd rather finish my tea," said the Hatter, with an anxious look at the Queen, who was reading the list of singers.

"You may go," said the King, and the Hatter hurriedly left the court, without even waiting to put his shoes on.

" - and just take his head off outside," the Queen added to one of the officers; but the Hatter was out of sight before the officer could get to the door.

"Call the next witness!" said the King.

The next witness was the Duchess' cook. She carried the pepper-box in her hand, and Alice guessed who it was, even before she got into the court by the way the people near the door began sneezing all at once.

"Give your evidence," said the King.

"Shan't," said the cook.

The King looked anxiously at the White Rabbit, who said in a low voice, "Your Majesty must cross-examine this witness."

"Well, if I must, I must," the King said with a melancholy air, and, after folding his arms and frowning at the cook till his eyes were nearly out of sight, he said in a deep voice, "What are tarts made of?"

"Pepper, mostly," said the cook.

"Treacle," said a sleepy voice behind her.

"Collar that Dormouse!" the Queen shrieked out. "Behead that Dormouse! Turn that Dormouse out of court! Suppress him! Pinch him! Off with his whiskers!"

For some minutes the whole court was in confusion, getting the Dormouse turned out, and, by the time they had settled down again, the cook had disappeared.

"Never mind!" said the King, with an air of great relief. "Call the next witness." And he added in an under-tone to the Queen, "Really, my dear, you must cross-examine the next witness. It quite makes my forehead ache!"

Alice watched the White Rabbit as he fumbled over the list, feeling very curious to see what the next witness would be like," - for they haven't got much evidence yet," she said to herself. Imagine her surprise, when the White Rabbit read out, at the top of his shrill little voice, the name "Alice!"

Questions/tasks

In your Learning Journal answer these questions and complete these activities:

What does Alice find when she enters the courtroom?
Why do the jury have to write their own names?
What does Bill write with?
What does the White Rabbit announce?
Why won't the Hatter remove his Hat when the King asks him to?
Why does the Dormouse become upset?
What is the Hatter's mood and behaviour like? Why is he like this?
Why does the Dormouse cause a commotion?
Who does the White Rabbit call at the end of the chapter?

Analytical question: how does Carroll mock the institution of the law in this chapter?

Creative Response: write the Mad Hatter's diary for this chapter, discussing his response to the King's questions.

Textual re-casting: write a court report on the proceedings.

Devise a flow-chart/spider diagram/storyboard of the major events of the chapter.

Write down in your responses to the characters and situations in the chapter, noting down your thoughts and feelings about the various things that happen. What do you think will happen next?

What reading strategies are you using to help you enjoy the book? How could you improve your reading?

See Answers to the questions at the back to mark your own work.

12 Alice's Evidence

Teaching points

Learning Objectives: To analyse the evidence in the trial and reach a verdict; To write an advisory and explanatory letter to the Court.

Key Words: Pronouns.

Starter activity: Students discuss meaning of 'advise' and 'explain' and generate their own criterion for advisory and 'explanatory' writing. These become other key words.

Activity One: Read Chapter 12 up to "Let the jury consider their verdict".

Activity Two: In groups students collate all the important evidence and reach a decision as to whether the Knave is guilty or innocent; you can make up evidence, half the group should opt to find evidence to make him guilty, and the other half of the group make up evidence to make him innocent. Hold a "mini-trial" in your group with a judge, appointed within the group, deciding the verdict.

Activity Three: Each student writes the Judge's Report to the Court explaining their findings and advising what to do next.

Activity Four: Finish reading the book. Students should explore and consider the points raised in the commentaries/discussion points as well as answering the questions at the end of the chapter as best they can.

Plenary: Peer Assessment and feedback.

The text

"Here!" cried Alice, quite forgetting in the flurry of the moment how large she had grown in the last few minutes, and she jumped up in such a hurry that she tipped over the jury-box with the edge of her skirt, upsetting all the jurymen on to the heads of the crowd below, and there they lay sprawling about, reminding her very much of a globe of gold-fish she had accidentally upset the week before.

> **Commentary:** Carroll points out in one version of the story that the jury members are: a frog, dormouse, rat, ferret, hedgehog, lizard, bantam cock, mole, duck, squirrel, storkling, mousling.

> **Discussion point:** how does Carroll generate comedy and suspense at this point in the book?

"Oh, I beg your pardon!" she exclaimed in a tone of great dismay, and began picking them up again as quickly as she could, for the accident of the gold-fish kept running in her head, and she had a vague sort of idea that they must be collected at once and put back into the jury-box, or they would die.

"The trial cannot proceed," said the King in a very grave voice, "until all the jurymen are back in their proper places - all," he repeated with great emphasis, looking hard at Alice as he said so.

Alice looked at the jury-box, and saw that, in her haste, she had put the Lizard in head downwards, and the poor little thing was waving its tail about in a melancholy way, being quite unable to move. She soon got it out again, and put it right; "not that it signifies much," she said to herself; "I should think it would be quite as much use in the trial one way up as the other."

As soon as the jury had a little recovered from the shock of being upset, and their slates and pencils had been found and handed back to them, they set to work very diligently to write out a history of the accident, all except the Lizard, who seemed too much overcome to do anything but sit with its mouth open, gazing up into the roof of the court.

"What do you know about this business?" the King said to Alice.

"Nothing," said Alice.

"Nothing whatever?" persisted the King.

"Nothing whatever," said Alice.

"That's very important," the King said, turning to the jury. They were just beginning to write this down on their slates, when the White Rabbit interrupted: "Unimportant, your Majesty means, of course," he said in a very respectful tone, but frowning and making faces at him as he spoke.

"Unimportant, of course, I meant," the King hastily said, and went on to himself in an undertone, "important - unimportant - unimportant - important -" as if he were trying which word sounded best.

Some of the jury wrote it down "important," and some "unimportant." Alice could see this, as she was near enough to look over their slates; "but it doesn't matter a bit," she thought to herself.

At this moment the King, who had been for some time busily writing in his note-book, called out "Silence!" and read out from his book, "Rule Forty-two. All persons more than a mile high to leave the court."

> **Commentary:** the number 42 had a special significance for Carroll. It is a nautical rule which is cited in Carroll's poem The Hunting of the Snark, Carroll cited his age as 42 in his poem "Phantasmgoria". In Through the Looking Glass, the White King sends 4,207 horses

and 7 is a factor of 42. Alice gives her age as 7 years 6 months, which multiplied make 42. The two books together contain 24 chapters, which doubled make 42. In the Hitch-Hiker's Guide to the Galaxy, the answer to the universe is 42 (Carroll L., Gardner M., 1990, p. 120)

Discussion: why is 42 so important in our culture as a number? Why do people give certain numbers superstitious qualities, e.g. 7 and 13 etc? What numbers are important to you? Consider the number of the places where you live and have lived; the ages that have real significance for you; the years in school which are important and what emotions phrases like "year 7" provoke in you. Consider the emotions numbers make you feel in different contexts.

Everybody looked at Alice.

"I'm not a mile high," said Alice.

"You are," said the King.

"Nearly two miles high," added the Queen.

"Well, I shan't go, at any rate," said Alice; "besides, that's not a regular rule: you invented it just now."

"It's the oldest rule in the book," said the King.

"Then it ought to be Number One," said Alice.

The King turned pale, and shut his notebook hastily. "Consider your verdict," he said to the jury, in a low trembling voice.

"There's more evidence to come yet, please your Majesty," said the White Rabbit, jumping up in a great hurry; "this paper has just been picked up."

"What's in it?" said the Queen.

"I haven't opened it yet," said the White Rabbit, "but it seems to be a letter, written by the prisoner to - to somebody."

"It must have been that," said the King, "unless it was written to nobody, which isn't usual, you know."

"Who is it directed to?" said one of the jurymen.

"It isn't directed at all," said the White Rabbit; "in fact, there's nothing written on the outside." He unfolded the paper as he spoke, and added, "It isn't a letter after all: it's a set of verses."

"Are they in the prisoner's handwriting?" asked another of the jurymen.

"No, they're not," said the White Rabbit, "and that's the queerest thing about it." (The jury all looked puzzled.)

"He must have imitated somebody else's hand," said the King. (The jury all brightened up again.)

"Please, your Majesty," said the Knave, "I didn't write it, and they can't write it, and they can't prove I did: there's no name signed at the end."

"If you didn't sign it," said the King, "that only makes the matter worse. You must have meant some mischief, or else you'd have signed your name like an honest man."

There was a general clapping of hands at this: it was the first really clever thing the King had said that day.

"That proves his guilt," said the Queen.

"It proves nothing of the sort!" said Alice. "Why, you don't even know what they're about!"

"Read them," said the King.

The White Rabbit put on his spectacles. "Where shall I begin, please your Majesty?" he asked.

"Begin at the beginning," the King said, gravely, "and go on till you come to the end: then stop."

These were the verses the White Rabbit read: -

"They told me you had been to her,
And mentioned me to him:
She gave me a good character,
But said I could not swim.

He sent them word I had not gone
(We know it to be true):
If she should push the matter on,
What would become of you?

I gave her one, they gave him two,
You gave us three or more;
They all returned from him to you,
Though they were mine before.

If I or she should chance to be
Involved in this affair,
He trusts to you to set them free,
Exactly as we were.

My notion was that you had been
(Before she had this fit)
An obstacle that came between
Him, and ourselves, and it.

Don't let him know she liked them best,
For this must ever be
A secret, kept from all the rest,
Between yourself and me."

Commentary: this nonsense poem, although it has the same first line as William Mee's "Alice Gray" (Carroll L., Gardner M., 1990, p. 122) does not resemble that poem, and is not really a parody. For me, it is the funniest poem in the book because it shows how language is ultimately a "game" of pronouns.

Discussion point: what feelings/thoughts does this poem provoke in you? Why do you think some people find it very funny?

"That's the most important piece of evidence we've heard yet," said the King, rubbing his hands; "so now let the jury -"

"If any one of them can explain it," said Alice, (she had grown so large in the last few minutes that she wasn't a bit afraid of interrupting him), "I'll give him sixpence. I don't believe there's an atom of meaning in it."

The jury all wrote down on their slates, "She doesn't believe there's an atom of meaning in it," but none of them attempted to explain the paper.

If there's no meaning in it," said the King, "that saves a world of trouble, you know, as we needn't try to find any. And yet I don't know," he went on, spreading out the verses on his knee, and looking at them with one eye; "I seem to see some meaning in them, after all. '- said I could not swim, -' you can't swim, can you?" he added, turning to the Knave.

The Knave shook his head sadly. "Do I look like it?" he said. (Which he certainly did not, being made entirely of cardboard.)

"All right, so far," said the King, and he went on muttering over the verses to himself: "'We know it to be true -' that's the jury, of course - 'If she should push the matter on' - that must be the Queen -' What would become of you?' - What, indeed! - 'I gave her one, they gave him two - ' why, that must be what he did with the tarts, you know -"

"But it goes on 'they all returned from him to you,'" said Alice.

"Why, there they are!" said the King triumphantly, pointing to the tarts on the table. "Nothing can be clearer than that. Then again - 'before she had this fit -' you never had fits, my dear, I think?" he said to the Queen.

"Never!" said the Queen furiously, throwing an inkstand at the Lizard as she spoke. (The unfortunate little Bill had left off writing on his slate with one finger, as he found it made no mark; but he now hastily began again, using the ink, that was trickling down his face, as long as it lasted.)

"Then the words don't fit you," said the King, looking round the court with a smile. There was a dead silence.

"It's a pun!" the King added in an angry tone, and everybody laughed. "Let the jury consider their verdict," the King said, for about the twentieth time that day.

"No, no!" said the Queen. "Sentence first-verdict afterwards."

"Stuff and nonsense!" said Alice loudly. "The idea of having the sentence first!"

"Hold your tongue!" said the Queen, turning purple.

"I won't!" said Alice.

"Off with her head!" the Queen shouted at the top of her voice. Nobody moved.

"Who cares for you?" said Alice, (she had grown to her full size by this time.) "You're nothing but a pack of cards!"

At this the whole pack rose up into the air, and came flying down upon her; she gave a little scream, half of fright and half of anger, and tried to beat them off, and found herself lying on the bank, with her head in the lap of her sister, who was gently brushing away some dead leaves that had fluttered down from the trees on to her face.

"Wake up, Alice dear!" said her sister; "why, what a long sleep you've had!"

"Oh, I've had such a curious dream!" said Alice, and she told her sister, as well as she could remember them, all these strange Adventures of hers that you have just been reading about; and when she had finished, her sister kissed her, and said, "It was a curious dream, dear, certainly: but now run in to your tea; it's getting late." So Alice gut up and ran off, thinking while she ran, as well she might, what a wonderful dream it had been.

But her sister sat still just as she left her, leaning her head on her hand, watching the setting sun, and thinking of little Alice and all her wonderful Adventures, till she too began dreaming after a fashion, and this was her dream: -

First, she dreamed of little Alice herself: - once again the tiny hands were clasped upon her knee, and the bright eager eyes were looking up into hers - she could hear the very tones of her voice, and see that queer little toss of her head, to keep back the wandering hair that would always get into her eyes - and still as she listened, or seemed to listen, the whole place around her became alive with the strange creatures of her little sister's dream.

The long grass rustled at her feet as the White Rabbit hurried by - the frightened Mouse splashed his way through the neighbouring pool - she could hear the rattle of the teacups as the March Hare and his friends shared their never-ending meal, and the shrill voice of the Queen ordering off her unfortunate guests to execution - once more the pig - baby was sneezing on the Duchess' knee, while plates and dishes crashed around it - once more the shriek of the Gryphon, the squeaking of the Lizard's slate-pencil, and the choking of the suppressed guinea-pigs, filled the air, mixed up with the distant sob of the miserable Mock Turtle.

So she sat on, with closed eyes, and half believed herself in Wonderland, though she knew she had but to open them again and all would change to dull reality - the grass would be only rustling in the wind, and the pool rippling to the waving of the reeds - the rattling teacups would change to tinkling sheep-bells, and the Queen's shrill cries to the voice of the shepherd boy - and the sneeze of the baby, the shriek of the Gryphon, and all the other queer noises, would change (she knew) to the confused clamour of the busy farm-yard - while the lowing of the cattle in the distance would take the place of the Mock Turtle's heavy sobs.

Lastly, she pictured to herself how this same little sister of hers would, in the after-time, be herself a grown woman; and how she would keep, through all her riper years, the simple and loving heart of her childhood: and how she would gather about her other little children, and make their eyes bright and eager with many a strange tale, perhaps even with the dream of Wonderland of long-ago: and how she would feel with all their simple sorrows, and find a pleasure in all their simple joys, remembering her own child - life, and the happy summer days.

Questions/tasks

In your Learning Journal answer these questions and complete these activities:

How and why does Alice disturb the jury?

What does Alice say she knows about the case and what is the King's response to her statement?

What does Rule 42 state?

What does Alice accuse the King of?

Why does the King believe the note proves the Knave's guilt?

What does the poem prove?

Why does Alice criticise the Queen?

How does Alice defeat the Queen and the creatures of Wonderland?

Where does Alice find herself when she wakes up?

What does Alice's sister imagine and why?

Analytical question: How does Carroll make this a surprising and dramatic end to the book?

Creative Response: Write Alice's sister's diary entry for this chapter.

Textual re-casting: Imagine you are Alice telling her story to her children in a much shorter version (no more than 1000 words) write her story in her own words as best you can.

Devise a flow-chart/spider diagram/storyboard of the major events of the chapter.

Write down in your responses to the characters and situations in the chapter, noting down your thoughts and feelings about the various things that happen. What do you think might happen next if the story were to continue?

What reading strategies are you using to help you enjoy the book? How could you improve your reading?

How successful an ending is this to the book?

See Answers to the questions at the back to mark your own work.

Teaching Points

Lesson 1

Learning objectives: To learn about planning stories and develop the ability to structure stories into a narrative. To develop their skill at using the five senses in writing.

Key Words: Imagination; dream; reality; alternative worlds and universes; parallel worlds; five senses.

Activity one: If possible take students outside (but you can do this in a classroom as well, but maybe the teacher will play or create some noises) Have them sit down in silence for five minutes, eyes closed, making a mental note of the things they can hear, feel, smell etc. They then write these down under the Five Senses headings. Close their eyes again and try to imagine each of those sounds etc. as something else (i.e. the rustling of leaves as someone shuffling papers etc.) Students then make a note of their imaginings. Close their eyes again and try to connect those things into a narrative with a clear beginning, middle and end. Students devise concept maps/spider diagrams of their narratives which should be called "Falling into My Dream World" in which these noises/smells/tastes/textures are experienced by the main character. The teacher should explain that using the five senses will make the stories much more "real".

Activity Two: Students make detailed narrative plans focused around certain key events that happen in their dream world. They should follow the structure of the Alice books, but having themselves entering a "dream world", encountering difficulties, building to a climax in which they are threatened, and then returning at the end of the "real" world, but not certain whether it is "real" or not.

Activity Three: Having devised a plan for their "dream" story, they should feedback ideas, using peer assessment to improve the plans.

Extension: Bring in detailed plan for next lesson. For each paragraph: what happens and what characters are involved?

Lesson 2

Learning Objective: To learn how to improve stories through planning; to develop writing skills. To develop powers of assessment.

Key Words: Narrative. Logic. Character. Vocabulary. Punctuation. Language Devices.

Starter: Referring back to key words from previous lessons, students brainstorm as many features as they can which they think might be key for an entertaining story.

Activity One: Students annotate their plans of "Falling into My Dream World" with these key features where they think they have been met. Peer assessment with students commenting other students' work with the two comments: "What I Learnt" (WIL) and "What I Want To Learn More About" (WIWT-LMA)

Activity Two: In pairs, students discuss the issues raised by WIL and WIWT-LMA. Students update their plans.

Activity Three: Begin first drafts of stories using "free writing"; students must write and keep writing, but it does not matter at this stage about the quality of what they are writing, the only rule is that they keep writing for 5-10 minutes. The teacher should guide three sessions of free writing in this way.

Activity Four: Brief self-assessment of free writing. More free writing to finish the story. Self-assessment and peer assessment of the rough versions of the stories using WIL and WIWT-LMA.

Activity Five: Students re-draft the stories for publication in an anthology of short stories entitled "Falling into My Dream World".

Eventual (!) Plenary: Publication of short stories and readings at the launch party of the new book.

Alice through the Looking Glass and What Alice Found There

By Lewis Carroll

Preface to the 1897 Edition

Enquiries have been so often addressed to me, as to whether any answer to the Hatter's Riddle can be imagined, that I may as well put on record here what seems to me to be an appropriate answer, viz. "Because it can produce a few notes, though they are very flat; and it is never put with the wrong end in front!" This, however, is merely an afterthought: the Riddle, as originally invented, had no answer at all. For this eighty-sixth thousand, fresh electrotypes have been taken from the woodblocks (which, never having been used for printing from, are in as good condition as when first cut in 1865), and the whole book has been set up afresh with new type. If the artistic qualities of this reissue fall short, in any particular, of those possessed by the original issue, it will not be for want of painstaking on the part of author, publisher or printer. I take this opportunity of announcing that the Nursery "Alice", hitherto priced at four shillings, net, is now to be had on the same terms as the ordinary shilling picture books – although I feel sure that it is, in every quality (except the text itself, on which I am not qualified to pronounce), greatly superior to them. Four shillings was a perfectly reasonable price to charge, considering the very heavy initial outlay I had incurred: still, as the Public have practically 4 Alice's Adventures in Wonderland said: "We will not give more than a shilling for a picture book, however artistically got up", I am content to reckon my outlay on the book as so much dead loss, and, rather than let the little ones, for whom it was written, go without it, I am selling it at a price which is, to me, much the same thing as giving it away. Christmas, 1896

> **Commentary:** Carroll's description of the chess problem in the book is accurate: the story in the book mostly follows the rules of chess, given that the rows of the chessboard are separated by brooks or streams., with the columns divided by hedges. Throughout Alice

remains on the White Queen's "file" – i.e. under the Queen's protection – except when she checkmates the Red King (Carroll L., Gardner M., 1990, p 133-134). You can find a full explanation of the chess game here: **http://www.smithsonianmag.com/arts-culture/the-64-square-grid-design-of-through-the-looking-glass-24546391/**

Discussion point: why and how does Carroll make the story correlate with a game of chess?

> *Child of the pure unclouded brow*
> *And dreaming eyes of wonder!*
> *Though time be fleet, and I and thou*
> *Are half a life asunder,*
> *Thy loving smile will surely hail*
> *The love-gift of a fairy-tale.*
>
> *I have not seen thy sunny face,*
> *Nor heard thy silver laughter;*
> *No thought of me shall find a place*
> *In thy young life's hereafter –*
> *Enough that now thou wilt not fail*
> *To listen to my fairy-tale.*
>
> *A tale begun in other days,*
> *When summer suns were glowing –*
> *A simple chime, that served to time*
> *The rhythm of our rowing –*
> *Whose echoes live in memory yet,*
> *Though envious years would say 'forget'.*
>
> *Come, hearken then, ere voice of dread,*
> *With bitter tidings laden,*
> *Shall summon to unwelcome bed*
> *A melancholy maiden!*
> *We are but older children, dear,*
> *Who fret to find our bedtime near.*
>
> *Without, the frost, the blinding snow,*
> *The storm-wind's moody madness –*
> *Within, the firelight's ruddy glow,*
> *And childhood's nest of gladness.*
> *The magic words shall hold thee fast:*
> *Thou shalt not heed the raving blast.*
>
> *And though the shadow of a sigh*
> *May tremble through the story,*
> *For 'happy summer days' gone by,*

And vanish'd summer glory –
It shall not touch with breath of bale
The pleasance of our fairy-tale.

Commentary: This poem is much sadder than the poem that prefaces the Wonderland story because Carroll is older, and broke off contact from the children he knew when they were younger. However, his 'child' friends, including Alice Liddell, continued to remember him fondly when they were adults.

Discussion point: why is this poem so sad? Given that it is often left out of children's editions, is it an appropriate beginning to the book do you think?

1 Looking-Glass house

Teaching points

Learning objectives: to develop students' knowledge of what makes an effective opening to a story; to understand story structure and genre.

Starter activity: what makes an effective opening to a story? What was interesting about the beginning of *Alice in Wonderland*?

Main activities: read the first chapter, answer the comprehension questions and highlight four elements in it which interest you, answering these questions: why are you interested in these sections? How are they similar and different from other openings of novels you have read, including *Alice in Wonderland*?

Students should explore and consider the points raised in the commentaries/discussion points as well as answering the questions at the end of the chapter as best they can.

Plenary: What have you learnt about the openings of stories?

The text

One thing was certain, that the *white* kitten had had nothing to do with it:—it was the black kitten's fault entirely. For the white kitten had been having its face washed by the old cat for the last quarter of an hour (and bearing it pretty well, considering); so you see that it *couldn't* have had any hand in the mischief.

The way Dinah washed her children's faces was this: first she held the poor thing down by its ear with one paw, and then with the other paw she rubbed its face all over, the wrong way, beginning at the nose: and just now, as I said, she was hard at work on the white kitten, which was lying quite still and trying to purr—no doubt feeling that it was all meant for its good.

But the black kitten had been finished with earlier in the afternoon, and so, while Alice was sitting curled up in a corner of the great arm-chair, half talking to herself and half asleep, the kitten had been having a grand game of romps with the ball of worsted Alice had been trying to wind up, and had been rolling it up and down till it had all come undone again; and there it was, spread over the hearth-rug, all knots and tangles, with the kitten running after its own tail in the middle.

'Oh, you wicked little thing!' cried Alice, catching up the kitten, and giving it a little kiss to make it understand that it was in disgrace. 'Really, Dinah ought to have taught you better manners! You *ought*, Dinah, you know you ought!' she added, looking reproachfully at the old cat, and speaking in as cross a voice as she could manage—and then she scrambled back into the arm-chair, taking the kitten and the worsted with her, and began winding up the ball again. But she didn't get on very fast, as she was talking all the time, sometimes to the kitten, and sometimes to herself. Kitty sat very demurely on her knee, pretending to watch the progress of the winding, and now and then putting out one paw and gently touching the ball, as if it would be glad to help, if it might.

'Do you know what to-morrow is, Kitty?' Alice began. 'You'd have guessed if you'd been up in the window with me—only Dinah was making you tidy, so you couldn't. I was watching the boys getting in sticks for the bonfire—and it wants plenty of sticks, Kitty! Only it got so cold, and it snowed so, they had to leave off. Never mind, Kitty, we'll go and see the bonfire to-morrow.' Here Alice wound two or three turns of the worsted round the kitten's neck, just to see how it would look: this led to a scramble, in which the ball rolled down upon the floor, and yards and yards of it got unwound again.

> **Commentary:** Carroll, in sharp contrast, to the *Wonderland* book, set in May, sets this story in mid-winter. There is a suggestion that tomorrow is Guy Fawkes' day, 5th November. Alice, we learn later, is seven and a half years old (Carroll L., Gardner M., 1990, p. 140).

> **Discussion point:** why did Carroll set the story in mid-winter? Discuss how the times of year affect stories you have read, think about winter time stories such as Christmas stories, and summer stories such as *Grease* etc.

'Do you know, I was so angry, Kitty,' Alice went on as soon as they were comfortably settled again, 'when I saw all the mischief you had been doing, I was very nearly opening the window, **and** putting you out into the snow! And you'd have deserved it, you little mischievous darling! What have you got to say for yourself? Now don't interrupt me!' she went on, holding up one finger. 'I'm going to tell you all your faults. Number one: you squeaked twice while Dinah was washing your face this morning. Now you can't deny it, Kitty: I heard you! What's that you say?' (pretending that the kitten was speaking.) 'Her paw went into your eye? Well, that's *your* fault, for keeping your eyes open—if you'd shut them tight up, it wouldn't have happened. Now don't make any more excuses, but listen! Number two: you pulled Snowdrop away by the tail just as I had put down the saucer of milk before her! What, you were thirsty, were you? How do you know she wasn't thirsty too? Now for number three: you unwound every bit of the worsted while I wasn't looking!

> **Commentary:** Snowdrop and Kitty are black and white kittens, suggesting the black and white pieces of the chessboard.

> **Discussion point:** what colour schemes does Carroll use his stories and why? Discuss more generally how colours affect stories, think about important colours in stories such as the Red Room in *Jane Eyre, Little Red Riding Hood, Charlie and the Chocolate Factory* etc. How and why does colour have such an effect in stories?

'That's three faults, Kitty, and you've not been punished for any of them yet. You know I'm saving up all your punishments for Wednesday week— Suppose they had saved up all *my* punishments!' she went on, talking more to herself than the kitten. 'What *would* they do at the end of a year? I should be sent to prison, I suppose, when the day came. Or—let me see— suppose each punishment was to be going without a dinner: then, when the miserable day came, I should have to go without fifty dinners at once! Well, I shouldn't mind *that* much! I'd far rather go without them than eat them!

'Do you hear the snow against the window-panes, Kitty? How nice and soft it sounds! Just as if some one was kissing the window all over outside. I wonder if the snow *loves* the trees and fields, that it kisses them so gently? And then it covers them up snug, you know, with a white quilt; and perhaps it says, "Go to sleep, darlings, till the summer comes again." And when they wake up in the summer, Kitty, they dress themselves all in green, and dance about—whenever the wind blows—oh, that's very pretty!' cried Alice, dropping the ball of worsted to clap her hands. 'And I do so *wish* it was true! I'm sure the woods look sleepy in the autumn, when the leaves are getting brown.

'Kitty, can you play chess? Now, don't smile, my dear, I'm asking it seriously. Because, when we were playing just now, you watched just as if you understood it: and when I said "Check!" you purred! Well, it *was* a nice check, Kitty, and really I might have won, if it hadn't been for that nasty Knight, that came wiggling down among my pieces. Kitty, dear, let's pretend—' And here I wish I could tell you half the things Alice used to say, beginning with her favourite phrase 'Let's pretend.' She had had quite a long argument with her sister only the day before—all because Alice had begun with 'Let's pretend we're kings and queens;' and her sister, who liked being very exact, had argued that they couldn't, because there were only two of them, and Alice had been reduced at last to say, 'Well, *you* can be one of them then, and *I'll* be all the rest.' And once she had really frightened her old nurse by shouting suddenly in her ear, 'Nurse! Do let's pretend that I'm a hungry hyaena, and you're a bone.'

But this is taking us away from Alice's speech to the kitten. 'Let's pretend that you're the Red Queen, Kitty! Do you know, I think if you sat up and folded your arms, you'd look exactly like her. Now do try, there's a dear!' And Alice got the Red Queen off the table, and set it up before the kitten as a model for it to imitate: however, the thing didn't succeed, principally,

Alice said, because the kitten wouldn't fold its arms properly. So, to punish it, she held it up to the Looking-glass, that it might see how sulky it was—'and if you're not good directly,' she added, 'I'll put you through into Looking-glass House. How would you like *that*?'

'Now, if you'll only attend, Kitty, and not talk so much, I'll tell you all my ideas about Looking-glass House. First, there's the room you can see through the glass—that's just the same as our drawing room, only the things go the other way.

> **Commentary:** Carroll cleverly suggests a mirror world by pointing out that in a mirror all asymmetrical objects "go the other way". There are many references in the story to these reversals: Tweedledee and Tweedledum are mirror-image twins, the White sings of squeezing a right foot into a left shoe, and there are references to corkscrews which are helixes. Carroll also liked to "invert" things: to turn them upside down. He "inverted" games, poems, and stories, turning serious things into parodies, problems and jokes. It is worth looking at Tenniel's pictures of Alice passing through the mirror too: **http://www.alice-in-wonderland.net/resources/pictures/through-the-looking-glass/** (Carroll L., Gardner M., 1990, p. 141).

> **Discussion point:** why and how does Carroll make this story so full of references to "mirror images" and things to do with "mirrors"? Why are people so obsessed with mirrors? Do some research into other literature which is influenced by mirrors: **https://www.theguardian.com/books/2010/oct/30/john-mullan-mirrors-literature-review**

I can see all of it when I get upon a chair—all but the bit behind the fireplace. Oh! I do so wish I could see *that* bit! I want so much to know whether they've a fire in the winter: you never *can* tell, you know, unless our fire smokes, and then smoke comes up in that room too—but that may be only pretence, just to make it look as if they had a fire. Well then, the books are something like our books, only the words go the wrong way; I know that, because I've held up one of our books to the glass, and then they hold up one in the other room.

'How would you like to live in Looking-glass House, Kitty? I wonder if they'd give you milk in there? Perhaps Looking-glass milk isn't good to drink—But oh, Kitty! now we come to the passage. You can just see a little *peep* of the passage in Looking-glass House, if you leave the door of our drawing-room wide open: and it's very like our passage as far as you can see, only you know it may be quite different on beyond. Oh, Kitty! how nice it would be if we could only get through into Looking-glass House! I'm sure it's got, oh! such beautiful things in it! Let's pretend there's a way of getting through into it, somehow, Kitty. Let's pretend the glass has got all soft like gauze, so that we can get through. Why, it's turning into a sort of mist now, I declare! It'll be easy enough to get through—' She was up on the chimney-piece while she said this, though she hardly knew how she had got there. And certainly the glass *was* beginning to melt away, just like a bright silvery mist.

In another moment Alice was through the glass, and had jumped lightly down into the Looking-glass room. The very first thing she did was to look whether there was a fire in the fireplace, and she was quite pleased to find that there was a real one, blazing away as brightly as the one she had left behind. 'So I shall be as warm here as I was in the old room,' thought Alice: 'warmer, in fact, because there'll be no one here to scold me away from the fire. Oh, what fun it'll be, when they see me through the glass in here, and can't get at me!'

Then she began looking about, and noticed that what could be seen from the old room was quite common and uninteresting, but that all the rest was as different as possible. For instance, the pictures on the wall next the fire seemed to be all alive, and the very clock on the chimney-piece (you know you can only see the back of it in the Looking-glass) had got the face of a little old man, and grinned at her.

'They don't keep this room so tidy as the other,' Alice thought to herself, as she noticed several of the chessmen down in the hearth among the cinders: but in another moment, with a little 'Oh!' of surprise, she was down on her hands and knees watching them. The chessmen were walking about, two and two!

'Here are the Red King and the Red Queen,' Alice said (in a whisper, for fear of frightening them), 'and there are the White King and the White Queen sitting on the edge of the shovel—and here are two castles walking arm in arm—I don't think they can hear me,' she went on, as she put her head closer down, 'and I'm nearly sure they can't see me. I feel somehow as if I were invisible—'

Here something began squeaking on the table behind Alice, and made her turn her head just in time to see one of the White Pawns roll over and begin kicking: she watched it with great curiosity to see what would happen next.

'It is the voice of my child!' the White Queen cried out as she rushed past the King, so violently that she knocked him over among the cinders. 'My precious Lily! My imperial kitten!' and she began scrambling wildly up the side of the fender.

'Imperial fiddlestick!' said the King, rubbing his nose, which had been hurt by the fall. He had a right to be a *little* annoyed with the Queen, for he was covered with ashes from head to foot.

Alice was very anxious to be of use, and, as the poor little Lily was nearly screaming herself into a fit, she hastily picked up the Queen and set her on the table by the side of her noisy little daughter.

The Queen gasped, and sat down: the rapid journey through the air had quite taken away her breath and for a minute or two she could do nothing but hug the little Lily in silence. As soon as she had recovered her breath a little, she called out to the White King, who was sitting sulkily among the ashes, 'Mind the volcano!'

'What volcano?' said the King, looking up anxiously into the fire, as if he thought that was the most likely place to find one.

'Blew—me—up,' panted the Queen, who was still a little out of breath. 'Mind you come up—the regular way—don't get blown up!'

Alice watched the White King as he slowly struggled up from bar to bar, till at last she said, 'Why, you'll be hours and hours getting to the table, at that rate. I'd far better help you, hadn't I?' But the King took no notice of the question: it was quite clear that he could neither hear her nor see her.

So Alice picked him up very gently, and lifted him across more slowly than she had lifted the Queen, that she mightn't take his breath away: but, before she put him on the table, she thought she might as well dust him a little, he was so covered with ashes.

She said afterwards that she had never seen in all her life such a face as the King made, when he found himself held in the air by an invisible hand, and being dusted: he was far too much astonished to cry out, but his eyes and his mouth went on getting larger and larger, and rounder and rounder, till her hand shook so with laughing that she nearly let him drop upon the floor.

'Oh! *please* don't make such faces, my dear!' she cried out, quite forgetting that the King couldn't hear her. 'You make me laugh so that I can hardly hold you! And don't keep your mouth so wide open! All the ashes will get into it—there, now I think you're tidy enough!' she added, as she smoothed his hair, and set him upon the table near the Queen.

The King immediately fell flat on his back, and lay perfectly still: and Alice was a little alarmed at what she had done, and went round the room to see if she could find any water to throw over him. However, she could find nothing but a bottle of ink, and when she got back with it she found he had recovered, and he and the Queen were talking together in a frightened whisper—so low, that Alice could hardly hear what they said.

The King was saying, 'I assure, you my dear, I turned cold to the very ends of my whiskers!'

To which the Queen replied, 'You haven't got any whiskers.'

'The horror of that moment,' the King went on, 'I shall never, *never* forget!'

'You will, though,' the Queen said, 'if you don't make a memorandum of it.'

Alice looked on with great interest as the King took an enormous memorandum-book out of his pocket, and began writing. A sudden thought struck her, and she took hold of the end of the pencil, which came some way over his shoulder, and began writing for him.

Commentary: Automatic writing was a craze in the 19th century, when people believed the dead could write by taking possession of a psychic person.

Discussion point: what do you think of automatic writing? Have a go at some free writing if you have not tried it; this is writing which is completely free, the only rule is that you must keep writing for a set amount of time, e.g. 5 minutes. What is the effect of this kind of writing? What is its value?

The poor King looked puzzled and unhappy, and struggled with the pencil for some time without saying anything; but Alice was too strong for him, and at last he panted out, 'My dear! I really *must* get a thinner pencil. I can't manage this one a bit; it writes all manner of things that I don't intend—'

'What manner of things?' said the Queen, looking over the book (in which Alice had put '*The White Knight is sliding down the poker. He balances very badly*') 'That's not a memorandum of *your* feelings!'

There was a book lying near Alice on the table, and while she sat watching the White King (for she was still a little anxious about him, and had the ink all ready to throw over him, in case he fainted again), she turned over the leaves, to find some part that she could read, '—for it's all in some language I don't know,' she said to herself.

It was like this.

> YKCOWREBBAJ

> sevot yhtils eht dna,gillirb sawT'
> ebaw eht ni elbmig dna eryg diD
>   ,sevogorob eht erew ysmim llA
>   .ebargtuo shtar emom eht dnA

She puzzled over this for some time, but at last a bright thought struck her. 'Why, it's a Looking-glass book, of course! And if I hold it up to a glass, the words will all go the right way again.'

This was the poem that Alice read.

JABBERWOCKY

'Twas brillig, and the slithy toves
 Did gyre and gimble in the wabe;
All mimsy were the borogoves,
And the mome raths outgrabe.

'Beware the Jabberwock, my son!
 The jaws that bite, the claws that catch!
Beware the Jubjub bird, and shun
The frumious Bandersnatch!'

He took his vorpal sword in hand:
 Long time the manxome foe he sought—
So rested he by the Tumtum tree,
 And stood awhile in thought.

And as in uffish thought he stood,
 The Jabberwock, with eyes of flame,
Came whiffling through the tulgey wood,
 And burbled as it came!

One, two! One, two! And through and through

The vorpal blade went snicker-snack!
He left it dead, and with its head
He went galumphing back.

'And hast thou slain the Jabberwock?
Come to my arms, my beamish boy!
O frabjous day! Callooh! Callay!'
He chortled in his joy.

'Twas brillig, and the slithy toves
Did gyre and gimble in the wabe;
All mimsy were the borogoves,
And the mome raths outgrabe.

> **Commentary:** This poem is possibly the most famous nonsense poem ever written. Carroll published the first verse in *Mischmasch*, a periodical he produced for his family in 1855, when he was twenty three (Carroll L., Gardner M., 1990, p. 148). You can find a detailed explanation of the poem here: `http://www.alice-in-wonderland.net/resources/analysis/poem-origins/jabberwocky/`

> **Discussion point:** what makes the poem so funny and nonsensical and yet conveying a strong sense of meaning as well?

'It seems very pretty,' she said when she had finished it, 'but it's *rather* hard to understand!' (You see she didn't like to confess, ever to herself, that she couldn't make it out at all.) 'Somehow it seems to fill my head with ideas—only I don't exactly know what they are! However, *somebody* killed *something*: that's clear, at any rate—'

'But oh!' thought Alice, suddenly jumping up, 'if I don't make haste I shall have to go back through the Looking-glass, before I've seen what the rest of the house is like! Let's have a look at the garden first!' She was out of the room in a moment, and ran down stairs—or, at least, it wasn't exactly running, but a new invention of hers for getting down stairs quickly and easily, as Alice said to herself. She just kept the tips of her fingers on the hand-rail, and floated gently down without even touching the stairs with her feet; then she floated on through the hall, and would have gone straight out at the door in the same way, if she hadn't caught hold of the door-post. She was getting a little giddy with so much floating in the air, and was rather glad to find herself walking again in the natural way.

Questions/tasks

In your Learning Journal answer these questions and complete these activities:

Why does Alice tell off the kitten?
Who does Alice imagine Kitty is?
What does she threaten to do to Kitty?
How does Alice enter the Looking-Glass World?
What does she find on the other side of the mirror?
What does she notice in the fireplace? How does Alice appear to the chess pieces?
Why is the White King so surprised?
What does Alice find strange about the books in the room?
How does Alice manage to read "Jabberwocky"?
What happens to Alice when she leaves the room?
Analytical question: how does Carroll make the mirror world such a strange place?
Creative Response: write the White King's diary for this chapter. Or write a translation of the poem "Jabberwocky".
Textual re-casting: write set of instructions for entering the mirror world and understanding it.
Devise a flow-chart/spider diagram/storyboard of the major events of the chapter.
Write down in your responses to the characters and situations in the chapter, noting down your thoughts and feelings about the various things that happen. What do you think will happen next?
What reading strategies are you using to help you enjoy the book? How could you improve your reading?

See Answers to the questions at the back to mark your own work.

2 The Garden of Live Flowers

Teaching points

Learning objectives: to develop students' knowledge of personification.

Starter activity: brainstorm all the times when writers and people generally personify objects, e.g. the table was groaning under the weight of the food. What objects are typically personified and why? Consider: doors, floors, cars, dolls etc. Look at the environment you are in, how might you personify the objects around you; what character would you give the different things around you?

Main activities: read the chapter and highlight how and why Carroll personifies objects in the story, exploring the effects of the personification.

If they have not done so already, students should explore and consider the points raised in the commentaries/discussion points as well as answering the questions at the end of the chapter as best they can.

Extension: compare and contrast with other personification you have encountered both in the novel and outside the text.

Plenary: What have you learnt about personification?

The text

'I should see the garden far better,' said Alice to herself, 'if I could get to the top of that hill: and here's a path that leads straight to it—at least, no, it doesn't do that—' (after going a few yards along the path, and turning several sharp corners), 'but I suppose it will at last. But how curiously it twists! It's more like a corkscrew than a path! Well, *this* turn goes to the hill, I suppose—no, it doesn't! This goes straight back to the house! Well then, I'll try it the other way.'

And so she did: wandering up and down, and trying turn after turn, but always coming back to the house, do what she would. Indeed, once, when she turned a corner rather more quickly than usual, she ran against it before she could stop herself.

'It's no use talking about it,' Alice said, looking up at the house and pretending it was arguing with her. 'I'm *not* going in again yet. I know I should have to get through the Looking-glass again—back into the old room—and there'd be an end of all my adventures!'

So, resolutely turning her back upon the house, she set out once more down the path, determined to keep straight on till she got to the hill. For a few minutes all went on well, and she was just saying, 'I really *shall* do it this time—' when the path gave a sudden twist and shook itself (as she described it afterwards), and the next moment she found herself actually walking in at the door.

'Oh, it's too bad!' she cried. 'I never saw such a house for getting in the way! Never!'

However, there was the hill full in sight, so there was nothing to be done but start again. This time she came upon a large flower-bed, with a border of daisies, and a willow-tree growing in the middle.

'O Tiger-lily,' said Alice, addressing herself to one that was waving gracefully about in the wind, 'I *wish* you could talk!'

> **Commentary:** the entire section about the talking flowers is a parody of section 22 of Tennyson's poem *Maud:* You can find the poem here: **http://www.englishverse.com/poems/maud**

> **Discussion point:** how does Carroll make this section funny? Consider how you might make personifying certain objects funny? For example, what might happen if you personified things like pieces of chewing gum, or objects like shoes, baths and insects? Why might the personification of these things be funny?

'We *can* talk,' said the Tiger-lily: 'when there's anybody worth talking to.'

Alice was so astonished that she could not speak for a minute: it quite seemed to take her breath away. At length, as the Tiger-lily only went on waving about, she spoke again, in a timid voice—almost in a whisper. 'And can *all* the flowers talk?'

'As well as *you* can,' said the Tiger-lily. 'And a great deal louder.'

'It isn't manners for us to begin, you know,' said the Rose, 'and I really was wondering when you'd speak! Said I to myself, "Her face has got *some* sense in it, though it's not a clever one!" Still, you're the right colour, and that goes a long way.'

'I don't care about the colour,' the Tiger-lily remarked. 'If only her petals curled up a little more, she'd be all right.'

Alice didn't like being criticised, so she began asking questions. 'Aren't you sometimes frightened at being planted out here, with nobody to take care of you?'

'There's the tree in the middle,' said the Rose: 'what else is it good for?'

'But what could it do, if any danger came?' Alice asked.

'It says "Bough-wough!"' cried a Daisy: 'that's why its branches are called boughs!'

'Didn't you know *that*?' cried another Daisy, and here they all began shouting together, till the air seemed quite full of little shrill voices. 'Silence, every one of you!' cried the Tiger-lily, waving itself passionately from side to side, and trembling with excitement. 'They know I can't get at them!' it panted, bending its quivering head towards Alice, 'or they wouldn't dare to do it!'

'Never mind!' Alice said in a soothing tone, and stooping down to the daisies, who were just beginning again, she whispered, 'If you don't hold your tongues, I'll pick you!'

There was silence in a moment, and several of the pink daisies turned white.

'That's right!' said the Tiger-lily. 'The daisies are worst of all. When one speaks, they all begin together, and it's enough to make one wither to hear the way they go on!'

'How is it you can all talk so nicely?' Alice said, hoping to get it into a better temper by a compliment. 'I've been in many gardens before, but none of the flowers could talk.'

'Put your hand down, and feel the ground,' said the Tiger-lily. 'Then you'll know why.'

Alice did so. 'It's very hard,' she said, 'but I don't see what that has to do with it.'

'In most gardens,' the Tiger-lily said, 'they make the beds too soft—so that the flowers are always asleep.'

This sounded a very good reason, and Alice was quite pleased to know it. 'I never thought of that before!' she said.

'It's *my* opinion that you never think *at all*,' the Rose said in a rather severe tone.

'I never saw anybody that looked stupider,' a Violet said, so suddenly, that Alice quite jumped; for it hadn't spoken before.

'Hold *your* tongue!' cried the Tiger-lily. 'As if *you* ever saw anybody! You keep your head under the leaves, and snore away there, till you know no more what's going on in the world, than if you were a bud!'

'Are there any more people in the garden besides me?' Alice said, not choosing to notice the Rose's last remark.

'There's one other flower in the garden that can move about like you,' said the Rose. 'I wonder how you do it—' ('You're always wondering,' said the Tiger-lily), 'but she's more bushy than you are.'

'Is she like me?' Alice asked eagerly, for the thought crossed her mind, 'There's another little girl in the garden, somewhere!'

'Well, she has the same awkward shape as you,' the Rose said, 'but she's redder—and her petals are shorter, I think.'

'Her petals are done up close, almost like a dahlia,' the Tiger-lily interrupted: 'not tumbled about anyhow, like yours.'

'But that's not *your* fault,' the Rose added kindly: 'you're beginning to fade, you know—and then one can't help one's petals getting a little untidy.'

Alice didn't like this idea at all: so, to change the subject, she asked 'Does she ever come out here?'

'I daresay you'll see her soon,' said the Rose. 'She's one of the thorny kind.'

'Where does she wear the thorns?' Alice asked with some curiosity.

'Why all round her head, of course,' the Rose replied. 'I was wondering *you* hadn't got some too. I thought it was the regular rule.'

'She's coming!' cried the Larkspur. 'I hear her footstep, thump, thump, thump, along the gravel-walk!'

Commentary: Compare this with the following stanza from Maud:

> There has fallen a splendid tear
> From the passion-flower at the gate.
> She is coming, my dove, my dear;
> She is coming, my life, my fate;
> The red rose cries, 'She is near, she is near;'
> And the white rose weeps, 'She is late;'
> The larkspur listens, 'I hear, I hear;'
> And the lily whispers, 'I wait.'

Discussion point: how and why does Carroll poke fun at the *Maud* poem? Can you think of any serious people, texts or situations that you might make funny? How would you make them funny?

Alice looked round eagerly, and found that it was the Red Queen. 'She's grown a good deal!' was her first remark. She had indeed: when Alice first found her in the ashes, she had been only three inches high—and here she was, half a head taller than Alice herself!

'It's the fresh air that does it,' said the Rose: 'wonderfully fine air it is, out here.'

'I think I'll go and meet her,' said Alice, for, though the flowers were interesting enough, she felt that it would be far grander to have a talk with a real Queen.

'You can't possibly do that,' said the Rose: '*I* should advise you to walk the other way.'

This sounded nonsense to Alice, so she said nothing, but set off at once towards the Red Queen. To her surprise, she lost sight of her in a moment, and found herself walking in at the front-door again.

A little provoked, she drew back, and after looking everywhere for the queen (whom she spied out at last, a long way off), she thought she would try the plan, this time, of walking in the opposite direction.

It succeeded beautifully.

> **Commentary:** Backward and forward are reversed by a mirror: walk towards a mirror and the image moves in the opposite direction (Carroll L., Gardner M., 1990, p. 161).

> **Discussion point:** how does Carroll create interest in the mirror world? Why has he invented a mirror world, do you think? What are his purposes? You can guess, we can never know for sure...

She had not been walking a minute before she found herself face to face with the Red Queen, and full in sight of the hill she had been so long aiming at.

'Where do you come from?' said the Red Queen. 'And where are you going? Look up, speak nicely, and don't twiddle your fingers all the time.'

> **Commentary:** Carroll wrote in his article "*Alice* on the Stage": "The Red Queen I pictured as a Fury, but be cold and calm; she must be formal and strict, yet not unkindly; pedantic to the tenth degree, the concentrated essence of all governesses". People have said that the Red Queen is based on the Liddell children's governess, Miss Prickett nicknamed "Pricks" (Carroll L., Gardner M., 1990, p. 161).

> **Discussion point:** who does the Red Queen remind you of? Is it a sexist portrait? What do you think of Carroll's suggestions? Do they chime with your thoughts? Do some research into "mean women" in literature: **http://www.huffingtonpost.com/10-mean-girls-in-literatu_b_3942456.html**

Alice attended to all these directions, and explained, as well as she could, that she had lost her way.

'I don't know what you mean by *your* way,' said the Queen: 'all the ways about here belong to *me*—but why did you come out here at all?' she added in a kinder tone. 'Curtsey while you're thinking what to say, it saves time.'

Alice wondered a little at this, but she was too much in awe of the Queen to disbelieve it. 'I'll try it when I go home,' she thought to herself, 'the next time I'm a little late for dinner.'

'It's time for you to answer now,' the Queen said, looking at her watch: 'open your mouth a *little* wider when you speak, and always say "your Majesty."'

'I only wanted to see what the garden was like, your Majesty—'

'That's right,' said the Queen, patting her on the head, which Alice didn't like at all, 'though, when you say "garden,"—*I've* seen gardens, compared with which this would be a wilderness.'

Alice didn't dare to argue the point, but went on: '—and I thought I'd try and find my way to the top of that hill—'

'When you say "hill,"' the Queen interrupted, '*I* could show you hills, in comparison with which you'd call that a valley.'

'No, I shouldn't,' said Alice, surprised into contradicting her at last: 'a hill *can't* be a valley, you know. That would be nonsense—'

The Red Queen shook her head, 'You may call it "nonsense" if you like,' she said, 'but *I've* heard nonsense, compared with which that would be as sensible as a dictionary!'

Alice curtseyed again, as she was afraid from the Queen's tone that she was a *little* offended: and they walked on in silence till they got to the top of the little hill.

For some minutes Alice stood without speaking, looking out in all directions over the country—and a most curious country it was. There were a number of tiny little brooks running straight across it from side to side, and the ground between was divided up into squares by a number of little green hedges, that reached from brook to brook.

'I declare it's marked out just like a large chessboard!' Alice said at last. 'There ought to be some men moving about somewhere—and so there are!' She added in a tone of delight, and her heart began to beat quick with excitement as she went on. 'It's a great huge game of chess that's being played—all over the world—if this *is* the world at all, you know. Oh, what fun it is! How I *wish* I was one of them! I wouldn't mind being a Pawn, if only I might join—though of course I should *like* to be a Queen, best.'

> **Commentary:** many writers have compared life to chess. You can start your researches here if you are interested: **https://en.wikipedia.org/wiki/Chess_in_the_arts**
>
> **Discussion point:** why do writers compare life to chess? Do some of your own research into this matter: **http://www.rd.com/culture/memorable-movie-quotes/**

She glanced rather shyly at the real Queen as she said this, but her companion only smiled pleasantly, and said, 'That's easily managed. You can be the White Queen's Pawn, if you like, as Lily's too young to play; and you're in the Second Square to begin with: when you get to the Eighth Square you'll be a Queen—' Just at this moment, somehow or other, they began to run.

Alice never could quite make out, in thinking it over afterwards, how it was that they began: all she remembers is, that they were running hand in hand, and the Queen went so fast that it was all she could do to keep up with her: and still the Queen kept crying 'Faster! Faster!' but Alice felt she *could not* go faster, though she had not breath left to say so.

The most curious part of the thing was, that the trees and the other things round them never changed their places at all: however fast they went, they never seemed to pass anything. 'I wonder if all the things move along with us?' thought poor puzzled Alice. And the Queen seemed to guess her thoughts, for she cried, 'Faster! Don't try to talk!'

Not that Alice had any idea of doing *that*. She felt as if she would never be able to talk again, she was getting so much out of breath: and still the Queen cried 'Faster! Faster!' and dragged her along. 'Are we nearly there?' Alice managed to pant out at last.

'Nearly there!' the Queen repeated. 'Why, we passed it ten minutes ago! Faster!' And they ran on for a time in silence, with the wind whistling in Alice's ears, and almost blowing her hair off her head, she fancied.

'Now! Now!' cried the Queen. 'Faster! Faster!' And they went so fast that at last they seemed to skim through the air, hardly touching the ground with their feet, till suddenly, just as Alice was getting quite exhausted, they stopped, and she found herself sitting on the ground, breathless and giddy.

The Queen propped her up against a tree, and said kindly, 'You may rest a little now.'

Alice looked round her in great surprise. 'Why, I do believe we've been under this tree the whole time! Everything's just as it was!'

'Of course it is,' said the Queen, 'what would you have it?'

'Well, in *our* country,' said Alice, still panting a little, 'you'd generally get to somewhere else—if you ran very fast for a long time, as we've been doing.'

'A slow sort of country!' said the Queen. 'Now, *here*, you see, it takes all the running *you* can do, to keep in the same place.

Commentary: this is one of the most quoted passages in the novel.

Discussion point: why is it so often quoted? What makes certain quotes so memorable? Do some research into memorable quotes: **http://www.rd.com/culture/memorable-movie-quotes/**

If you want to get somewhere else, you must run at least twice as fast as that!'

'I'd rather not try, please!' said Alice. 'I'm quite content to stay here—only I *am* so hot and thirsty!'

'I know what *you'd* like!' the Queen said good-naturedly, taking a little box out of her pocket. 'Have a biscuit?'

Alice thought it would not be civil to say 'No,' though it wasn't at all what she wanted. So she took it, and ate it as well as she could: and it was *very* dry; and she thought she had never been so nearly choked in all her life.

'While you're refreshing yourself,' said the Queen, 'I'll just take the measurements.' And she took a ribbon out of her pocket, marked in inches, and began measuring the ground, and sticking little pegs in here and there.

'At the end of two yards,' she said, putting in a peg to mark the distance, 'I shall give you your directions—have another biscuit?'

'No, thank you,' said Alice: 'one's *quite* enough!'

'Thirst quenched, I hope?' said the Queen.

Alice did not know what to say to this, but luckily the Queen did not wait for an answer, but went on. 'At the end of *three* yards I shall repeat them—for fear of your forgetting them. At the end of *four*, I shall say good-bye. And at the end of *five*, I shall go!'

She had got all the pegs put in by this time, and Alice looked on with great interest as she returned to the tree, and then began slowly walking down the row.

At the two-yard peg she faced round, and said, 'A pawn goes two squares in its first move, you know. So you'll go *very* quickly through the Third Square—by railway, I should think—and you'll find yourself in the Fourth Square in no time. Well, *that* square belongs to Tweedledum and Tweedledee—the Fifth is mostly water—the Sixth belongs to Humpty Dumpty—But you make no remark?'

'I—I didn't know I had to make one—just then,' Alice faltered out.

'You *should* have said, "It's extremely kind of you to tell me all this"—however, we'll suppose it said—the Seventh Square is all forest—however, one of the Knights will show you the way—and in the Eighth Square we shall be Queens together, and it's all feasting and fun!' Alice got up and curtseyed, and sat down again.

At the next peg the Queen turned again, and this time she said, 'Speak in French when you can't think of the English for a thing—turn out your toes as you walk—and remember who you are!' She did not wait for Alice to curtsey this time, but walked on quickly to the next peg, where she turned for a moment to say 'good-bye,' and then hurried on to the last.

How it happened, Alice never knew, but exactly as she came to the last peg, she was gone. Whether she vanished into the air, or whether she ran quickly into the wood ('and she *can* run very fast!' thought Alice), there was no way of guessing, but she was gone, and Alice began to remember that she was a Pawn, and that it would soon be time for her to move.

This is a colourful and helpful workbook based on this chapter:
http://www.k12reader.com/literature/through_the_looking_g lass.pdf

Questions/tasks

In your Learning Journal answer these questions and complete these activities:

Why does Alice climb the hill?
What does Alice find frustrating?
What is surprising about the flowers?
Who protects the flowers and how?
How do the Rose and the Violet treat Alice?
Who else is in the garden?
How does Alice manage to reach her and why does she reach her this way?
What does the Red Queen say the hill is like and what is Alice's response

to this?

What does Alice realise about the countryside?

How does Alice join the game?

What is strange about their running?

What does the Red Queen explain about the game?

Analytical question: how does Carroll present Alice as a misguided and confused explorer in this chapter?

Creative Response: write Alice's diary for this chapter, outlining how she comes to understand, after much confusion, the rules of the mirror world.

Write a story/poem/play in which you explore life as a game of chess.

Textual re-casting: write a gardening manual for looking after the Flower Garden.

Devise a flow-chart/spider diagram/storyboard of the major events of the chapter.

Write down in your responses to the characters and situations in the chapter, noting down your thoughts and feelings about the various things that happen. What do you think will happen next?

What reading strategies are you using to help you enjoy the book? How could you improve your reading?

See Answers to the questions at the back to mark your own work.

3 Looking-Glass Insects

Teaching points

Learning objectives: to develop students' knowledge of nouns, noun phrases and "proper nouns" in particular.

Starter activity: spider diagram what you know about nouns. What are nouns, why are they used, and what are their effects? Consider the proper noun of your name and other people's names. What is the effect of your name upon you, and other people? What do you think, feel and see when people say your name?

Main activities: read the chapter and highlight how and why Carroll uses "proper nouns" (names) in this chapter. Consider why he capitalizes the "Gnat" and other objects. What discussion does Alice have about names, and what do you think is interesting about names? Have a go at the textual re-casting exercise at the end of the chapter.

If they have not done so already, students should explore and consider the points raised in the commentaries/discussion points as well as answering the questions at the end of the chapter as best they can.

Extension: do some research about the role names play in your life, consider what names create feelings of joy, sadness, fear, worry, excitement in your life, and write an essay on the role of names in your life.

Plenary: What have you learnt about nouns?

The text

Of course the first thing to do was to make a grand survey of the country she was going to travel through. 'It's something very like learning geography,' thought Alice, as she stood on tiptoe in hopes of being able to see a little further. 'Principal rivers—there *are* none. Principal mountains—I'm on the only one, but I don't think it's got any name. Principal towns—why, what *are* those creatures, making honey down there? They can't be bees—nobody ever saw bees a mile off, you know—' and for some time she stood silent, watching one of them that was bustling about among the flowers, poking its proboscis into them, 'just as if it was a regular bee,' thought Alice.

However, this was anything but a regular bee: in fact it was an elephant—as Alice soon found out, though the idea quite took her breath away at first. 'And what enormous flowers they must be!' was her next idea. 'Something like cottages with the roofs taken off, and stalks put to them—and what quantities of honey they must make! I think I'll go down and—no, I won't *just* yet,' she went on, checking herself just as she was beginning to run down the hill, and trying to find some excuse for turning shy so suddenly. 'It'll never do to go down among them without a good long branch to brush them away—and what fun it'll be when they ask me how I like my walk. I shall say—"Oh, I like it well enough—"' (here came the favourite little toss of the head), '"only it was so dusty and hot, and the elephants did tease so!"'

'I think I'll go down the other way,' she said after a pause: 'and perhaps I may visit the elephants later on. Besides, I do so want to get into the Third Square!'

So with this excuse she ran down the hill and jumped over the first of the six little brooks.

$$* \quad * \quad * \quad * \quad * \quad * \quad *$$

$$* \quad * \quad * \quad * \quad * \quad *$$

$$* \quad * \quad * \quad * \quad * \quad * \quad *$$

Commentary: The six little brooks are the six horizontal lines separating Alice from the 8th square where she will be queened. Each time she crosses a line, the crossing is marked in the story by three rows of dots. Her first move is 2 squares, the only long journey a pawn can do. Here she leaps into the third square and then the train takes her to the 4th (Carroll L., Gardner M., 1990, p. 169).

Discussion point: How does the chess game bring excitement to the story? Can you think of other stories where games play an important role? Think about stories like *The Hunger Games*. Why and how do games make stories exciting?

'Tickets, please!' said the Guard, putting his head in at the window. In a moment everybody was holding out a ticket: they were about the same size as the people, and quite seemed to fill the carriage.

'Now then! Show your ticket, child!' the Guard went on, looking angrily at Alice. And a great many voices all said together ('like the chorus of a song,' thought Alice), 'Don't keep him waiting, child! Why, his time is worth a thousand pounds a minute!'

'I'm afraid I haven't got one,' Alice said in a frightened tone: 'there wasn't a ticket-office where I came from.' And again the chorus of voices went on. 'There wasn't room for one where she came from. The land there is worth a thousand pounds an inch!'

'Don't make excuses,' said the Guard: 'you should have bought one from the engine-driver.' And once more the chorus of voices went on with 'The man that drives the engine. Why, the smoke alone is worth a thousand pounds a puff!'

> **Commentary:** it is believed that this phrase refers to an advertising catchphrase popular at the time for Beecham's pills: "worth a guinea a box" but there is much debate about this (Carroll L., Gardner M., 1990, p. 170).

> **Discussion point:** How are money and valuable things represented in the books?

Alice thought to herself, 'Then there's no use in speaking.' The voices didn't join in this time, as she hadn't spoken, but to her great surprise, they all *thought* in chorus (I hope you understand what *thinking in chorus* means—for I must confess that *I* don't), 'Better say nothing at all. Language is worth a thousand pounds a word!'

'I shall dream about a thousand pounds tonight, I know I shall!' thought Alice.

All this time the Guard was looking at her, first through a telescope, then through a microscope, and then through an opera-glass. At last he said, 'You're travelling the wrong way,' and shut up the window and went away.

'So young a child,' said the gentleman sitting opposite to her (he was dressed in white paper), 'ought to know which way she's going, even if she doesn't know her own name!'

A Goat, that was sitting next to the gentleman in white, shut his eyes and said in a loud voice, 'She ought to know her way to the ticket-office, even if she doesn't know her alphabet!'

There was a Beetle sitting next to the Goat (it was a very queer carriage-full of passengers altogether), and, as the rule seemed to be that they should all speak in turn, *he* went on with 'She'll have to go back from here as luggage!'

Alice couldn't see who was sitting beyond the Beetle, but a hoarse voice spoke next. 'Change engines—' it said, and was obliged to leave off.

'It sounds like a horse,' Alice thought to herself. And an extremely small voice, close to her ear, said, 'You might make a joke on that—something about "horse" and "hoarse," you know.'

Then a very gentle voice in the distance said, 'She must be labelled "Lass, with care," you know—'

And after that other voices went on ('What a number of people there are in the carriage!' thought Alice), saying, 'She must go by post, as she's got a head **(Victorian slang for postage stamp)** on her—' 'She must be sent as a message by the telegraph—' 'She must draw the train herself the rest of the way—' and so on.

But the gentleman dressed in white paper leaned forwards and whispered in her ear, 'Never mind what they all say, my dear, but take a return-ticket every time the train stops.'

'Indeed I shan't!' Alice said rather impatiently. 'I don't belong to this railway journey at all—I was in a wood just now—and I wish I could get back there.'

'You might make a joke on *that*,' said the little voice close to her ear: 'something about "you *would* if you could," you know.'

'Don't tease so,' said Alice, looking about in vain to see where the voice came from; 'if you're so anxious to have a joke made, why don't you make one yourself?'

The little voice sighed deeply: it was *very* unhappy, evidently, and Alice would have said something pitying to comfort it, 'If it would only sigh like other people!' she thought. But this was such a wonderfully small sigh, that she wouldn't have heard it at all, if it hadn't come *quite* close to her ear. The consequence of this was that it tickled her ear very much, and quite took off her thoughts from the unhappiness of the poor little creature.

'I know you are a friend,' the little voice went on; 'a dear friend, and an old friend. And you won't hurt me, though I *am* an insect.'

'What kind of insect?' Alice inquired a little anxiously. What she really wanted to know was, whether it could sting or not, but she thought this wouldn't be quite a civil question to ask.

'What, then you don't—' the little voice began, when it was drowned by a shrill scream from the engine, and everybody jumped up in alarm, Alice among the rest.

The Horse, who had put his head out of the window, quietly drew it in and said, 'It's only a brook we have to jump over.' Everybody seemed satisfied with this, though Alice felt a little nervous at the idea of trains jumping at all. 'However, it'll take us into the Fourth Square, that's some comfort!' she said to herself. In another moment she felt the carriage rise straight up into the air, and in her fright she caught at the thing nearest to her hand, which happened to be the Goat's beard.

* * * * * * *

* * * * * *

* * * * * * *

But the beard seemed to melt away as she touched it, and she found herself sitting quietly under a tree—while the Gnat (for that was the insect she had been talking to) was balancing itself on a twig just over her head, and fanning her with its wings.

It certainly was a *very* large Gnat: 'about the size of a chicken,' Alice thought. Still, she couldn't feel nervous with it, after they had been talking together so long.

'—then you don't like all insects?' the Gnat went on, as quietly as if nothing had happened.

'I like them when they can talk,' Alice said. 'None of them ever talk, where *I* come from.'

'What sort of insects do you rejoice in, where *you* come from?' the Gnat inquired.

'I don't *rejoice* in insects at all,' Alice explained, 'because I'm rather afraid of them—at least the large kinds. But I can tell you the names of some of them.'

'Of course they answer to their names?' the Gnat remarked carelessly.

'I never knew them to do it.'

'What's the use of their having names,' the Gnat said, 'if they won't answer to them?'

'No use to *them*,' said Alice; 'but it's useful to the people who name them, I suppose. If not, why do things have names at all?'

'I can't say,' the Gnat replied. 'Further on, in the wood down there, they've got no names—however, go on with your list of insects: you're wasting time.'

'Well, there's the Horse-fly,' Alice began, counting off the names on her fingers.

'All right,' said the Gnat: 'half way up that bush, you'll see a Rocking-horse-fly, if you look. It's made entirely of wood, and gets about by swinging itself from branch to branch.'

'What does it live on?' Alice asked, with great curiosity.

'Sap and sawdust,' said the Gnat. 'Go on with the list.'

Alice looked up at the Rocking-horse-fly with great interest, and made up her mind that it must have been just repainted, it looked so bright and sticky; and then she went on.

'And there's the Dragon-fly.'

'Look on the branch above your head,' said the Gnat, 'and there you'll find a snap-dragon-fly. Its body is made of plum-pudding, its wings of holly-leaves, and its head is a raisin burning in brandy.'

> **Commentary:** Snapdragon (or flapdragon) is the name of a game that Victorian children liked during Christmas in which a shallow bowl is filled with brandy, raisins are thrown in it, and the brandy set on fire. Players try and snatch the raisins amidst the flames and pop them into their mouths still burning. The burning raisins were also called snapdragons (Carroll L., Gardner M., 1990, p. 174).

Discussion point: why might this game be fun but now permitted nowadays? What role do games play in this book?

'And what does it live on?'

'Frumenty and mince pie,' the Gnat replied; 'and it makes its nest in a Christmas box.'

'And then there's the Butterfly,' Alice went on, after she had taken a good look at the insect with its head on fire, and had thought to herself, 'I wonder if that's the reason insects are so fond of flying into candles— because they want to turn into Snap-dragon-flies!'

'Crawling at your feet,' said the Gnat (Alice drew her feet back in some alarm), 'you may observe a Bread-and-Butterfly. Its wings are thin slices of Bread-and-butter, its body is a crust, and its head is a lump of sugar.'

'And what does *it* live on?'

'Weak tea with cream in it.'

A new difficulty came into Alice's head. 'Supposing it couldn't find any?' she suggested.

'Then it would die, of course.'

'But that must happen very often,' Alice remarked thoughtfully.

'It always happens,' said the Gnat.

After this, Alice was silent for a minute or two, pondering. The Gnat amused itself meanwhile by humming round and round her head: at last it settled again and remarked, 'I suppose you don't want to lose your name?'

'No, indeed,' Alice said, a little anxiously.

'And yet I don't know,' the Gnat went on in a careless tone: 'only think how convenient it would be if you could manage to go home without it! For instance, if the governess wanted to call you to your lessons, she would call out "come here—," and there she would have to leave off, because there wouldn't be any name for her to call, and of course you wouldn't have to go, you know.'

'That would never do, I'm sure,' said Alice: 'the governess would never think of excusing me lessons for that. If she couldn't remember my name, she'd call me "Miss!" as the servants do.'

'Well, if she said "Miss," and didn't say anything more,' the Gnat remarked, 'of course you'd miss your lessons. That's a joke. I wish *you* had made it.'

'Why do you wish *I* had made it?' Alice asked. 'It's a very bad one.'

But the Gnat only sighed deeply, while two large tears came rolling down its cheeks.

'You shouldn't make jokes,' Alice said, 'if it makes you so unhappy.'

Then came another of those melancholy little sighs, and this time the poor Gnat really seemed to have sighed itself away, for, when Alice looked up, there was nothing whatever to be seen on the twig, and, as she was getting quite chilly with sitting still so long, she got up and walked on.

She very soon came to an open field, with a wood on the other side of it: it looked much darker than the last wood, and Alice felt a *little* timid about going into it. However, on second thoughts, she made up her mind to go on: 'for I certainly won't go *back*,' she thought to herself, and this was the only way to the Eighth Square.

> **Commentary:** Alice can't go back because pawns can't go back in chess.

> **Discussion point:** In what ways is Alice a pawn both literally and metaphorically in this book?

'This must be the wood,' she said thoughtfully to herself, 'where things have no names. I wonder what'll become of *my* name when I go in? I shouldn't like to lose it at all—because they'd have to give me another, and it would be almost certain to be an ugly one. But then the fun would be trying to find the creature that had got my old name! That's just like the advertisements, you know, when people lose dogs—"*answers to the name of 'Dash:' had on a brass collar*"—just fancy calling everything you met "Alice," till one of them answered! Only they wouldn't answer at all, if they were wise.'

She was rambling on in this way when she reached the wood: it looked very cool and shady. 'Well, at any rate it's a great comfort,' she said as she stepped under the trees, 'after being so hot, to get into the—into *what*?' she went on, rather surprised at not being able to think of the word. 'I mean to get under the—under the—under *this*, you know!' putting her hand on the trunk of the tree. 'What *does* it call itself, I wonder? I do believe it's got no name—why, to be sure it hasn't!'

She stood silent for a minute, thinking: then she suddenly began again. 'Then it really *has* happened, after all! And now, who am I? I *will* remember, if I can! I'm determined to do it!' But being determined didn't help much, and all she could say, after a great deal of puzzling, was, 'L, I *know* it begins with L!'

> **Commentary:** the theme of forgetting comes up a few times in the books, and the theme of forgetting one's name comes up frequently in Carroll's writing (Carroll L., Gardner M., 1990, p. 177).

> **Discussion point:** why and how is forgetting such an important idea in the Alice books as a whole?

Just then a Fawn **(a young deer)** came wandering by: it looked at Alice with its large gentle eyes, but didn't seem at all frightened. 'Here then! Here then!' Alice said, as she held out her hand and tried to stroke it; but it only started back a little, and then stood looking at her again.

'What do you call yourself?' the Fawn said at last. Such a soft sweet voice it had!

'I wish I knew!' thought poor Alice. She answered, rather sadly, 'Nothing, just now.'

'Think again,' it said: 'that won't do.'

Alice thought, but nothing came of it. 'Please, would you tell me what *you* call yourself?' she said timidly. 'I think that might help a little.'

'I'll tell you, if you'll move a little further on,' the Fawn said. 'I can't remember here.'

So they walked on together though the wood, Alice with her arms clasped lovingly round the soft neck of the Fawn, till they came out into another open field, and here the Fawn gave a sudden bound into the air, and shook itself free from Alice's arms. 'I'm a Fawn!' it cried out in a voice of delight, 'and, dear me! you're a human child!' A sudden look of alarm came into its beautiful brown eyes, and in another moment it had darted away at full speed.

> **Commentary:** the wood in which things have no name is the universe itself: in other words, the relationship between the things of the world and words is arbitrary, or "by chance". This is a major insight of linguists and philosophers like Saussure and Wittgenstein (Carroll L., Gardner M., 1990, p. 178).

> **Discussion point:** why is the universe like the wood in this book?

Alice stood looking after it, almost ready to cry with vexation at having lost her dear little fellow-traveller so suddenly. 'However, I know my name now.' she said, 'that's *some* comfort. Alice—Alice—I won't forget it again. And now, which of these finger-posts ought I to follow, I wonder?'

It was not a very difficult question to answer, as there was only one road through the wood, and the two finger-posts both pointed along it. 'I'll settle it,' Alice said to herself, 'when the road divides and they point different ways.'

But this did not seem likely to happen. She went on and on, a long way, but wherever the road divided there were sure to be two finger-posts pointing the same way, one marked 'TO TWEEDLEDUM'S HOUSE' and the other 'TO THE HOUSE OF TWEEDLEDEE.'

'I do believe,' said Alice at last, 'that they live in the same house! I wonder I never thought of that before—But I can't stay there long. I'll just call and say "how d'you do?" and ask them the way out of the wood. If I could only get to the Eighth Square before it gets dark!' So she wandered on, talking to herself as she went, till, on turning a sharp corner, she came upon two fat little men, so suddenly that she could not help starting back, but in another moment she recovered herself, feeling sure that they must be.

Questions/tasks

In your Learning Journal answer these questions and complete these activities:

What do the elephants appear to be doing in the distance?

Where does Alice suddenly find herself in and what problem does she feel she has?

Who is in the carriage and what do they say about Alice?

Why does the train jump?

What voice does Alice hear in her ear?

What does the Gnat say will happen to Alice when she enters the wood?
What does happen to Alice when she enters the wood?
Where does Alice head towards in the wood?
Analytical question: how does Carroll explore issues about language and evolution in this chapter?
Creative Response: write the Fawn's diary for this chapter, outlining its reaction to Alice and the wood.
Textual re-casting: write an article about the power of names in your life; names you've been given, both good and bad by your parents, family, friends, school teachers etc.
Devise a flow-chart/spider diagram/storyboard of the major events of the chapter.
Write down in your responses to the characters and situations in the chapter, noting down your thoughts and feelings about the various things that happen. What do you think will happen next?
What reading strategies are you using to help you enjoy the book? How could you improve your reading?

See Answers to the questions at the back to mark your own work.

4 Tweedledum And Tweedledee

Teaching points

Learning objectives: to develop students' knowledge of verbs, and dynamic verbs.
Starter activity: spider diagram what you know about verbs. What are verbs, why are they used, and what are their effects? Consider verbs you like and dislike: e.g. to run, to jump, to dance, to work, to worry. What is the effect of different sentence structures connected with verbs upon you? Consider, for example, how verbs affect you when they are structured in declarative sentences (a statement), interrogatives (a question) and imperative sentences (orders), e.g. the verb 'to work', 'I work' (declarative), 'are you working?' (interrogative), 'Work hard!' (imperative). How would you feel when people said these different sentences to you? What have you learnt about the effects of verbs and sentence structures by doing this exercise?
Main activities: read the chapter and highlight the interesting use of verbs in the chapter, particularly when Alice and the Tweedle twins use verbs. What are the effects of sentence structures upon the verbs used (declarative, interrogative, imperatives)?
If they have not done so already, students should explore and consider the points raised in the commentaries/discussion points as well as answering the questions at the end of the chapter as best they can.
Extension: do some research about the role verbs play in your life, are there particular verbs you really like or dislike? Why? Are there sentence structures that you say to yourself and other people which affect you a great

deal, such as 'work', 'understand', 'go'.

Plenary: What have you learnt about verbs?

The text

They were standing under a tree, each with an arm round the other's neck, and Alice knew which was which in a moment, because one of them had 'DUM' embroidered on his collar, and the other 'DEE.' 'I suppose they've each got "TWEEDLE" round at the back of the collar,' she said to herself.

They stood so still that she quite forgot they were alive, and she was just looking round to see if the word "TWEEDLE" was written at the back of each collar, when she was startled by a voice coming from the one marked 'DUM.'

'If you think we're wax-works,' he said, 'you ought to pay, you know. Wax-works weren't made to be looked at for nothing, nohow!'

'Contrariwise,' added the one marked 'DEE,' 'if you think we're alive, you ought to speak.'

'I'm sure I'm very sorry,' was all Alice could say; for the words of the old song kept ringing through her head like the ticking of a clock, and she could hardly help saying them out loud:—

> '*Tweedledum and Tweedledee*
> *Agreed to have a battle;*
> *For Tweedledum said Tweedledee*
> *Had spoiled his nice new rattle.*
>
> *Just then flew down a monstrous crow,*
> *As black as a tar-barrel;*
> *Which frightened both the heroes so,*
> *They quite forgot their quarrel.*'

Commentary: In the 1720s, there was a terrible rivalry between the composers Handel and Battista. John Byrom wrote a poem about it:

> *Some say, compared to Bononcini*
> *That Mynheer Handel's but a ninny;*
> *Other aver that he to Handel*
> *Is scarcely fit to hold a candle;*
> *Strange all this difference should be*
> *Twixt tweedled-dum and tweedled-dee.*

Discussion point: why do rivalries seem funny to outsiders but not to the rivals themselves? Can you think of any examples of famous rivalries between very similar people, e.g. sportspeople? Why do similar people hate each other especially?

'I know what you're thinking about,' said Tweedledum: 'but it isn't so, nohow.'

'Contrariwise,' continued Tweedledee, 'if it was so, it might be; and if it were so, it would be; but as it isn't, it ain't. That's logic.'

'I was thinking,' Alice said very politely, 'which is the best way out of this wood: it's getting so dark. Would you tell me, please?'

But the little men only looked at each other and grinned.

They looked so exactly like a couple of great schoolboys, that Alice couldn't help pointing her finger at Tweedledum, and saying 'First Boy!'

'Nohow!' Tweedledum cried out briskly, and shut his mouth up again with a snap.

'Next Boy!' said Alice, passing on to Tweedledee, though she felt quite certain he would only shout out 'Contrariwise!' and so he did.

'You've been wrong!' cried Tweedledum. 'The first thing in a visit is to say "How d'ye do?" and shake hands!' And here the two brothers gave each other a hug, and then they held out the two hands that were free, to shake hands with her.

> **Commentary:** Tweedledum and Tweedledee are what geometers call "enantiomorphs", mirror-image forms of each other. See Tenniel's pictures of them here: **https://en.wikipedia.org/wiki/Tweedledum_and_Tweedle dee**

> **Discussion point:** why do Carroll and John Tenniel, the first artist for the Alice books, make them enantiomorphs? What is the effect of this?

Alice did not like shaking hands with either of them first, for fear of hurting the other one's feelings; so, as the best way out of the difficulty, she took hold of both hands at once: the next moment they were dancing round in a ring. This seemed quite natural (she remembered afterwards), and she was not even surprised to hear music playing: it seemed to come from the tree under which they were dancing, and it was done (as well as she could make it out) by the branches rubbing one across the other, like fiddles and fiddle-sticks.

'But it certainly *was* funny,' (Alice said afterwards, when she was telling her sister the history of all this,) 'to find myself singing "*Here we go round the mulberry bush.*" I don't know when I began it, but somehow I felt as if I'd been singing it a long long time!'

The other two dancers were fat, and very soon out of breath. 'Four times round is enough for one dance,' Tweedledum panted out, and they left off dancing as suddenly as they had begun: the music stopped at the same moment.

Then they let go of Alice's hands, and stood looking at her for a minute: there was a rather awkward pause, as Alice didn't know how to begin a conversation with people she had just been dancing with. 'It would never do to say "How d'ye do?" *now*,' she said to herself: 'we seem to have got beyond that, somehow!'

'I hope you're not much tired?' she said at last.

'Nohow. And thank you *very* much for asking,' said Tweedledum.

'So *much* obliged!' added Tweedledee. 'You like poetry?'

'Ye-es, pretty well—*some* poetry,' Alice said doubtfully. 'Would you tell me which road leads out of the wood?'

'What shall I repeat to her?' said Tweedledee, looking round at Tweedledum with great solemn eyes, and not noticing Alice's question.

'"*The Walrus and the Carpenter*" is the longest,' Tweedledum replied, giving his brother an affectionate hug.

Tweedledee began instantly:

> *'The sun was shining—'*

Here Alice ventured to interrupt him. 'If it's *very* long,' she said, as politely as she could, 'would you please tell me first which road—'

Tweedledee smiled gently, and began again:

> *'The sun was shining on the sea,*
>   *Shining with all his might:*
> *He did his very best to make*
>   *The billows smooth and bright—*
> *And this was odd, because it was*
>   *The middle of the night.*
>
> *The moon was shining sulkily,*
>   *Because she thought the sun*
> *Had got no business to be there*
>   *After the day was done—*
> *"It's very rude of him," she said,*
>   *"To come and spoil the fun!"*
>
> *The sea was wet as wet could be,*
>   *The sands were dry as dry.*
> *You could not see a cloud, because*
>   *No cloud was in the sky:*
> *No birds were flying over head—*
>   *There were no birds to fly.*
>
> *The Walrus and the Carpenter*
>   *Were walking close at hand;*
> *They wept like anything to see*
>   *Such quantities of sand:*
> *"If this were only cleared away,"*
>   *They said, "it would be grand!"*
>
> *"If seven maids with seven mops*
>   *Swept it for half a year,*
> *Do you suppose," the Walrus said,*
>   *"That they could get it clear?"*

"I doubt it," said the Carpenter,
And shed a bitter tear.

"O Oysters, come and walk with us!"
The Walrus did beseech.
"A pleasant walk, a pleasant talk,
Along the briny beach:
We cannot do with more than four,
To give a hand to each."

The eldest Oyster looked at him.
But never a word he said:
The eldest Oyster winked his eye,
And shook his heavy head—
Meaning to say he did not choose
To leave the oyster-bed.

But four young oysters hurried up,
All eager for the treat:
Their coats were brushed, their faces washed,
Their shoes were clean and neat—
And this was odd, because, you know,
They hadn't any feet.

Four other Oysters followed them,
And yet another four;
And thick and fast they came at last,
And more, and more, and more—
All hopping through the frothy waves,
And scrambling to the shore.

The Walrus and the Carpenter
Walked on a mile or so,
And then they rested on a rock
Conveniently low:
And all the little Oysters stood
And waited in a row.

"The time has come," the Walrus said,
"To talk of many things:
Of shoes—and ships—and sealing-wax—
Of cabbages—and kings—
And why the sea is boiling hot—
And whether pigs have wings."

"But wait a bit," the Oysters cried,
"Before we have our chat;

For some of us are out of breath,
 And all of us are fat!"
"No hurry!" said the Carpenter.
 They thanked him much for that.

"A loaf of bread," the Walrus said,
 "Is what we chiefly need:
Pepper and vinegar besides
 Are very good indeed—
Now if you're ready Oysters dear,
 We can begin to feed."

"But not on us!" the Oysters cried,
 Turning a little blue,
"After such kindness, that would be
 A dismal thing to do!"
"The night is fine," the Walrus said
 "Do you admire the view?

"It was so kind of you to come!
 And you are very nice!"
The Carpenter said nothing but
 "Cut us another slice:
I wish you were not quite so deaf—
 I've had to ask you twice!"

"It seems a shame," the Walrus said,
 "To play them such a trick,
After we've brought them out so far,
 And made them trot so quick!"
The Carpenter said nothing but
 "The butter's spread too thick!"

"I weep for you," the Walrus said.
 "I deeply sympathize."
With sobs and tears he sorted out
 Those of the largest size.
Holding his pocket handkerchief
 Before his streaming eyes.

"O Oysters," said the Carpenter.
 "You've had a pleasant run!
Shall we be trotting home again?"
 But answer came there none—
And that was scarcely odd, because
 They'd eaten every one.'

Commentary: once again we see Carroll showing the brutal side of life in the way that the Walrus and the Carpenter treat the oysters.

Discussion point: How and why does Carroll show the cruel side of life in this poem? How does he generate comedy and pathos?

'I like the Walrus best,' said Alice: 'because you see he was a *little* sorry for the poor oysters.'

'He ate more than the Carpenter, though,' said Tweedledee. 'You see he held his handkerchief in front, so that the Carpenter couldn't count how many he took: contrariwise.'

'That was mean!' Alice said indignantly. 'Then I like the Carpenter best— if he didn't eat so many as the Walrus.'

'But he ate as many as he could get,' said Tweedledum.

This was a puzzler.

Commentary: Alice here faces the traditional ethical dilemma of having to judge someone in terms of what they have done (their acts) or what they are thinking (their intentions).

Discussion point: What do you think about this moral dilemma? Should we judge people's actions or their intentions?

After a pause, Alice began, 'Well! They were *both* very unpleasant characters—' Here she checked herself in some alarm, at hearing something that sounded to her like the puffing of a large steam-engine in the wood near them, though she feared it was more likely to be a wild beast. 'Are there any lions or tigers about here?' she asked timidly.

'It's only the Red King snoring,' said Tweedledee.

'Come and look at him!' the brothers cried, and they each took one of Alice's hands, and led her up to where the King was sleeping.

'Isn't he a *lovely* sight?' said Tweedledum.

Alice couldn't say honestly that he was. He had a tall red night-cap on, with a tassel, and he was lying crumpled up into a sort of untidy heap, and snoring loud—'fit to snore his head off!' as Tweedledum remarked.

'I'm afraid he'll catch cold with lying on the damp grass,' said Alice, who was a very thoughtful little girl.

'He's dreaming now,' said Tweedledee: 'and what do you think he's dreaming about?'

Alice said 'Nobody can guess that.'

'Why, about *you!*' Tweedledee exclaimed, clapping his hands triumphantly. 'And if he left off dreaming about you, where do you suppose you'd be?'

'Where I am now, of course,' said Alice.

'Not you!' Tweedledee retorted contemptuously. 'You'd be nowhere. Why, you're only a sort of thing in his dream!'

Commentary: Here the Red King's dream throws up a particularly important philosophical problem: how do we know we are not living in a dream? The Tweedle brothers defend the philosopher Bishop Berkeley's view that all material objects, including ourselves, are "sort of things" in the mind of God, i.e. we are living in God's "dream" if you like. Alice takes Samuel Johnson's view that you hurt your foot if you kick a large stone (Carroll L., Gardner M., 1990, p. 189).

Discussion point: what is reality? How do we know that we are not living in a dream? Do some research into this and hold a debate: **https://en.wikipedia.org/wiki/Dream_argument**

'If that there King was to wake,' added Tweedledum, 'you'd go out—bang!—just like a candle!'

'I shouldn't!' Alice exclaimed indignantly. 'Besides, if *I'm* only a sort of thing in his dream, what are *you*, I should like to know?'

'Ditto' said Tweedledum.

'Ditto, ditto' cried Tweedledee.

He shouted this so loud that Alice couldn't help saying, 'Hush! You'll be waking him, I'm afraid, if you make so much noise.'

'Well, it no use *your* talking about waking him,' said Tweedledum, 'when you're only one of the things in his dream. You know very well you're not real.'

'I *am* real!' said Alice and began to cry.

'You won't make yourself a bit realler by crying,' Tweedledee remarked: 'there's nothing to cry about.'

'If I wasn't real,' Alice said—half-laughing through her tears, it all seemed so ridiculous—'I shouldn't be able to cry.'

'I hope you don't suppose those are real tears?' Tweedledum interrupted in a tone of great contempt.

'I know they're talking nonsense,' Alice thought to herself: 'and it's foolish to cry about it.' So she brushed away her tears, and went on as cheerfully as she could. 'At any rate I'd better be getting out of the wood, for really it's coming on very dark. Do you think it's going to rain?'

Tweedledum spread a large umbrella over himself and his brother, and looked up into it. 'No, I don't think it is,' he said: 'at least—not under *here*. Nohow.'

'But it may rain *outside*?'

'It may—if it chooses,' said Tweedledee: 'we've no objection. Contrariwise.'

'Selfish things!' thought Alice, and she was just going to say 'Good-night' and leave them, when Tweedledum sprang out from under the umbrella and seized her by the wrist.

'Do you see *that*?' he said, in a voice choking with passion, and his eyes grew large and yellow all in a moment, as he pointed with a trembling finger at a small white thing lying under the tree.

'It's only a rattle,' Alice said, after a careful examination of the little white thing. 'Not a rattle-*snake*, you know,' she added hastily, thinking that he was frightened: 'only an old rattle—quite old and broken.'

'I knew it was!' cried Tweedledum, beginning to stamp about wildly and tear his hair. 'It's spoilt, of course!' Here he looked at Tweedledee, who immediately sat down on the ground, and tried to hide himself under the umbrella.

Alice laid her hand upon his arm, and said in a soothing tone, 'You needn't be so angry about an old rattle.'

'But it isn't old!' Tweedledum cried, in a greater fury than ever. 'It's new, I tell you—I bought it yesterday—my nice new RATTLE!' and his voice rose to a perfect scream.

All this time Tweedledee was trying his best to fold up the umbrella, with himself in it: which was such an extraordinary thing to do, that it quite took off Alice's attention from the angry brother. But he couldn't quite succeed, and it ended in his rolling over, bundled up in the umbrella, with only his head out: and there he lay, opening and shutting his mouth and his large eyes—'looking more like a fish than anything else,' Alice thought.

'Of course you agree to have a battle?' Tweedledum said in a calmer tone.

'I suppose so,' the other sulkily replied, as he crawled out of the umbrella: 'only *she* must help us to dress up, you know.'

So the two brothers went off hand-in-hand into the wood, and returned in a minute with their arms full of things—such as bolsters, blankets, hearth-rugs, table-cloths, dish-covers and coal-scuttles. 'I hope you're a good hand at pinning and tying strings?' Tweedledum remarked. 'Every one of these things has got to go on, somehow or other.'

Alice said afterwards she had never seen such a fuss made about anything in all her life—the way those two bustled about—and the quantity of things they put on—and the trouble they gave her in tying strings and fastening buttons—'Really they'll be more like bundles of old clothes than anything else, by the time they're ready!' she said to herself, as she arranged a bolster round the neck of Tweedledee, 'to keep his head from being cut off,' as he said.

'You know,' he added very gravely, 'it's one of the most serious things that can possibly happen to one in a battle—to get one's head cut off.'

Alice laughed aloud: but she managed to turn it into a cough, for fear of hurting his feelings.

'Do I look very pale?' said Tweedledum, coming up to have his helmet tied on. (He *called* it a helmet, though it certainly looked much more like a saucepan.)

'Well—yes—a *little*,' Alice replied gently.

'I'm very brave generally,' he went on in a low voice: 'only to-day I happen to have a headache.'

'And *I've* got a toothache!' said Tweedledee, who had overheard the remark. 'I'm far worse off than you!'

'Then you'd better not fight to-day,' said Alice, thinking it a good opportunity to make peace.

'We *must* have a bit of a fight, but I don't care about going on long,' said Tweedledum. 'What's the time now?'

Tweedledee looked at his watch, and said 'Half-past four.'

'Let's fight till six, and then have dinner,' said Tweedledum.

'Very well,' the other said, rather sadly: 'and *she* can watch us—only you'd better not come *very* close,' he added: 'I generally hit everything I can see—

when I get really excited.'

'And *I* hit everything within reach,' cried Tweedledum, 'whether I can see it or not!'

Alice laughed. 'You must hit the *trees* pretty often, I should think,' she said.

Tweedledum looked round him with a satisfied smile. 'I don't suppose,' he said, 'there'll be a tree left standing, for ever so far round, by the time we've finished!'

'And all about a rattle!' said Alice, still hoping to make them a *little* ashamed of fighting for such a trifle.

'I shouldn't have minded it so much,' said Tweedledum, 'if it hadn't been a new one.'

'I wish the monstrous crow would come!' thought Alice.

'There's only one sword, you know,' Tweedledum said to his brother: 'but you can have the umbrella—it's quite as sharp. Only we must begin quick. It's getting as dark as it can.'

'And darker,' said Tweedledee.

It was getting dark so suddenly that Alice thought there must be a thunderstorm coming on. 'What a thick black cloud that is!' she said. 'And how fast it comes! Why, I do believe it's got wings!'

'It's the crow!' Tweedledum cried out in a shrill voice of alarm: and the two brothers took to their heels and were out of sight in a moment.

Alice ran a little way into the wood, and stopped under a large tree. 'It can never get at me *here*,' she thought: 'it's far too large to squeeze itself in among the trees. But I wish it wouldn't flap its wings so—it makes quite a hurricane in the wood—here's somebody's shawl being blown away!'

> **Commentary:** One critic argues that the crow represents an eclipse, when the moon covers the sun, which superstitions say suggest the end of the world. In other myths, crows represent the messengers of doom. They are generally gloomy animals.

> **Discussion point:** what does the crow represent at the end of this chapter do you think? Do some research into crows and write an article about them: **https://en.wikipedia.org/wiki/Corvus**

Questions/tasks

In your Learning Journal answer these questions and complete these activities:

How do Tweedledee and Tweedledum stand?

What does Alice's poem about them describe?

What is their response to Alice's questions about how to get out of the wood?

What is the poem "The Walrus and the Carpenter" about?

Who does Alice prefer in the poem and why? How are her opinions challenged?

Who does Alice see sleeping under a tree and what does Tweedledee say about him?

What do the twins fight over and how are they distracted?

Analytical question: how does Carroll create both humour and menace in this chapter?

Creative Response: write the twins' diaries for this chapter.

Textual re-casting: write a poem about how we might all be living in someone else's dream.

Devise a flow-chart/spider diagram/storyboard of the major events of the chapter.

Write down in your responses to the characters and situations in the chapter, noting down your thoughts and feelings about the various things that happen. What do you think will happen next?

What reading strategies are you using to help you enjoy the book? How could you improve your reading?

See Answers to the questions at the back to mark your own work.

5 Wool and Water

Teaching points

Learning objectives: to develop students' knowledge of adjectives, and emotive adjectives.

Starter activity: spider diagram what you know about adjectives. What are adjectives, why are they used, and what are their effects? Consider adjectives you like and dislike: e.g. good, brilliant, nice, smelly, generous, chocolatey. Explore and discuss particularly emotive adjectives in your life such as adjectives like "stupid", "lazy", "clever". Why are these adjectives so emotive and powerful?

Main activities: read the chapter and highlight the interesting use of adjectives in the chapter, such as "untidy", "dark", "crooked", "lovely". Why are these such important adjectives in the chapter and what do these adjectives make you think, feel and see?

If they have not done so already, students should explore and consider the points raised in the commentaries/discussion points as well as answering the questions at the end of the chapter as best they can.

Extension (very difficult one!): The chapter contains a strange incident where time is reversed (the Queen's finger hurts before she pricks it); how is language used to create a sense of time happening in reverse? Consider the use of adjectives and other word classes when analysing this.

Extension: do some research about the role verbs play in your life, are there particular verbs you really like or dislike? Why? Are there sentence structures that you say to yourself and other people which affect you a great deal, such as 'work', 'understand', 'go'.

Plenary: What have you learnt about adjectives?

The text

She caught the shawl as she spoke, and looked about for the owner: in another moment the White Queen came running wildly through the wood, with both arms stretched out wide, as if she were flying, and Alice very civilly went to meet her with the shawl.

> **Commentary:** By running wildly to QB4 (the chess board place), the White Queen arrives on the square directly west of Alice; this copies the way the Queen chess piece behaves. The Queen is careless and does not realise that she could checkmate the Red King by moving to K3. In his article "Alice on Stage", Carroll writes that the Queen is "gentle, fat and pale; helpless as an infant; and with a slow, maundering, bewildered air about her just suggesting imbecility, but never quite passing into it..." (Carroll L., Gardner M., 1990, p. 194).

> **Discussion point:** what do you think of the character of the White Queen? How are queens and women generally represented in Carroll's work?

'I'm very glad I happened to be in the way,' Alice said, as she helped her to put on her shawl again.

The White Queen only looked at her in a helpless frightened sort of way, and kept repeating something in a whisper to herself that sounded like 'bread-and-butter, bread-and-butter,' and Alice felt that if there was to be any conversation at all, she must manage it herself. So she began rather timidly: 'Am I addressing the White Queen?'

> **Commentary:** "Bread and butter, bread and butter" was a phrase used in Victorian times to ward off bees (Carroll L., Gardner M., 1990, p. 195).

> **Discussion point:** How does Carroll generate humour here?

'Well, yes, if you call that a-dressing,' The Queen said. 'It isn't *my* notion of the thing, at all.'

Alice thought it would never do to have an argument at the very beginning of their conversation, so she smiled and said, 'If your Majesty will only tell me the right way to begin, I'll do it as well as I can.'

'But I don't want it done at all!' groaned the poor Queen. 'I've been a-dressing myself for the last two hours.'

It would have been all the better, as it seemed to Alice, if she had got some one else to dress her, she was so dreadfully untidy. 'Every single thing's crooked,' Alice thought to herself, 'and she's all over pins!—may I put your shawl straight for you?' she added aloud.

'I don't know what's the matter with it!' the Queen said, in a melancholy voice. 'It's out of temper, I think. I've pinned it here, and I've pinned it there, but there's no pleasing it!'

'It *can't* go straight, you know, if you pin it all on one side,' Alice said, as she gently put it right for her; 'and, dear me, what a state your hair is in!'

'The brush has got entangled in it!' the Queen said with a sigh. 'And I lost the comb yesterday.'

Alice carefully released the brush, and did her best to get the hair into order. 'Come, you look rather better now!' she said, after altering most of the pins. 'But really you should have a lady's maid!'

'I'm sure I'll take you with pleasure!' the Queen said. 'Twopence a week, and jam every other day.'

Alice couldn't help laughing, as she said, 'I don't want you to hire *me*— and I don't care for jam.'

'It's very good jam,' said the Queen.

'Well, I don't want any *to-day*, at any rate.'

'You couldn't have it if you *did* want it,' the Queen said. 'The rule is, jam to-morrow and jam yesterday—but never jam to-day.'

'It *must* come sometimes to "jam to-day,"' Alice objected.

'No, it can't,' said the Queen. 'It's jam every *other* day: to-day isn't any *other* day, you know.'

'I don't understand you,' said Alice. 'It's dreadfully confusing!'

'That's the effect of living backwards,' the Queen said kindly: 'it always makes one a little giddy at first—'

'Living backwards!' Alice repeated in great astonishment. 'I never heard of such a thing!'

'—but there's one great advantage in it, that one's memory works both ways.'

'I'm sure *mine* only works one way,' Alice remarked. 'I can't remember things before they happen.'

'It's a poor sort of memory that only works backwards,' the Queen remarked.

'What sort of things do *you* remember best?' Alice ventured to ask.

'Oh, things that happened the week after next,' the Queen replied in a careless tone. 'For instance, now,' she went on, sticking a large piece of plaster [band-aid] on her finger as she spoke, 'there's the King's Messenger.

> **Commentary:** the King's Messenger, as the illustrations by Tenniel make clear, is the Mad Hatter, who is being punished for a crime he has yet to commit because in the Mirror world time goes both ways (Carroll L., Gardner M., 1990, p. 199).

> **Discussion point:** why is the King's Messenger the Hatter? Why is he being punished? What would happen is time went both ways in our world?

He's in prison now, being punished: and the trial doesn't even begin till next Wednesday: and of course the crime comes last of all.'

'Suppose he never commits the crime?' said Alice.

'That would be all the better, wouldn't it?' the Queen said, as she bound the plaster round her finger with a bit of ribbon.

Alice felt there was no denying *that*. 'Of course it would be all the better,' she said: 'but it wouldn't be all the better his being punished.'

'You're wrong *there*, at any rate,' said the Queen: 'were *you* ever punished?'

'Only for faults,' said Alice.

'And you were all the better for it, I know!' the Queen said triumphantly.

'Yes, but then I *had* done the things I was punished for,' said Alice: 'that makes all the difference.'

'But if you *hadn't* done them,' the Queen said, 'that would have been better still; better, and better, and better!' Her voice went higher with each 'better,' till it got quite to a squeak at last.

Alice was just beginning to say 'There's a mistake somewhere—,' when the Queen began screaming so loud that she had to leave the sentence unfinished. 'Oh, oh, oh!' shouted the Queen, shaking her hand about as if she wanted to shake it off. 'My finger's bleeding! Oh, oh, oh, oh!'

Her screams were so exactly like the whistle of a steam-engine, that Alice had to hold both her hands over her ears.

'What *is* the matter?' she said, as soon as there was a chance of making herself heard. 'Have you pricked your finger?'

'I haven't pricked it *yet*,' the Queen said, 'but I soon shall—oh, oh, oh!'

'When do you expect to do it?' Alice asked, feeling very much inclined to laugh.

'When I fasten my shawl again,' the poor Queen groaned out: 'the brooch will come undone directly. Oh, oh!' As she said the words the brooch flew open, and the Queen clutched wildly at it, and tried to clasp it again.

'Take care!' cried Alice. 'You're holding it all crooked!' And she caught at the brooch; but it was too late: the pin had slipped, and the Queen had pricked her finger.

'That accounts for the bleeding, you see,' she said to Alice with a smile. 'Now you understand the way things happen here.'

'But why don't you scream now?' Alice asked, holding her hands ready to put over her ears again.

'Why, I've done all the screaming already,' said the Queen. 'What would be the good of having it all over again?'

By this time it was getting light. 'The crow must have flown away, I think,' said Alice: 'I'm so glad it's gone. I thought it was the night coming on.'

'I wish *I* could manage to be glad!' the Queen said. 'Only I never can remember the rule. You must be very happy, living in this wood, and being glad whenever you like!'

'Only it is so *very* lonely here!' Alice said in a melancholy voice; and at the thought of her loneliness two large tears came rolling down her cheeks.

'Oh, don't go on like that!' cried the poor Queen, wringing her hands in despair. 'Consider what a great girl you are. Consider what a long way you've come to-day. Consider what o'clock it is. Consider anything, only don't cry!'

Alice could not help laughing at this, even in the midst of her tears. 'Can *you* keep from crying by considering things?' she asked.

'That's the way it's done,' the Queen said with great decision: 'nobody can do two things at once, you know. Let's consider your age to begin with—

how old are you?'

> **Commentary:** Carroll heeded this advice: he talks about working on maths problems in the night as a way not thinking naughty and wicked thoughts (Carroll L., Gardner M., 1990, p. 199).

> **Discussion point:** Do you think it is a good idea to distract yourself when you are having bad thoughts? How do you distract yourself if you are feeling "bad"?

'I'm seven and a half exactly.'

'You needn't say "exactually,"' the Queen remarked: 'I can believe it without that. Now I'll give *you* something to believe. I'm just one hundred and one, five months and a day.'

'I can't believe *that*!' said Alice.

'Can't you?' the Queen said in a pitying tone. 'Try again: draw a long breath, and shut your eyes.'

Alice laughed. 'There's no use trying,' she said: 'one *can't* believe impossible things.'

'I daresay you haven't had much practice,' said the Queen. 'When I was your age, I always did it for half-an-hour a day. Why, sometimes I've believed as many as six impossible things before breakfast. There goes the shawl again!'

The brooch had come undone as she spoke, and a sudden gust of wind blew the Queen's shawl across a little brook. The Queen spread out her arms again, and went flying after it, and this time she succeeded in catching it for herself. 'I've got it!' she cried in a triumphant tone. 'Now you shall see me pin it on again, all by myself!'

'Then I hope your finger is better now?' Alice said very politely, as she crossed the little brook after the Queen.

> **Commentary:** Alice moves one square to Q5 just as the Queen has just done.

> **Discussion point:** what is happening in the chess game at this point? How is Carroll generating tension and comedy here?

*   *   *   *   *   *   *

*   *   *   *   *   *

*   *   *   *   *   *   *

'Oh, much better!' cried the Queen, her voice rising to a squeak as she went on. 'Much be-etter! Be-etter! Be-e-e-etter! Be-e-ehh!' The last word ended in a long bleat, so like a sheep that Alice quite started.

She looked at the Queen, who seemed to have suddenly wrapped herself up in wool. Alice rubbed her eyes, and looked again. She couldn't make out what had happened at all. Was she in a shop? And was that really—was it really a *sheep* that was sitting on the other side of the counter? Rub as she could, she could make nothing more of it: she was in a little dark shop, leaning with her elbows on the counter, and opposite to her was an old

Sheep, sitting in an arm-chair knitting, and every now and then leaving off to look at her through a great pair of spectacles.

> **Commentary:** Tenniel's picture is a rendition of a real small grocery shop at 83 St. Aldate's Street, Oxford, but he reverses the shop because we are in the Mirror world. The shop is now called the Alice in Wonderland shop (Carroll L., Gardner M., 1990, p. 200). You can find the picture here: **https://en.wikipedia.org/wiki/Alice's_Shop#/media/File:J ohn_Tenniel_Alice_and_the_Knitting_Sheep.jpeg** and an article about the shop here: **https://en.wikipedia.org/wiki/Alice's_Shop**

> **Discussion point:** what role does the shop play in the story here?

'What is it you want to buy?' the Sheep said at last, looking up for a moment from her knitting.

'I don't *quite* know yet,' Alice said, very gently. 'I should like to look all round me first, if I might.'

'You may look in front of you, and on both sides, if you like,' said the Sheep: 'but you can't look *all* round you—unless you've got eyes at the back of your head.'

But these, as it happened, Alice had *not* got: so she contented herself with turning round, looking at the shelves as she came to them.

The shop seemed to be full of all manner of curious things—but the oddest part of it all was, that whenever she looked hard at any shelf, to make out exactly what it had on it, that particular shelf was always quite empty: though the others round it were crowded as full as they could hold.

'Things flow about so here!' she said at last in a plaintive tone, after she had spent a minute or so in vainly pursuing a large bright thing, that looked sometimes like a doll and sometimes like a work-box, and was always in the shelf next above the one she was looking at. 'And this one is the most provoking of all—but I'll tell you what—' she added, as a sudden thought struck her, 'I'll follow it up to the very top shelf of all. It'll puzzle it to go through the ceiling, I expect!'

But even this plan failed: the 'thing' went through the ceiling as quietly as possible, as if it were quite used to it.

'Are you a child or a teetotum **(a spinning top with numbers or letters on it indicating what a player should do in a game)**?' the Sheep said, as she took up another pair of needles. 'You'll make me giddy soon, if you go on turning round like that.' She was now working with fourteen pairs at once, and Alice couldn't help looking at her in great astonishment.

'How *can* she knit with so many?' the puzzled child thought to herself. 'She gets more and more like a porcupine every minute!'

'Can you row?' the Sheep asked, handing her a pair of knitting-needles as she spoke.

'Yes, a little—but not on land—and not with needles—' Alice was beginning to say, when suddenly the needles turned into oars in her hands, and she found they were in a little boat, gliding along between banks: so there was nothing for it but to do her best.

'Feather!' cried the Sheep, as she took up another pair of needles.

> **Commentary:** in the poem at the beginning of *Alice in Wonderland*, Alice is described as having little skill at rowing. The Sheep is asking Alice to turn her oar blades horizontally as she moves them back for the next "catch" so that the lower edge of the blade will not drag through the water (Carroll L., Gardner M., 1990, p. 202).

> **Discussion point:** what role do boats, rowing and water play in the stories?

This didn't sound like a remark that needed any answer, so Alice said nothing, but pulled away. There was something very queer about the water, she thought, as every now and then the oars got fast in it, and would hardly come out again.

'Feather! Feather!' the Sheep cried again, taking more needles. 'You'll be catching a crab directly.'

> **Commentary:** *Catching a crab* is rowing slang for a bad stroke in which the oar is dipped so deeply in the water that the boat's motion, if fast enough, can send the oar handle against the rower's chest with enough force to unseat him (Carroll L., Gardner M., 1990, p. 202).

> **Discussion point:** how is suspense generated here?

'A dear little crab!' thought Alice. 'I should like that.'

'Didn't you hear me say "Feather"?' the Sheep cried angrily, taking up quite a bunch of needles.

'Indeed I did,' said Alice: 'you've said it very often—and very loud. Please, where *are* the crabs?'

'In the water, of course!' said the Sheep, sticking some of the needles into her hair, as her hands were full. 'Feather, I say!'

'*Why* do you say "feather" so often?' Alice asked at last, rather vexed. 'I'm not a bird!'

'You are,' said the Sheep: 'you're a little goose.'

This offended Alice a little, so there was no more conversation for a minute or two, while the boat glided gently on, sometimes among beds of weeds (which made the oars stick fast in the water, worse then ever), and sometimes under trees, but always with the same tall river-banks frowning over their heads.

'Oh, please! There are some scented rushes!' Alice cried in a sudden transport of delight. 'There really are—and *such* beauties!'

'You needn't say "please" to *me* about 'em,' the Sheep said, without looking up from her knitting: 'I didn't put 'em there, and I'm not going to take 'em away.'

'No, but I meant—please, may we wait and pick some?' Alice pleaded. 'If you don't mind stopping the boat for a minute.'

'How am *I* to stop it?' said the Sheep. 'If you leave off rowing, it'll stop of itself.'

So the boat was left to drift down the stream as it would, till it glided gently in among the waving rushes. And then the little sleeves were carefully rolled up, and the little arms were plunged in elbow-deep to get the rushes a good long way down before breaking them off—and for a while Alice forgot all about the Sheep and the knitting, as she bent over the side of the boat, with just the ends of her tangled hair dipping into the water—while with bright eager eyes she caught at one bunch after another of the darling scented rushes.

'I only hope the boat won't tipple over!' she said to herself. 'Oh, *what* a lovely one! Only I couldn't quite reach it.' 'And it certainly *did* seem a little provoking ('almost as if it happened on purpose,' she thought) that, though she managed to pick plenty of beautiful rushes as the boat glided by, there was always a more lovely one that she couldn't reach.

'The prettiest are always further!' she said at last, with a sigh at the obstinacy of the rushes in growing so far off, as, with flushed cheeks and dripping hair and hands, she scrambled back into her place, and began to arrange her new-found treasures.

What mattered it to her just then that the rushes had begun to fade, and to lose all their scent and beauty, from the very moment that she picked them?

> **Commentary:** Gardner suggests that Carroll thought of these dream-rushes as symbols of child-friends (Carroll L., Gardner M., 1990, p. 204).

> **Discussion point:** what do the dream-rushes suggest in your mind?

Even real scented rushes, you know, last only a very little while—and these, being dream-rushes, melted away almost like snow, as they lay in heaps at her feet—but Alice hardly noticed this, there were so many other curious things to think about.

They hadn't gone much farther before the blade of one of the oars got fast in the water and *wouldn't* come out again (so Alice explained it afterwards), and the consequence was that the handle of it caught her under the chin, and, in spite of a series of little shrieks of 'Oh, oh, oh!' from poor Alice, it swept her straight off the seat, and down among the heap of rushes.

However, she wasn't hurt, and was soon up again: the Sheep went on with her knitting all the while, just as if nothing had happened. 'That was a nice crab you caught!' she remarked, as Alice got back into her place, very much relieved to find herself still in the boat.

'Was it? I didn't see it,' Said Alice, peeping cautiously over the side of the boat into the dark water. 'I wish it hadn't let go—I should so like to see a little crab to take home with me!' But the Sheep only laughed scornfully, and went on with her knitting.

'Are there many crabs here?' said Alice.

'Crabs, and all sorts of things,' said the Sheep: 'plenty of choice, only make up your mind. Now, what *do* you want to buy?'

'To buy!' Alice echoed in a tone that was half astonished and half frightened—for the oars, and the boat, and the river, had vanished all in a moment, and she was back again in the little dark shop.

'I should like to buy an egg, please,' she said timidly. 'How do you sell them?'

'Fivepence farthing for one—Twopence for two,' the Sheep replied.

'Then two are cheaper than one?' Alice said in a surprised tone, taking out her purse.

'Only you *must* eat them both, if you buy two,' said the Sheep.

'Then I'll have *one*, please,' said Alice, as she put the money down on the counter. For she thought to herself, 'They mightn't be at all nice, you know.'

The Sheep took the money, and put it away in a box: then she said 'I never put things into people's hands—that would never do—you must get it for yourself.' And so saying, she went off to the other end of the shop, and set the egg upright on a shelf.

> **Commentary:** Students at Oxford in Carroll's day often complained that if you ordered one boiled egg for breakfast you usually received two, one good, one bad. The Sheep's movement to the other end of the shop is shown on the chessboard by the move of the White Queen to KB8. The dots show that Alice has crossed the brook by advancing to Q6. She is now on the square to the right of the White King, although she does not meet him until after Humpty Dumpty.

> **Discussion point:** what common complaints do students have?

'I wonder *why* it wouldn't do?' thought Alice, as she groped her way among the tables and chairs, for the shop was very dark towards the end. 'The egg seems to get further away the more I walk towards it. Let me see, is this a chair? Why, it's got branches, I declare! How very odd to find trees growing here! And actually here's a little brook! Well, this is the very queerest shop I ever saw!'

$$* \quad * \quad * \quad * \quad * \quad * \quad *$$

$$* \quad * \quad * \quad * \quad * \quad *$$

$$* \quad * \quad * \quad * \quad * \quad * \quad *$$

So she went on, wondering more and more at every step, as everything turned into a tree the moment she came up to it, and she quite expected the egg to do the same.

Questions/tasks

In your Learning Journal answer these questions and complete these activities:

Who does Alice bump into and why?

What job does the White Queen offer her and what perks does it have?

What is going to happen to the King's Messenger according to the White

Queen?

What happens to the Queen when she crosses the brook?

Where does Alice suddenly find herself and what is odd about this place?

What activity does Alice do with the Sheep and where does she find herself again?

What does Alice pay for and why does this purchase pose a problem?

Analytical question: how does Carroll make the shop such a mysterious and magical place?

Creative response: write Alice's diary for this chapter and previous ones if necessary, outlining her thoughts and feelings about the characters and situations she has encountered.

Textual re-casting: write an advertisement for the shop.

Devise a flow-chart/spider diagram/storyboard of the major events of the chapter.

Write down in your responses to the characters and situations in the chapter, noting down your thoughts and feelings about the various things that happen. What do you think will happen next?

What reading strategies are you using to help you enjoy the book? How could you improve your reading?

See Answers to the questions at the back to mark your own work.

6 Humpty Dumpty

Teaching points

Learning objectives: to develop students' knowledge of interpretation and working out the meaning of things.

Starter activity: what texts and things do you find difficult to understand? Consider everything in your life from poems, to people, to long books, to TV shows, blogs, social media etc. What skills do you use to work out the meaning of things when you don't understand? E.g. asking other people to explain things, to guess the meanings of things and test out whether you're correct etc.

Main activities: read the chapter. What do you think of Humpty Dumpty's interpretation of "Jabberwocky"? Why is his interpretation ridiculous? What would be your interpretation of the poem?

If they have not done so already, students should explore and consider the points raised in the commentaries/discussion points as well as answering the questions at the end of the chapter as best they can.

Extension: write your own nonsense poem and then write a very serious interpretation of it.

Plenary: What have you learnt about interpreting things?

The text

However, the egg only got larger and larger, and more and more human: when she had come within a few yards of it, she saw that it had eyes and a nose and mouth; and when she had come close to it, she saw clearly that it was HUMPTY DUMPTY himself. 'It can't be anybody else!' she said to herself. 'I'm as certain of it, as if his name were written all over his face.'

It might have been written a hundred times, easily, on that enormous face. Humpty Dumpty was sitting with his legs crossed, like a Turk, on the top of a high wall—such a narrow one that Alice quite wondered how he could keep his balance—and, as his eyes were steadily fixed in the opposite direction, and he didn't take the least notice of her, she thought he must be a stuffed figure after all.

'And how exactly like an egg he is!' she said aloud, standing with her hands ready to catch him, for she was every moment expecting him to fall.

'It's *very* provoking,' Humpty Dumpty said after a long silence, looking away from Alice as he spoke, 'to be called an egg—*Very!*'

'I said you *looked* like an egg, Sir,' Alice gently explained. 'And some eggs are very pretty, you know' she added, hoping to turn her remark into a sort of a compliment.

'Some people,' said Humpty Dumpty, looking away from her as usual, 'have no more sense than a baby!'

Alice didn't know what to say to this: it wasn't at all like conversation, she thought, as he never said anything to *her*; in fact, his last remark was evidently addressed to a tree—so she stood and softly repeated to herself:—

> '*Humpty Dumpty sat on a wall:*
> *Humpty Dumpty had a great fall.*
> *All the King's horses and all the King's men*
> *Couldn't put Humpty Dumpty in his place again.*'

Commentary: The Humpty Dumpty episode, like the stories about the Jack of Hearts, the Tweedle twins, and the Lion and the Unicorn, take the ideas/characters from nursery rhymes and turn them on their heads.

Discussion point: how and why does Carroll play around with familiar nursery rhymes?

'That last line is much too long for the poetry,' she added, almost out loud, forgetting that Humpty Dumpty would hear her.

'Don't stand there chattering to yourself like that,' Humpty Dumpty said, looking at her for the first time, 'but tell me your name and your business.'

'My *name* is Alice, but—'

'It's a stupid enough name!' Humpty Dumpty interrupted impatiently. 'What does it mean?'

'*Must* a name mean something?' Alice asked doubtfully.

'Of course it must,' Humpty Dumpty said with a short laugh: '*my* name means the shape I am—and a good handsome shape it is, too. With a name like yours, you might be any shape, almost.'

'Why do you sit out here all alone?' said Alice, not wishing to begin an argument.

'Why, because there's nobody with me!' cried Humpty Dumpty. 'Did you think I didn't know the answer to *that*? Ask another.'

'Don't you think you'd be safer down on the ground?' Alice went on, not with any idea of making another riddle, but simply in her good-natured anxiety for the queer creature. 'That wall is so *very* narrow!'

'What tremendously easy riddles you ask!' Humpty Dumpty growled out. 'Of course I don't think so! Why, if ever I *did* fall off—which there's no chance of—but *if* I did—' Here he pursed his lips and looked so solemn and grand that Alice could hardly help laughing. '*If* I did fall,' he went on, '*The King has promised me—with his very own mouth—to—to—*'

'To send all his horses and all his men,' Alice interrupted, rather unwisely.

'Now I declare that's too bad!' Humpty Dumpty cried, breaking into a sudden passion. 'You've been listening at doors—and behind trees—and down chimneys—or you couldn't have known it!'

'I haven't, indeed!' Alice said very gently. 'It's in a book.'

'Ah, well! They may write such things in a *book*,' Humpty Dumpty said in a calmer tone. 'That's what you call a History of England, that is. Now, take a good look at me! I'm one that has spoken to a King, *I* am: mayhap you'll never see such another: and to show you I'm not proud, you may shake hands with me!'

> **Commentary:** Humpty Dumpty is very proud and suffers because "pride goeth before a fall". This is a typical example of "hubris": thinking too highly of yourself and thereby suffering as a result (Carroll L., Gardner M., 1990, p. 209).
>
> **Discussion point:** how does Carroll explore the theme of pride and hubris in the stories? Do some research into hubris in literature and life: **https://en.wikipedia.org/wiki/Hubris**

And he grinned almost from ear to ear, as he leant forwards (and as nearly as possible fell off the wall in doing so) and offered Alice his hand. She watched him a little anxiously as she took it. 'If he smiled much more, the ends of his mouth might meet behind,' she thought: 'and then I don't know what would happen to his head! I'm afraid it would come off!'

'Yes, all his horses and all his men,' Humpty Dumpty went on. 'They'd pick me up again in a minute, *they* would! However, this conversation is going on a little too fast: let's go back to the last remark but one.'

'I'm afraid I can't quite remember it,' Alice said very politely.

'In that case we start fresh,' said Humpty Dumpty, 'and it's my turn to choose a subject—' ('He talks about it just as if it was a game!' thought Alice.) 'So here's a question for you. How old did you say you were?'

Alice made a short calculation, and said 'Seven years and six months.'

'Wrong!' Humpty Dumpty exclaimed triumphantly. 'You never said a word like it!'

'I though you meant "How old *are* you?"' Alice explained.

'If I'd meant that, I'd have said it,' said Humpty Dumpty.

Alice didn't want to begin another argument, so she said nothing.

'Seven years and six months!' Humpty Dumpty repeated thoughtfully. 'An uncomfortable sort of age. Now if you'd asked *my* advice, I'd have said "Leave off at seven"—but it's too late now.'

'I never ask advice about growing,' Alice said indignantly.

'Too proud?' the other inquired.

Alice felt even more indignant at this suggestion. 'I mean,' she said, 'that one can't help growing older.'

'*One* can't, perhaps,' said Humpty Dumpty, 'but *two* can. With proper assistance, you might have left off at seven.'

'What a beautiful belt you've got on!' Alice suddenly remarked.

(They had had quite enough of the subject of age, she thought: and if they really were to take turns in choosing subjects, it was her turn now.) 'At least,' she corrected herself on second thoughts, 'a beautiful cravat, I should have said—no, a belt, I mean—I beg your pardon!' she added in dismay, for Humpty Dumpty looked thoroughly offended, and she began to wish she hadn't chosen that subject. 'If I only knew,' she thought to herself, 'which was neck and which was waist!'

Evidently Humpty Dumpty was very angry, though he said nothing for a minute or two. When he *did* speak again, it was in a deep growl.

'It is a—*most*—*provoking*—thing,' he said at last, 'when a person doesn't know a cravat from a belt!'

'I know it's very ignorant of me,' Alice said, in so humble a tone that Humpty Dumpty relented.

'It's a cravat, child, and a beautiful one, as you say. It's a present from the White King and Queen. There now!'

'Is it really?' said Alice, quite pleased to find that she *had* chosen a good subject, after all.

'They gave it me,' Humpty Dumpty continued thoughtfully, as he crossed one knee over the other and clasped his hands round it, 'they gave it me—for an un-birthday present.'

'I beg your pardon?' Alice said with a puzzled air.

'I'm not offended,' said Humpty Dumpty.

'I mean, what *is* an un-birthday present?'

'A present given when it isn't your birthday, of course.'

Alice considered a little. 'I like birthday presents best,' she said at last.

'You don't know what you're talking about!' cried Humpty Dumpty. 'How many days are there in a year?'

'Three hundred and sixty-five,' said Alice.

'And how many birthdays have you?'

'One.'

'And if you take one from three hundred and sixty-five, what remains?'

'Three hundred and sixty-four, of course.'

Humpty Dumpty looked doubtful. 'I'd rather see that done on paper,' he said.

Commentary: Humpty Dumpty is a philologist. The dictionary says: "Philology is the study of language in written historical sources; it is a combination of literary criticism, history, and linguistics. It is more commonly defined as the study of literary texts and written records, the establishment of their authenticity and their original form, and the determination of their meaning." He is also a philosopher skilled in the study of language (Carroll L., Gardner M., 1990, p. 212).

Discussion point: what do you think about Humpty Dumpty's knowledge and points?

Alice couldn't help smiling as she took out her memorandum-book, and worked the sum for him:

$$365$$
$$1$$
$$364$$
_____

Humpty Dumpty took the book, and looked at it carefully. 'That seems to be done right—' he began.

'You're holding it upside down!' Alice interrupted.

'To be sure I was!' Humpty Dumpty said gaily, as she turned it round for him. 'I thought it looked a little queer. As I was saying, that *seems* to be done right—though I haven't time to look it over thoroughly just now—and that shows that there are three hundred and sixty-four days when you might get un-birthday presents—'

'Certainly,' said Alice.

'And only *one* for birthday presents, you know. There's glory for you!'

'I don't know what you mean by "glory,"' Alice said.

Humpty Dumpty smiled contemptuously. 'Of course you don't—till I tell you. I meant "there's a nice knock-down argument for you!"'

'But "glory" doesn't mean "a nice knock-down argument,"' Alice objected.

'When *I* use a word,' Humpty Dumpty said in rather a scornful tone, 'it means just what I choose it to mean—neither more nor less.'

'The question is,' said Alice, 'whether you *can* make words mean so many different things.'

'The question is,' said Humpty Dumpty, 'which is to be master—that's all.'

Commentary: Humpty Dumpty's point of view was known in the Middle Ages as nominalism, the idea that universal terms do not refer to objective existences but are nothing more than verbal utterances, words. William of Occam defended this view, as do some modern philosophers (Carroll L., Gardner M., 1990, p. 215).

Discussion point: what do you think of Humpty Dumpty's views on language? How does Carroll generate interest and tension in the narrative here? Do some research into nominalism: **https://en.wikipedia.org/wiki/Nominalism**

Alice was too much puzzled to say anything, so after a minute Humpty

Dumpty began again. 'They've a temper, some of them—particularly verbs, they're the proudest—adjectives you can do anything with, but not verbs—however, *I* can manage the whole lot of them! Impenetrability! That's what *I* say!'

'Would you tell me, please,' said Alice 'what that means?'

'Now you talk like a reasonable child,' said Humpty Dumpty, looking very much pleased. 'I meant by "impenetrability" that we've had enough of that subject, and it would be just as well if you'd mention what you mean to do next, as I suppose you don't mean to stop here all the rest of your life.'

'That's a great deal to make one word mean,' Alice said in a thoughtful tone.

'When I make a word do a lot of work like that,' said Humpty Dumpty, 'I always pay it extra.'

'Oh!' said Alice. She was too much puzzled to make any other remark.

'Ah, you should see 'em come round me of a Saturday night,' Humpty Dumpty went on, wagging his head gravely from side to side: 'for to get their wages, you know.'

(Alice didn't venture to ask what he paid them with; and so you see I can't tell *you*.)

'You seem very clever at explaining words, Sir,' said Alice. 'Would you kindly tell me the meaning of the poem called "Jabberwocky"?'

'Let's hear it,' said Humpty Dumpty. 'I can explain all the poems that were ever invented—and a good many that haven't been invented just yet.'

This sounded very hopeful, so Alice repeated the first verse:

> *'Twas brillig, and the slithy toves*
> *Did gyre and gimble in the wabe;*
> *All mimsy were the borogoves,*
> *And the mome raths outgrabe.*

'That's enough to begin with,' Humpty Dumpty interrupted: 'there are plenty of hard words there. "*Brillig*" means four o'clock in the afternoon—the time when you begin *broiling* things for dinner.'

'That'll do very well,' said Alice: 'and "*slithy*"?'

'Well, "*slithy*" means "lithe and slimy." "Lithe" is the same as "active." You see it's like a portmanteau—there are two meanings packed up into one word.'

'I see it now,' Alice remarked thoughtfully: 'and what are "*toves*"?'

'Well, "*toves*" are something like badgers—they're something like lizards—and they're something like corkscrews.'

'They must be very curious looking creatures.'

'They are that,' said Humpty Dumpty: 'also they make their nests under sun-dials—also they live on cheese.'

'And what's the "*gyre*" and to "*gimble*"?'

'To "*gyre*" is to go round and round like a gyroscope. To "*gimble*" is to make holes like a gimlet.'

'And "*the wabe*" is the grass-plot round a sun-dial, I suppose?' said Alice, surprised at her own ingenuity.

'Of course it is. It's called "*wabe*," you know, because it goes a long way before it, and a long way behind it—'

'And a long way beyond it on each side,' Alice added.

'Exactly so. Well, then, "*mimsy*" is "flimsy and miserable" (there's another portmanteau for you). And a "*borogove*" is a thin shabby-looking bird with its feathers sticking out all round—something like a live mop.'

'And then "*mome raths*"?' said Alice. 'I'm afraid I'm giving you a great deal of trouble.'

'Well, a "*rath*" is a sort of green pig: but "*mome*" I'm not certain about. I think it's short for "from home"—meaning that they'd lost their way, you know.'

'And what does "*outgrabe*" mean?'

'Well, "*outgrabing*" is something between bellowing and whistling, with a kind of sneeze in the middle: however, you'll hear it done, maybe—down in the wood yonder—and when you've once heard it you'll be *quite* content. Who's been repeating all that hard stuff to you?'

'I read it in a book,' said Alice. 'But I had some poetry repeated to me, much easier than that, by—Tweedledee, I think it was.'

'As to poetry, you know,' said Humpty Dumpty, stretching out one of his great hands, '*I* can repeat poetry as well as other folk, if it comes to that—'

'Oh, it needn't come to that!' Alice hastily said, hoping to keep him from beginning.

'The piece I'm going to repeat,' he went on without noticing her remark, 'was written entirely for your amusement.'

Alice felt that in that case she really *ought* to listen to it, so she sat down, and said 'Thank you' rather sadly.

> *'In winter, when the fields are white,*
> *I sing this song for your delight—*

only I don't sing it,' he added, as an explanation.

'I see you don't,' said Alice.

'If you can *see* whether I'm singing or not, you've sharper eyes than most.' Humpty Dumpty remarked severely. Alice was silent.

> *'In spring, when woods are getting green,*
> *I'll try and tell you what I mean.'*

'Thank you very much,' said Alice.

> *'In summer, when the days are long,*
> *Perhaps you'll understand the song:*
> *In autumn, when the leaves are brown,*
> *Take pen and ink, and write it down. '*

'I will, if I can remember it so long,' said Alice.

'You needn't go on making remarks like that,' Humpty Dumpty said: 'they're not sensible, and they put me out.'

> *I sent a message to the fish:*
> *I told them "This is what I wish."*
>
> *The little fishes of the sea,*
> *They sent an answer back to me.*
>
> *The little fishes' answer was*
> *"We cannot do it, Sir, because—"*

'I'm afraid I don't quite understand,' said Alice.
'It gets easier further on,' Humpty Dumpty replied.

> *I sent to them again to say*
> *"It will be better to obey."*
>
> *The fishes answered with a grin,*
> *"Why, what a temper you are in!"*
>
> *I told them once, I told them twice:*
> *They would not listen to advice.*
>
> *I took a kettle large and new,*
> *Fit for the deed I had to do.*
>
> *My heart went hop, my heart went thump;*
> *I filled the kettle at the pump.*
>
> *Then some one came to me and said,*
> *"The little fishes are in bed."*
>
> *I said to him, I said it plain,*
> *"Then you must wake them up again."*
>
> *I said it very loud and clear;*
> *I went and shouted in his ear.'*

Humpty Dumpty raised his voice almost to a scream as he repeated this verse, and Alice thought with a shudder, 'I wouldn't have been the messenger for *anything*!'

> *'But he was very stiff and proud;*
> *He said "You needn't shout so loud!"*
>
> *And he was very proud and stiff;*

He said "I'd go and wake them, if—"

I took a corkscrew from the shelf:
I went to wake them up myself.

And when I found the door was locked,
I pulled and pushed and kicked and knocked.

And when I found the door was shut,
I tried to turn the handle, but—'
There was a long pause.

Commentary: the poem may have been inspired by "Summer Days" by Mark Wilks Call:

> *In Summer, when the days were long,*
> *We walked together in the wood:*
> *Our heart was light, our step was strong;*
> *Sweet flutterings were there in our blood,*
> *In Summer, when the days were long.*
>
> *We strayed from morn till evening caine;*
> *We gathered flowers, and wove us crowns;*
> *We walked 'mid poppies red as flame;*
> *Or sat upon the yellow downs,*
> *And always wished our life the same.*
>
> *In Summer, when the days were long,*
> *We leaped the hedgerow, crossed the brook;*
> *And still her voice flowed forth in song,*
> *Or else she read some graceful book,*
> *In Summer, when the days were long.*
>
> *And then we sat beneath the trees,*
> *With shadows lessening in the noon;*
> *And, in the sunlight and the breeze,*
> *We feasted, many a gorgeous June,*
> *While larks were singing o'er the leas.*
>
> *In Summer, when the days were long,*
> *On dainty chicken, snow-white bread,*
> *We feasted, with no grace but song.*
> *We plucked wild strawberries, ripe and red,*
> *In Summer, when the days were long.*
>
> *We loved, and yet we knew it not;*
> *For loving seemed like breathing then.*
> *We found a heaven in every spot,*
> *Saw angels too, in all good men,*
> *And dreamed of God in grove and grot.*

In Summer, when the days are long,
Alone I wander, muse alone.
I see her not; but that old song
Under the fragrant wind is blown,
In Summer, when the days are long.

Alone I wander in the wood;
But one fair spirit hears my sighs;
And half I see, so glad and good,
The honest daylight of her eyes,
That charmed me under earlier skies.

In Summer, when the days are long,
I love her as we loved of old;
My heart is light, my step is strong;
For love brings back those hours of gold,
In Summer, when the days are long.

Discussion point: how and why was Carroll possibly influenced by this poem, do you think? Some critics have said that this is the worst poem in the *Alice* books, what do you think?

'Is that all?' Alice timidly asked.

'That's all,' said Humpty Dumpty. 'Good-bye.'

This was rather sudden, Alice thought: but, after such a *very* strong hint that she ought to be going, she felt that it would hardly be civil to stay. So she got up, and held out her hand. 'Good-bye, till we meet again!' she said as cheerfully as she could.

'I shouldn't know you again if we *did* meet,' Humpty Dumpty replied in a discontented tone, giving her one of his fingers to shake; 'you're so exactly like other people.'

'The face is what one goes by, generally,' Alice remarked in a thoughtful tone.

'That's just what I complain of,' said Humpty Dumpty. 'Your face is the same as everybody has—the two eyes, so—' (marking their places in the air with this thumb) 'nose in the middle, mouth under. It's always the same. Now if you had the two eyes on the same side of the nose, for instance—or the mouth at the top—that would be *some* help.'

'It wouldn't look nice,' Alice objected. But Humpty Dumpty only shut his eyes and said 'Wait till you've tried.'

Alice waited a minute to see if he would speak again, but as he never opened his eyes or took any further notice of her, she said 'Good-bye!' once more, and, getting no answer to this, she quietly walked away: but she couldn't help saying to herself as she went, 'Of all the unsatisfactory—' (she repeated this aloud, as it was a great comfort to have such a long word to say) 'of all the unsatisfactory people I *ever* met—' She never finished the sentence, for at this moment a heavy crash shook the forest from end to end.

Questions/tasks

In your Learning Journal answer these questions and complete these activities:

What does the egg grow into?
What does Humpty say about Alice's name and why?
How does Alice anger Humpty?
What is troubling about Humpty's conversation?
What is an un-birthday?
What poem does Humpty explain for Alice and how convincing his explanation?
How does Humpty's poem annoy Alice?
What noise does Alice hear in the wood?
Analytical question: how does Carroll make Humpty such a troubling and entertaining character?
Creative response: write Humpty's story, outlining his thoughts and feelings about Alice, and the things that happen in the nursery rhyme.
Textual re-casting: turn the Humpty Dumpty nursery rhyme into a news report.
Devise a flow-chart/spider diagram/storyboard of the major events of the chapter.
Write down in your responses to the characters and situations in the chapter, noting down your thoughts and feelings about the various things that happen. What do you think will happen next?
What reading strategies are you using to help you enjoy the book? How could you improve your reading?

See Answers to the questions at the back to mark your own work.

7 The Lion and the Unicorn

Teaching points

Learning objectives: to develop students' knowledge of why misunderstandings can be the source of very effective and sometimes funny stories.
Starter activity: spider diagram some misunderstandings in your own life; when have you been mistaken for someone else, when you have misunderstood an instruction, when you have found misunderstandings confusing, scary, funny etc. Think comedies where misunderstandings play a key role, e.g. a comic character is mistaken for someone important; Shakespeare's plays are full of these: **https://www.bl.uk/shakespeare/articles/an-introduction-to-shakespeares-comedy**
Think of serious stories where misunderstandings play a central role, e.g.

innocent people being wrongly accused of crime etc:
https://www.bl.uk/shakespeare/articles/misunderstanding-in-othello

Main activities: read the chapter, and note down how misunderstandings happen in the story and what effect they have. Why do you think Carroll was obsessed with misunderstandings? Consider other misunderstandings which are important in the *Alice* books; devise a poster which shows misunderstandings in the stories, and explains the effects they have.

If they have not done so already, students should explore and consider the points raised in the commentaries/discussion points as well as answering the questions at the end of the chapter as best they can.

Plenary: What have you learnt about misunderstandings in stories?

The text

The next moment soldiers came running through the wood, at first in twos and threes, then ten or twenty together, and at last in such crowds that they seemed to fill the whole forest. Alice got behind a tree, for fear of being run over, and watched them go by.

She thought that in all her life she had never seen soldiers so uncertain on their feet: they were always tripping over something or other, and whenever one went down, several more always fell over him, so that the ground was soon covered with little heaps of men.

Then came the horses. Having four feet, these managed rather better than the foot-soldiers: but even *they* stumbled now and then; and it seemed to be a regular rule that, whenever a horse stumbled the rider fell off instantly. The confusion got worse every moment, and Alice was very glad to get out of the wood into an open place, where she found the White King seated on the ground, busily writing in his memorandum-book.

'I've sent them all!' the King cried in a tone of delight, on seeing Alice. 'Did you happen to meet any soldiers, my dear, as you came through the wood?'

'Yes, I did,' said Alice: 'several thousand, I should think.'

'Four thousand two hundred and seven, that's the exact number,' the King said, referring to his book. 'I couldn't send all the horses, you know, because two of them are wanted in the game. And I haven't sent the two Messengers, either. They're both gone to the town. Just look along the road, and tell me if you can see either of them.'

'I see nobody on the road,' said Alice.

'I only wish *I* had such eyes,' the King remarked in a fretful tone. 'To be able to see Nobody! And at that distance, too! Why, it's as much as *I* can do to see real people, by this light!'

> **Commentary:** Lewis Carroll, like many mathematicians, treated "nothing", the number zero, as "something". Here we find the unexecuted Nobody walking along the road, and later we learn that Nobody walks slower or faster than the Messenger. As a character,

Nobody appears at the Mad Hatter's tea party when Alice said "Nobody asked your opinion" to the Mad Hatter. He appears again in Chapter 12 of *Alice in Wonderland* when the White Rabbit shows a letter in which the Knave of Hearts has written to "somebody", to which the King replies, "Unless it was written to nobody which isn't usual, you know" (Carroll L., Gardner M., 1990, p. 223). There is also famous incident in the story of Odysseus in which he tricks a one-eyed giant by saying he is "Nobody": **http://www.greekboston.com/culture/mythology/odysseus -tricked-polyphemus/**

Discussion point: what is the role of "nobody" in the Alice stories? Why is the idea of being a "nobody" so haunting and upsetting for some people?

All this was lost on Alice, who was still looking intently along the road, shading her eyes with one hand. 'I see somebody now!' she exclaimed at last. 'But he's coming very slowly—and what curious attitudes he goes into!' (For the messenger kept skipping up and down, and wriggling like an eel, as he came along, with his great hands spread out like fans on each side.)

'Not at all,' said the King. 'He's an Anglo-Saxon Messenger—and those are Anglo-Saxon **(English, but also the study of Old English, which was Anglo-Saxon)** attitudes. He only does them when he's happy. His name is Haigha.' (He pronounced it so as to rhyme with 'mayor.')

'I love my love with an H,' Alice couldn't help beginning, 'because he is Happy. I hate him with an H, because he is Hideous. I fed him with—with—with Ham-sandwiches and Hay. His name is Haigha, and he lives—'

'He lives on the Hill,' the King remarked simply, without the least idea that he was joining in the game, while Alice was still hesitating for the name of a town beginning with H. 'The other Messenger's called Hatta. I must have *two*, you know—to come and go. One to come, and one to go.'

Commentary: "Hatta" is the Mad Hatter again newly released from prison, who appears several times in the book in different guises. The other character, Haigha, is the March Hare. (Carroll L., Gardner M., 1990, p. 223) "I love my love with an A" was a popular word game in Victorian England. You can find out more here: **http://www.fresnostate.edu/folklore/ballads/BGMG667.ht ml**

Discussion point: what is the role of the Mad Hatter in the books? Why and how does he keep reappearing, do you think? Why and how does the March Hare keep reappearing as well?

'I beg your pardon?' said Alice.

'It isn't respectable to beg,' said the King.

'I only meant that I didn't understand,' said Alice. 'Why one to come and one to go?'

'Didn't I tell you?' the King repeated impatiently. 'I must have *two*—to fetch and carry. One to fetch, and one to carry.'

At this moment the Messenger arrived: he was far too much out of breath to say a word, and could only wave his hands about, and make the most fearful faces at the poor King.

'This young lady loves you with an H,' the King said, introducing Alice in the hope of turning off the Messenger's attention from himself—but it was no use—the Anglo-Saxon attitudes only got more extraordinary every moment, while the great eyes rolled wildly from side to side.

'You alarm me!' said the King. 'I feel faint—Give me a ham sandwich!'

On which the Messenger, to Alice's great amusement, opened a bag that hung round his neck, and handed a sandwich to the King, who devoured it greedily.

'Another sandwich!' said the King.

'There's nothing but hay left now,' the Messenger said, peeping into the bag.

'Hay, then,' the King murmured in a faint whisper.

Alice was glad to see that it revived him a good deal. 'There's nothing like eating hay when you're faint,' he remarked to her, as he munched away.

'I should think throwing cold water over you would be better,' Alice suggested: 'or some sal-volatile.'

'I didn't say there was nothing *better*,' the King replied. 'I said there was nothing *like* it.' Which Alice did not venture to deny.

> **Commentary:** taking phrases literally is something the characters behind the looking-glass do, and creates the humour in the books (Carroll L., Gardner M., 1990, p. 225).

> **Discussion point:** how does Carroll create humour in the books? Why is it funny when the characters take the phrases literally? Discuss what it means to be "literal-minded" and why this can be a problem in life. Some people on the autistic spectrum can struggle because of this. Do some research: **http://aspiewriter.com/2015/07/the-literal-minded-asd-child-taking-what-you-say-literally.html**

'Who did you pass on the road?' the King went on, holding out his hand to the Messenger for some more hay.

'Nobody,' said the Messenger.

'Quite right,' said the King: 'this young lady saw him too. So of course Nobody walks slower than you.'

'I do my best,' the Messenger said in a sulky tone. 'I'm sure nobody walks much faster than I do!'

'He can't do that,' said the King, 'or else he'd have been here first. However, now you've got your breath, you may tell us what's happened in the town.'

'I'll whisper it,' said the Messenger, putting his hands to his mouth in the shape of a trumpet, and stooping so as to get close to the King's ear. Alice was sorry for this, as she wanted to hear the news too. However, instead of whispering, he simply shouted at the top of his voice 'They're at it again!'

'Do you call *that* a whisper?' cried the poor King, jumping up and shaking himself. 'If you do such a thing again, I'll have you buttered! It went through and through my head like an earthquake!'

'It would have to be a very tiny earthquake!' thought Alice. 'Who are at it again?' she ventured to ask.

'Why the Lion and the Unicorn, of course,' said the King.

'Fighting for the crown?'

'Yes, to be sure,' said the King: 'and the best of the joke is, that it's *my* crown all the while! Let's run and see them.' And they trotted off, Alice repeating to herself, as she ran, the words of the old song:—

> *'The Lion and the Unicorn were fighting for the crown:*
> *The Lion beat the Unicorn all round the town.*
> *Some gave them white bread, some gave them brown;*
> *Some gave them plum-cake and drummed them out of town.'*

'Does—the one—that wins—get the crown?' she asked, as well as she could, for the run was putting her quite out of breath.

'Dear me, no!' said the King. 'What an idea!'

'Would you—be good enough,' Alice panted out, after running a little further, 'to stop a minute—just to get—one's breath again?'

'I'm *good* enough,' the King said, 'only I'm not strong enough. You see, a minute goes by so fearfully quick. You might as well try to stop a Bandersnatch!'

> **Commentary:** The rivalry between the Lion and the Unicorn goes back thousands of years. Some critics suggest that the Lion and the Unicorn incident is a satire on the rivalry between two very famous politicians Benjamin Disraeli and William Gladstone (Carroll L., Gardner M., 1990, p. 226), you read more about them at this BBC website:
> **http://www.bbc.co.uk/history/british/victorians/disraeli_ gladstone_01.shtml**
>
> **Discussion point:** why are the Lion and the Unicorn such terrible rivals? What is the effect of their rivalry here? Think about other people who are rivals in your own life and in stories. Do some research: https://famousrivalries.wordpress.com/. Why do rivalries create such great stories?

Notice also how the White King breaks the rules of the chess game by rushing to see the fight.

Alice had no more breath for talking, so they trotted on in silence, till they came in sight of a great crowd, in the middle of which the Lion and Unicorn were fighting. They were in such a cloud of dust, that at first Alice could not make out which was which: but she soon managed to distinguish the Unicorn by his horn.

They placed themselves close to where Hatta, the other messenger, was standing watching the fight, with a cup of tea in one hand and a piece of bread-and-butter in the other.

'He's only just out of prison, and he hadn't finished his tea when he was sent in,' Haigha whispered to Alice: 'and they only give them oyster-shells in there—so you see he's very hungry and thirsty. How are you, dear child?' he went on, putting his arm affectionately round Hatta's neck.

Hatta looked round and nodded, and went on with his bread and butter.

'Were you happy in prison, dear child?' said Haigha.

Hatta looked round once more, and this time a tear or two trickled down his cheek: but not a word would he say.

'Speak, can't you!' Haigha cried impatiently. But Hatta only munched away, and drank some more tea.

'Speak, won't you!' cried the King. 'How are they getting on with the fight?'

Hatta made a desperate effort, and swallowed a large piece of bread-and-butter. 'They're getting on very well,' he said in a choking voice: 'each of them has been down about eighty-seven times.'

'Then I suppose they'll soon bring the white bread and the brown?' Alice ventured to remark.

'It's waiting for 'em now,' said Hatta: 'this is a bit of it as I'm eating.'

There was a pause in the fight just then, and the Lion and the Unicorn sat down, panting, while the King called out 'Ten minutes allowed for refreshments!' Haigha and Hatta set to work at once, carrying rough trays of white and brown bread. Alice took a piece to taste, but it was *very* dry.

'I don't think they'll fight any more to-day,' the King said to Hatta: 'go and order the drums to begin.' And Hatta went bounding away like a grasshopper.

For a minute or two Alice stood silent, watching him. Suddenly she brightened up. 'Look, look!' she cried, pointing eagerly. 'There's the White Queen running across the country! She came flying out of the wood over yonder—How fast those Queens *can* run!'

> **Commentary:** the White Queen does not have to run; she could take the Knight, but he cannot take her. Thus, Carroll suggests her stupidity and panic (Carroll L., Gardner M., 1990, p. 228).

> **Discussion point:** how does Carroll generate comedy and drama here? Discuss the role "panic" plays in people's lives, considering your own life and other people's you know: have you seen people panic? Or worry for no reason? What happened in these situations? Why did the panic occur? What was the outcome of it?

'There's some enemy after her, no doubt,' the King said, without even looking round. 'That wood's full of them.'

'But aren't you going to run and help her?' Alice asked, very much surprised at his taking it so quietly.

'No use, no use!' said the King. 'She runs so fearfully quick. You might as well try to catch a Bandersnatch! But I'll make a memorandum about her, if you like—She's a dear good creature,' he repeated softly to himself, as he opened his memorandum-book. 'Do you spell "creature" with a double "e"?'

At this moment the Unicorn sauntered by them, with his hands in his pockets. 'I had the best of it this time?' he said to the King, just glancing at him as he passed.

'A little—a little,' the King replied, rather nervously. 'You shouldn't have run him through with your horn, you know.'

'It didn't hurt him,' the Unicorn said carelessly, and he was going on, when his eye happened to fall upon Alice: he turned round rather instantly, and stood for some time looking at her with an air of the deepest disgust.

'What—is—this?' he said at last.

'This is a child!' Haigha replied eagerly, coming in front of Alice to introduce her, and spreading out both his hands towards her in an Anglo-Saxon attitude. 'We only found it to-day. It's as large as life, and twice as natural!'

> **Commentary:** "As large as life and *quite* as natural!" was a common phrase in Carroll's time. Carroll put in the word "twice" to add humour.

> **Discussion point:** how does Carroll play around with well-worn phrases in the books and why does he do it?

'I always thought they were fabulous monsters!' said the Unicorn. 'Is it alive?'

'It can talk,' said Haigha, solemnly.

The Unicorn looked dreamily at Alice, and said 'Talk, child.'

Alice could not help her lips curling up into a smile as she began: 'Do you know, I always thought Unicorns were fabulous monsters, too! I never saw one alive before!'

'Well, now that we *have* seen each other,' said the Unicorn, 'if you'll believe in me, I'll believe in you. Is that a bargain?'

'Yes, if you like,' said Alice.

'Come, fetch out the plum-cake, old man!' the Unicorn went on, turning from her to the King. 'None of your brown bread for me!'

'Certainly—certainly!' the King muttered, and beckoned to Haigha. 'Open the bag!' he whispered. 'Quick! Not that one—that's full of hay!'

Haigha took a large cake out of the bag, and gave it to Alice to hold, while he got out a dish and carving-knife. How they all came out of it Alice couldn't guess. It was just like a conjuring-trick, she thought.

The Lion had joined them while this was going on: he looked very tired and sleepy, and his eyes were half shut. 'What's this!' he said, blinking lazily at Alice, and speaking in a deep hollow tone that sounded like the tolling of a great bell.

'Ah, what *is* it, now?' the Unicorn cried eagerly. 'You'll never guess! *I* couldn't.'

The Lion looked at Alice wearily. 'Are you animal—vegetable—or mineral?' he said, yawning at every other word.

'It's a fabulous monster!' the Unicorn cried out, before Alice could reply.

'Then hand round the plum-cake, Monster,' the Lion said, lying down and putting his chin on his paws. 'And sit down, both of you,' (to the King and the Unicorn): 'fair play with the cake, you know!'

The King was evidently very uncomfortable at having to sit down between the two great creatures; but there was no other place for him.

'What a fight we might have for the crown, *now!*' the Unicorn said, looking slyly up at the crown, which the poor King was nearly shaking off his head, he trembled so much.

'I should win easy,' said the Lion.

'I'm not so sure of that,' said the Unicorn.

'Why, I beat you all round the town, you chicken!' the Lion replied angrily, half getting up as he spoke.

Here the King interrupted, to prevent the quarrel going on: he was very nervous, and his voice quite quivered. 'All round the town?' he said. 'That's a good long way. Did you go by the old bridge, or the market-place? You get the best view by the old bridge.'

'I'm sure I don't know,' the Lion growled out as he lay down again. 'There was too much dust to see anything. What a time the Monster is, cutting up that cake!'

Alice had seated herself on the bank of a little brook, with the great dish on her knees, and was sawing away diligently with the knife. 'It's very provoking!' she said, in reply to the Lion (she was getting quite used to being called 'the Monster'). 'I've cut several slices already, but they always join on again!'

'You don't know how to manage Looking-glass cakes,' the Unicorn remarked. 'Hand it round first, and cut it afterwards.'

This sounded nonsense, but Alice very obediently got up, and carried the dish round, and the cake divided itself into three pieces as she did so. '*Now* cut it up,' said the Lion, as she returned to her place with the empty dish.

'I say, this isn't fair!' cried the Unicorn, as Alice sat with the knife in her hand, very much puzzled how to begin. 'The Monster has given the Lion twice as much as me!'

> **Commentary:** The idea of the "lion's share" comes from one of Aesop's fables in which a lion helps divide the spoils from a hunt by saying that he should have one-fourth because of his rank, another fourth for his greater bravery, a third quarter for his wife and children. As for the remaining fourth, anyone who wants to argue with him about it is free to do so (Carroll L., Gardner M., 1990, p. 231).

> **Discussion point:** how does Carroll play around with familiar fables in the books? Do some research into fables and consider why they are so popular as stories.

'She's kept none for herself, anyhow,' said the Lion. 'Do you like plum-cake, Monster?'

But before Alice could answer him, the drums began.

Where the noise came from, she couldn't make out: the air seemed full of it, and it rang through and through her head till she felt quite deafened. She started to her feet and sprang across the little brook in her terror,

*   *   *   *   *   *   *

*   *   *   *   *   *

*   *   *   *   *   *   *

and had just time to see the Lion and the Unicorn rise to their feet, with angry looks at being interrupted in their feast, before she dropped to her knees, and put her hands over her ears, vainly trying to shut out the dreadful uproar.

'If *that* doesn't "drum them out of town,"' she thought to herself, 'nothing ever will!'

Questions/tasks

In your Learning Journal answer these questions and complete these activities:

What characters does the King ask Alice about? Why does Alice's reply confuse the king?

What discussion do the King and Haigha (the March Hare) have about Nobody? Why is this funny?

What happens in Alice's rhyme about the Lion and the Unicorn?

Why does the White King believe it is pointless for Alice to follow the White Queen?

Who does the Unicorn think Alice is?

What causes Alice to run off in terror?

Analytical question: why and how does Carroll use nursery rhymes in the books?

Creative Response: write Alice's diary for this chapter, noting her reactions to the White King and the Lion and the Unicorn.

Textual re-casting: re-write the Lion and the Unicorn poem as a plan for a computer game or a storyboard for an action-comedy movie.

Devise a flow-chart/spider diagram/storyboard of the major events of the chapter.

Write down in your responses to the characters and situations in the chapter, noting down your thoughts and feelings about the various things that happen. What do you think will happen next?

What reading strategies are you using to help you enjoy the book? How could you improve your reading?

See Answers to the questions at the back to mark your own work.

8 'It's my own Invention'

Teaching points

Learning objectives: to develop students' knowledge of how authors create sympathetic characters.

Starter activity: consider what characters you find sympathetic in stories and why. What techniques do writers use to make their characters sympathetic? Consider what writers make their sympathetic characters do (e.g. rescue people), have done to them (e.g. being bullied/treated unfairly), how they describe them (the language they use to make them seem vivid and real) and how they make them "relatable" to their readership, consider how age/gender/ethnicity/religion/sexuality all play a role in making characters sympathetic. E.g. most children's books have children as the main characters to make their readership identify with them. However, many adult Hollywood films contain white male young characters as their "heroes" but actually their audience may well not be this age/gender/ethnicity/race etc. Why do Hollywood films and the mainstream media focus upon these sorts of characters as their main protagonists? Can you think of any "unusual" protagonists, e.g. disabled, gay, old etc? What is the effect of having them as main characters? Do they create more or less sympathy in the audience?

Main activities: read the chapter, noting down how Carroll makes both Alice and the White Knight sympathetic characters, then answer this question: "How and why does Carroll generate sympathy (or not) for the White Knight in this chapter?" Consider: what the White Knight does, how he is described, his dialogue, the comedy he generates, his responses to Alice, and his "long goodbye".

If they have not done so already, students should explore and consider the points raised in the commentaries/discussion points as well as answering the questions at the end of the chapter as best they can.

Plenary: What have you learnt about sympathetic characters?

The text

After a while the noise seemed gradually to die away, till all was dead silence, and Alice lifted up her head in some alarm. There was no one to be seen, and her first thought was that she must have been dreaming about the Lion and the Unicorn and those queer Anglo-Saxon Messengers. However, there was the great dish still lying at her feet, on which she had tried to cut the plum-cake, 'So I wasn't dreaming, after all,' she said to herself, 'unless—unless we're all part of the same dream. Only I do hope it's *my* dream, and not the Red King's! I don't like belonging to another person's dream,' she went on in a rather complaining tone: 'I've a great mind to go and wake him, and see what happens!'

At this moment her thoughts were interrupted by a loud shouting of 'Ahoy! Ahoy! Check!' and a Knight dressed in crimson armour came galloping down upon her, brandishing a great club. Just as he reached her, the horse stopped suddenly: 'You're my prisoner!' the Knight cried, as he tumbled off his horse.

Startled as she was, Alice was more frightened for him than for herself at the moment, and watched him with some anxiety as he mounted again. As soon as he was comfortably in the saddle, he began once more 'You're my—' but here another voice broke in 'Ahoy! Ahoy! Check!' and Alice looked round in some surprise for the new enemy.

This time it was a White Knight. He drew up at Alice's side, and tumbled off his horse just as the Red Knight had done: then he got on again, and the two Knights sat and looked at each other for some time without speaking. Alice looked from one to the other in some bewilderment.

> **Commentary:** The Red Knight moves to K2, a good move in a traditional chess game because he checks the White King and attacks the White Queen. The Queen will be lost unless the Red Knight can be removed from the board. The White Knight however checks his own King by landing on the square, but defeats the Red Knight by landing on his square. Many critics think that the White Knight represents Carroll himself, like the Knight he had shaggy hair, mild blue eyes and a kind and gentle face. Like the Knight he was fond of gadgets and a "great hand at inventing things". Only the White Knight seems to genuinely like Alice and he speaks to her politely. (Carroll L., Gardner M., 1990, p. 234-36).

> **Discussion point:** why might the White Knight represent Carroll? What role do the Knights play in the books? Look at Tenniel's picture of the White Knight on his horse: what objects on the horse relate to objects in the book. This is the picture: **http://www.alice-in-wonderland.net/wp-content/uploads/2book38.jpg**

'She's *my* prisoner, you know!' the Red Knight said at last.

'Yes, but then *I* came and rescued her!' the White Knight replied.

'Well, we must fight for her, then,' said the Red Knight, as he took up his helmet (which hung from the saddle, and was something the shape of a horse's head), and put it on.

'You will observe the Rules of Battle, of course?' the White Knight remarked, putting on his helmet too.

'I always do,' said the Red Knight, and they began banging away at each other with such fury that Alice got behind a tree to be out of the way of the blows.

'I wonder, now, what the Rules of Battle are,' she said to herself, as she watched the fight, timidly peeping out from her hiding-place: 'one Rule seems to be, that if one Knight hits the other, he knocks him off his horse, and if he misses, he tumbles off himself—and another Rule seems to be that they hold their clubs with their arms, as if they were Punch and Judy— What a noise they make when they tumble! Just like a whole set of fire-irons falling into the fender! And how quiet the horses are! They let them get on and off them just as if they were tables!'

Another Rule of Battle, that Alice had not noticed, seemed to be that they always fell on their heads, and the battle ended with their both falling off in this way, side by side: when they got up again, they shook hands, and then the Red Knight mounted and galloped off.

'It was a glorious victory, wasn't it?' said the White Knight, as he came up panting.

'I don't know,' Alice said doubtfully. 'I don't want to be anybody's prisoner. I want to be a Queen.'

'So you will, when you've crossed the next brook,' said the White Knight. 'I'll see you safe to the end of the wood—and then I must go back, you know. That's the end of my move.'

'Thank you very much,' said Alice. 'May I help you off with your helmet?' It was evidently more than he could manage by himself; however, she managed to shake him out of it at last.

'Now one can breathe more easily,' said the Knight, putting back his shaggy hair with both hands, and turning his gentle face and large mild eyes to Alice. She thought she had never seen such a strange-looking soldier in all her life.

He was dressed in tin armour, which seemed to fit him very badly, and he had a queer-shaped little deal box fastened across his shoulder, upside-down, and with the lid hanging open. Alice looked at it with great curiosity.

'I see you're admiring my little box.' the Knight said in a friendly tone. 'It's my own invention—to keep clothes and sandwiches in. You see I carry it upside-down, so that the rain can't get in.'

'But the things can get *out*,' Alice gently remarked. 'Do you know the lid's open?'

'I didn't know it,' the Knight said, a shade of vexation passing over his face. 'Then all the things must have fallen out! And the box is no use without them.' He unfastened it as he spoke, and was just going to throw it into the bushes, when a sudden thought seemed to strike him, and he hung it carefully on a tree. 'Can you guess why I did that?' he said to Alice.

Alice shook her head.

'In hopes some bees may make a nest in it—then I should get the honey.'

'But you've got a bee-hive—or something like one—fastened to the saddle,' said Alice.

'Yes, it's a very good bee-hive,' the Knight said in a discontented tone, 'one of the best kind. But not a single bee has come near it yet. And the other thing is a mouse-trap. I suppose the mice keep the bees out—or the bees keep the mice out, I don't know which.'

'I was wondering what the mouse-trap was for,' said Alice. 'It isn't very likely there would be any mice on the horse's back.'

'Not very likely, perhaps,' said the Knight: 'but if they *do* come, I don't choose to have them running all about.'

'You see,' he went on after a pause, 'it's as well to be provided for *everything*. That's the reason the horse has all those anklets round his feet.'

'But what are they for?' Alice asked in a tone of great curiosity.

'To guard against the bites of sharks,' the Knight replied. 'It's an invention of my own. And now help me on. I'll go with you to the end of the wood—What's the dish for?'

'It's meant for plum-cake,' said Alice.

'We'd better take it with us,' the Knight said. 'It'll come in handy if we find any plum-cake. Help me to get it into this bag.'

This took a very long time to manage, though Alice held the bag open very carefully, because the Knight was so *very* awkward in putting in the dish: the first two or three times that he tried he fell in himself instead. 'It's rather a tight fit, you see,' he said, as they got it in a last; 'There are so many candlesticks in the bag.' And he hung it to the saddle, which was already loaded with bunches of carrots, and fire-irons, and many other things.

'I hope you've got your hair well fastened on?' he continued, as they set off.

'Only in the usual way,' Alice said, smiling.

'That's hardly enough,' he said, anxiously. 'You see the wind is so *very* strong here. It's as strong as soup.'

'Have you invented a plan for keeping the hair from being blown off?' Alice enquired.

'Not yet,' said the Knight. 'But I've got a plan for keeping it from *falling* off.'

'I should like to hear it, very much.'

'First you take an upright stick,' said the Knight. 'Then you make your hair creep up it, like a fruit-tree. Now the reason hair falls off is because it hangs *down*—things never fall *upwards*, you know. It's a plan of my own invention. You may try it if you like.'

It didn't sound a comfortable plan, Alice thought, and for a few minutes she walked on in silence, puzzling over the idea, and every now and then stopping to help the poor Knight, who certainly was *not* a good rider.

Whenever the horse stopped (which it did very often), he fell off in front; and whenever it went on again (which it generally did rather suddenly), he fell off behind. Otherwise he kept on pretty well, except that he had a habit of now and then falling off sideways; and as he generally did this on the side on which Alice was walking, she soon found that it was the best plan not to walk *quite* close to the horse.

'I'm afraid you've not had much practice in riding,' she ventured to say, as she was helping him up from his fifth tumble.

The Knight looked very much surprised, and a little offended at the remark. 'What makes you say that?' he asked, as he scrambled back into the saddle, keeping hold of Alice's hair with one hand, to save himself from falling over on the other side.

'Because people don't fall off quite so often, when they've had much practice.'

'I've had plenty of practice,' the Knight said very gravely: 'plenty of practice!'

Alice could think of nothing better to say than 'Indeed?' but she said it as heartily as she could. They went on a little way in silence after this, the Knight with his eyes shut, muttering to himself, and Alice watching anxiously for the next tumble.

'The great art of riding,' the Knight suddenly began in a loud voice, waving his right arm as he spoke, 'is to keep—' Here the sentence ended as suddenly as it had begun, as the Knight fell heavily on the top of his head exactly in the path where Alice was walking. She was quite frightened this time, and said in an anxious tone, as she picked him up, 'I hope no bones are broken?'

'None to speak of,' the Knight said, as if he didn't mind breaking two or three of them. 'The great art of riding, as I was saying, is—to keep your balance properly. Like this, you know—'

He let go the bridle, and stretched out both his arms to show Alice what he meant, and this time he fell flat on his back, right under the horse's feet.

'Plenty of practice!' he went on repeating, all the time that Alice was getting him on his feet again. 'Plenty of practice!'

'It's too ridiculous!' cried Alice, losing all her patience this time. 'You ought to have a wooden horse on wheels, that you ought!'

'Does that kind go smoothly?' the Knight asked in a tone of great interest, clasping his arms round the horse's neck as he spoke, just in time to save himself from tumbling off again.

'Much more smoothly than a live horse,' Alice said, with a little scream of laughter, in spite of all she could do to prevent it.

'I'll get one,' the Knight said thoughtfully to himself. 'One or two— several.'

There was a short silence after this, and then the Knight went on again. 'I'm a great hand at inventing things. Now, I daresay you noticed, that last time you picked me up, that I was looking rather thoughtful?'

'You *were* a little grave,' said Alice.

'Well, just then I was inventing a new way of getting over a gate—would you like to hear it?'

'Very much indeed,' Alice said politely.

'I'll tell you how I came to think of it,' said the Knight. 'You see, I said to myself, "The only difficulty is with the feet: the *head* is high enough already." Now, first I put my head on the top of the gate—then I stand on my head—then the feet are high enough, you see—then I'm over, you see.'

'Yes, I suppose you'd be over when that was done,' Alice said thoughtfully: 'but don't you think it would be rather hard?'

'I haven't tried it yet,' the Knight said, gravely: 'so I can't tell for certain— but I'm afraid it *would* be a little hard.'

He looked so vexed at the idea, that Alice changed the subject hastily. 'What a curious helmet you've got!' she said cheerfully. 'Is that your invention too?'

The Knight looked down proudly at his helmet, which hung from the saddle. 'Yes,' he said, 'but I've invented a better one than that—like a sugar loaf **(in Carroll's day refined sugar was formed into cones called sugar loafs, cone-shaped hills/hats are also referred to as sugar loafs)**. When I used to wear it, if I fell off the horse, it always touched the ground directly. So I had a *very* little way to fall, you see—But there *was* the danger of falling *into* it, to be sure. That happened to me once—and the worst of it was, before I could get out again, the other White Knight came and put it on. He thought it was his own helmet.'

The knight looked so solemn about it that Alice did not dare to laugh. 'I'm afraid you must have hurt him,' she said in a trembling voice, 'being on the top of his head.'

'I had to kick him, of course,' the Knight said, very seriously. 'And then he took the helmet off again—but it took hours and hours to get me out. I was as fast as—as lightning, you know.'

'But that's a different kind of fastness,' Alice objected.

The Knight shook his head. 'It was all kinds of fastness with me, I can assure you!' he said. He raised his hands in some excitement as he said this, and instantly rolled out of the saddle, and fell headlong into a deep ditch.

Alice ran to the side of the ditch to look for him. She was rather startled by the fall, as for some time he had kept on very well, and she was afraid that he really *was* hurt this time. However, though she could see nothing but the soles of his feet, she was much relieved to hear that he was talking on in his usual tone. 'All kinds of fastness,' he repeated: 'but it was careless of him to put another man's helmet on—with the man in it, too.'

'How *can* you go on talking so quietly, head downwards?' Alice asked, as she dragged him out by the feet, and laid him in a heap on the bank.

The Knight looked surprised at the question. 'What does it matter where my body happens to be?' he said. 'My mind goes on working all the same. In fact, the more head downwards I am, the more I keep inventing new things.'

'Now the cleverest thing of the sort that I ever did,' he went on after a pause, 'was inventing a new pudding during the meat-course.'

'In time to have it cooked for the next course?' said Alice. 'Well, not the *next* course,' the Knight said in a slow thoughtful tone: 'no, certainly not the next *course.*'

'Then it would have to be the next day. I suppose you wouldn't have two pudding-courses in one dinner?'

'Well, not the *next* day,' the Knight repeated as before: 'not the next *day*. In fact,' he went on, holding his head down, and his voice getting lower and lower, 'I don't believe that pudding ever *was* cooked! In fact, I don't believe that pudding ever *will* be cooked! And yet it was a very clever pudding to invent.'

'What did you mean it to be made of?' Alice asked, hoping to cheer him up, for the poor Knight seemed quite low-spirited about it.

'It began with blotting paper,' the Knight answered with a groan.

'That wouldn't be very nice, I'm afraid—'

'Not very nice *alone*,' he interrupted, quite eagerly: 'but you've no idea what a difference it makes mixing it with other things—such as gunpowder and sealing-wax. And here I must leave you.' They had just come to the end of the wood.

Alice could only look puzzled: she was thinking of the pudding.

'You are sad,' the Knight said in an anxious tone: 'let me sing you a song to comfort you.'

'Is it very long?' Alice asked, for she had heard a good deal of poetry that day.

'It's long,' said the Knight, 'but very, *very* beautiful. Everybody that hears me sing it—either it brings the *tears* into their eyes, or else—'

'Or else what?' said Alice, for the Knight had made a sudden pause.

'Or else it doesn't, you know. The name of the song is called "*Haddocks' Eyes*."'

> **Commentary:** According to "two-valued logic", this would be called an example of the law of "excluded middle": a statement is either true or false, with no third alternative. Much of what follows would make sense to students of logic and semantics (Carroll L., Gardner M., 1990, p. 243). You can find out more about Carroll's interest in logic here: **https://www.bl.uk/collection-items/lewis-carrolls-the-game-of-logic**; there is more on inventions in the chapter here: **http://www.victorianweb.org/authors/carroll/ansay.html**

> **Discussion point:** how does Carroll use logic in the books? What effects does it create?

'Oh, that's the name of the song, is it?' Alice said, trying to feel interested.

'No, you don't understand,' the Knight said, looking a little vexed. 'That's what the name is *called*. The name really *is* "*The Aged Aged Man*."'

'Then I ought to have said "That's what the *song* is called"?' Alice corrected herself.

'No, you oughtn't: that's quite another thing! The *song* is called "*Ways and Means*": but that's only what it's *called*, you know!'

'Well, what *is* the song, then?' said Alice, who was by this time completely bewildered.

'I was coming to that,' the Knight said. 'The song really *is* "*A-sitting On A Gate*": and the tune's my own invention.'

So saying, he stopped his horse and let the reins fall on its neck: then, slowly beating time with one hand, and with a faint smile lighting up his gentle foolish face, as if he enjoyed the music of his song, he began.

Of all the strange things that Alice saw in her journey Through The Looking-Glass, this was the one that she always remembered most clearly. Years afterwards she could bring the whole scene back again, as if it had been only yesterday—the mild blue eyes and kindly smile of the Knight— the setting sun gleaming through his hair, and shining on his armour in a blaze of light that quite dazzled her—the horse quietly moving about, with the reins hanging loose on his neck, cropping the grass at her feet—and the black shadows of the forest behind—all this she took in like a picture, as, with one hand shading her eyes, she leant against a tree, watching the strange pair, and listening, in a half dream, to the melancholy music of the song.

'But the tune *isn't* his own invention,' she said to herself: 'it's "*I give thee all, I can no more*."' She stood and listened very attentively, but no tears came into her eyes.

> *I'll tell thee everything I can;*
> *There's little to relate.*
> *I saw an aged aged man,*
> *A-sitting on a gate.*

"Who are you, aged man?" I said,
 "and how is it you live?"
And his answer trickled through my head
Like water through a sieve.

He said "I look for butterflies
 That sleep among the wheat:
I make them into mutton-pies,
 And sell them in the street.
I sell them unto men," he said,
 "Who sail on stormy seas;
And that's the way I get my bread—
 A trifle, if you please."

But I was thinking of a plan
 To dye one's whiskers green,
And always use so large a fan
 That they could not be seen.
So, having no reply to give
 To what the old man said,
I cried, "Come, tell me how you live!"
 And thumped him on the head.

His accents mild took up the tale:
 He said "I go my ways,
And when I find a mountain-rill,
 I set it in a blaze;
And thence they make a stuff they call
 Rolands' Macassar Oil—
Yet twopence-halfpenny is all
 They give me for my toil."

But I was thinking of a way
 To feed oneself on batter,
And so go on from day to day
 Getting a little fatter.
I shook him well from side to side,
 Until his face was blue:
"Come, tell me how you live," I cried,
 "And what it is you do!"

He said "I hunt for haddocks' eyes
 Among the heather bright,
And work them into waistcoat-buttons
 In the silent night.
And these I do not sell for gold
 Or coin of silvery shine

But for a copper halfpenny,
And that will purchase nine.

"I sometimes dig for buttered rolls,
Or set limed twigs **(twigs smeared with bird lime to catch birds)** for crabs;
I sometimes search the grassy knolls
For wheels of Hansom-cabs **(Covered carriages with two wheels and a raised seat for the driver at the back)**.
And that's the way" (he gave a wink)
"By which I get my wealth—
And very gladly will I drink
Your Honour's noble health."

I heard him then, for I had just
Completed my design
To keep the Menai bridge (a bridge in Wales) from rust
By boiling it in wine.
I thanked him much for telling me
The way he got his wealth,
But chiefly for his wish that he
Might drink my noble health.

And now, if e'er by chance I put
My fingers into glue
Or madly squeeze a right-hand foot
Into a left-hand shoe **(an unlucky thing to do according to superstition)**,
Or if I drop upon my toe
A very heavy weight,
I weep, for it reminds me so,
Of that old man I used to know—

Whose look was mild, whose speech was slow,
Whose hair was whiter than the snow,
Whose face was very like a crow,
With eyes, like cinders, all aglow,
Who seemed distracted with his woe,
Who rocked his body to and fro,
And muttered mumblingly and low,
As if his mouth were full of dough,
Who snorted like a buffalo—
That summer evening, long ago,
A-sitting on a gate.'

Commentary: This poem, according to Carroll himself, is a parody of William Wordsworth's lyric poem 'Resolution and Independence'

which you can find here:
https://www.poetryfoundation.org/poems-and-poets/poems/detail/45545

> **Discussion point:** how and why does Carroll parody Wordsworth's poem?

As the Knight sang the last words of the ballad, he gathered up the reins, and turned his horse's head along the road by which they had come. 'You've only a few yards to go,' he said, 'down the hill and over that little brook, and then you'll be a Queen—But you'll stay and see me off first?' he added as Alice turned with an eager look in the direction to which he pointed. 'I shan't be long. You'll wait and wave your handkerchief when I get to that turn in the road? I think it'll encourage me, you see.'

'Of course I'll wait,' said Alice: 'and thank you very much for coming so far—and for the song—I liked it very much.'

'I hope so,' the Knight said doubtfully: 'but you didn't cry so much as I thought you would.'

So they shook hands, and then the Knight rode slowly away into the forest. 'It won't take long to see him *off*, I expect,' Alice said to herself, as she stood watching him. 'There he goes! Right on his head as usual! However, he gets on again pretty easily—that comes of having so many things hung round the horse—' So she went on talking to herself, as she watched the horse walking leisurely along the road, and the Knight tumbling off, first on one side and then on the other. After the fourth or fifth tumble he reached the turn, and then she waved her handkerchief to him, and waited till he was out of sight.

> **Commentary:** the White Knight has returned to KB5, the square he occupied before capturing the Red Knight. Because Knight's moves are L-shaped, his move is a "turn in the road". It is a sad episode because it represents, in a way, Carroll saying goodbye to Alice (Carroll L., Gardner M., 1990, p. 248).

> **Discussion point:** how and why is this a moving moment in the book?

'I hope it encouraged him,' she said, as she turned to run down the hill: 'and now for the last brook, and to be a Queen! How grand it sounds!' A very few steps brought her to the edge of the brook.

> **Commentary:** this is where Carroll originally intended the Wasp in a Wig episode to go. His illustrator, Tenniel, said he should leave it out. The whole episode can be read here: **http://www.alice-in-wonderland.net/resources/chapters-script/a-wasp-in-a-wig/**

> **Discussion point:** After reading the Wasp in a Wig, do you think it was a wise decision to leave the episode out?

'The Eighth Square at last!' she cried as she bounded across,

* * * * * * *

* * * * * *

* * * * * * *

and threw herself down to rest on a lawn as soft as moss, with little flower-beds dotted about it here and there. 'Oh, how glad I am to get here! And what *is* this on my head?' she exclaimed in a tone of dismay, as she put her hands up to something very heavy, and fitted tight all round her head.

'But how *can* it have got there without my knowing it?' she said to herself, as she lifted it off, and set it on her lap to make out what it could possibly be.

It was a golden crown.

> **Commentary:** Alice has leaped the last brook and is now on Q8, the last square of the queen's file. In chess, a pawn which reaches the end of the board can become any piece; most players choose the Queen, the most powerful character in a chess game (Carroll L., Gardner M., 1990, p. 249).

> **Discussion point:** how does Carroll create tension here? What is the effect of assuming a powerful role like being a Queen? Think of the effect that achieving a new role has upon people; consider "overnight celebrities", people who are suddenly promoted or win the lottery etc. Why do some people find it so difficult to assume a new role?

Questions/tasks

In your Learning Journal answer these questions and complete these activities:

What does Alice wonder as the drum beat dies down?
Who comes to Alice's rescue when the Red Knight puts her in "check"?
What news does the White Knight tell Alice?
What is odd about the White Knight and his horse?
How does Alice offend the White Knight?
What has the White Knight invented?
How does Alice say goodbye to the Knight? What is the mood here?
What happens when Alice jumps over the brook?
Analytical question: how does Carroll use the game of chess in the book? What effects are achieved by putting Alice in a chess game?
Creative Response: write your poem, story or play about life being a chess game.
Textual re-casting: re-write the Alice books as a set of instructions for a game.
Devise a flow-chart/spider diagram/storyboard of the major events of the chapter.
Write down in your responses to the characters and situations in the

chapter, noting down your thoughts and feelings about the various things that happen. What do you think will happen next?

What reading strategies are you using to help you enjoy the book? How could you improve your reading?

See Answers to the questions at the back to mark your own work.

9 Queen Alice

Teaching points

Learning objectives: to develop students' knowledge of what makes powerful characters in life and in stories.

Starter activity: who are the most powerful characters in your life? Why do they have so much power? How do they use that power? What is power? Who are the most powerful characters in stories you have read? How are powerful characters in stories similar and different to powerful characters in "real life"?

Main activities: read the chapter and consider how and why Carroll depicts powerful characters in it. Consider how he represents Alice now that she is a Queen: has she become a more powerful character? If so, why and how is she more powerful? Devise a visual organiser which shows the power that Alice gains and loses during both books; it could be in the form of a draft. Why is Alice continuously gaining and losing power in the stories? What authorial techniques does Carroll use to represent power?

If they have not done so already, students should explore and consider the points raised in the commentaries/discussion points as well as answering the questions at the end of the chapter as best they can.

Plenary: What have you learnt about power?

The text

'Well, this *is* grand!' said Alice. 'I never expected I should be a Queen so soon—and I'll tell you what it is, your majesty,' she went on in a severe tone (she was always rather fond of scolding herself), 'it'll never do for you to be lolling about on the grass like that! Queens have to be dignified, you know!'

So she got up and walked about—rather stiffly just at first, as she was afraid that the crown might come off: but she comforted herself with the thought that there was nobody to see her, 'and if I really am a Queen,' she said as she sat down again, 'I shall be able to manage it quite well in time.'

Everything was happening so oddly that she didn't feel a bit surprised at finding the Red Queen and the White Queen sitting close to her, one on each side: she would have liked very much to ask them how they came there, but she feared it would not be quite civil. However, there would be no harm, she thought, in asking if the game was over. 'Please, would you tell me—' she began, looking timidly at the Red Queen.

Commentary: The Red Queen has moved to the King's square so Alice now has a Queen on either side. The White King is placed in check by this move but does not notice it (Carroll L., Gardner M., 1990, p. 250).

Discussion point: how is Carroll building to an unexpected climax here?

'Speak when you're spoken to!' The Queen sharply interrupted her.

'But if everybody obeyed that rule,' said Alice, who was always ready for a little argument, 'and if you only spoke when you were spoken to, and the other person always waited for *you* to begin, you see nobody would ever say anything, so that—'

'Ridiculous!' cried the Queen. 'Why, don't you see, child—' here she broke off with a frown, and, after thinking for a minute, suddenly changed the subject of the conversation. 'What do you mean by "If you really are a Queen"? What right have you to call yourself so? You can't be a Queen, you know, till you've passed the proper examination. And the sooner we begin it, the better.'

'I only said "if"!' poor Alice pleaded in a piteous tone.

The two Queens looked at each other, and the Red Queen remarked, with a little shudder, 'She *says* she only said "if"—'

'But she said a great deal more than that!' the White Queen moaned, wringing her hands. 'Oh, ever so much more than that!'

'So you did, you know,' the Red Queen said to Alice. 'Always speak the truth—think before you speak—and write it down afterwards.'

'I'm sure I didn't mean—' Alice was beginning, but the Red Queen interrupted her impatiently.

'That's just what I complain of! You *should* have meant! What do you suppose is the use of child without any meaning? Even a joke should have some meaning—and a child's more important than a joke, I hope. You couldn't deny that, even if you tried with both hands.'

'I don't deny things with my *hands*,' Alice objected.

'Nobody said you did,' said the Red Queen. 'I said you couldn't if you tried.'

'She's in that state of mind,' said the White Queen, 'that she wants to deny *something*—only she doesn't know what to deny!'

'A nasty, vicious temper,' the Red Queen remarked; and then there was an uncomfortable silence for a minute or two.

The Red Queen broke the silence by saying to the White Queen, 'I invite you to Alice's dinner-party this afternoon.'

The White Queen smiled feebly, and said 'And I invite *you*.'

'I didn't know I was to have a party at all,' said Alice; 'but if there is to be one, I think *I* ought to invite the guests.'

'We gave you the opportunity of doing it,' the Red Queen remarked: 'but I daresay you've not had many lessons in manners yet?'

'Manners are not taught in lessons,' said Alice. 'Lessons teach you to do sums, and things of that sort.'

'And you do Addition?' the White Queen asked. 'What's one and one and one and one and one and one and one and one and one and one?'

'I don't know,' said Alice. 'I lost count.'

'She can't do Addition,' the Red Queen interrupted. 'Can you do Subtraction? Take nine from eight.'

'Nine from eight I can't, you know,' Alice replied very readily: 'but—'

'She can't do Subtraction,' said the White Queen. 'Can you do Division? Divide a loaf by a knife—what's the answer to that?'

'I suppose—' Alice was beginning, but the Red Queen answered for her. 'Bread-and-butter, of course. Try another Subtraction sum. Take a bone from a dog: what remains?'

Alice considered. 'The bone wouldn't remain, of course, if I took it—and the dog wouldn't remain; it would come to bite me—and I'm sure *I* shouldn't remain!'

'Then you think nothing would remain?' said the Red Queen.

'I think that's the answer.'

'Wrong, as usual,' said the Red Queen: 'the dog's temper would remain.'

'But I don't see how—'

'Why, look here!' the Red Queen cried. 'The dog would lose its temper, wouldn't it?'

'Perhaps it would,' Alice replied cautiously.

'Then if the dog went away, its temper would remain!' the Queen exclaimed triumphantly.

Alice said, as gravely as she could, 'They might go different ways.' But she couldn't help thinking to herself, 'What dreadful nonsense we *are* talking!'

'She can't do sums a *bit*!' the Queens said together, with great emphasis.

'Can *you* do sums?' Alice said, turning suddenly on the White Queen, for she didn't like being found fault with so much.

The Queen gasped and shut her eyes. 'I can do Addition, if you give me time—but I can't do Subtraction, under *any* circumstances!'

'Of course you know your A B C?' said the Red Queen.

'To be sure I do.' said Alice.

'So do I,' the White Queen whispered: 'we'll often say it over together, dear. And I'll tell you a secret—I can read words of one letter! Isn't *that* grand! However, don't be discouraged. You'll come to it in time.'

Here the Red Queen began again. 'Can you answer useful questions?' she said. 'How is bread made?'

'I know *that*!' Alice cried eagerly. 'You take some flour—'

'Where do you pick the flower?' the White Queen asked. 'In a garden, or in the hedges?'

'Well, it isn't *picked* at all,' Alice explained: 'it's *ground*—'

'How many acres of ground?' said the White Queen. 'You mustn't leave out so many things.'

'Fan her head!' the Red Queen anxiously interrupted. 'She'll be feverish after so much thinking.' So they set to work and fanned her with bunches of leaves, till she had to beg them to leave off, it blew her hair about so.

'She's all right again now,' said the Red Queen. 'Do you know Languages?

What's the French for fiddle-de-dee?'

'Fiddle-de-dee's not English,' Alice replied gravely.

'Who ever said it was?' said the Red Queen.

Alice thought she saw a way out of the difficulty this time. 'If you'll tell me what language "fiddle-de-dee" is, I'll tell you the French for it!' she exclaimed triumphantly.

But the Red Queen drew herself up rather stiffly, and said 'Queens never make bargains.'

'I wish Queens never asked questions,' Alice thought to herself.

'Don't let us quarrel,' the White Queen said in an anxious tone. 'What is the cause of lightning?'

'The cause of lightning,' Alice said very decidedly, for she felt quite certain about this, 'is the thunder—no, no!' she hastily corrected herself. 'I meant the other way.'

'It's too late to correct it,' said the Red Queen: 'when you've once said a thing, that fixes it, and you must take the consequences.'

'Which reminds me—' the White Queen said, looking down and nervously clasping and unclasping her hands, 'we had *such* a thunderstorm last Tuesday—I mean one of the last set of Tuesdays, you know.'

> **Commentary:** For some bizarre reason, Carroll particularly liked Tuesdays! On Tuesday 10th April 1877, he wrote in his diary: "Spend the day in London. It was (like so many Tuesdays in my life) a very enjoyable day" (Carroll L., Gardner M., 1990, p. 255).

> **Discussion point:** what is your favourite day of the week and why? Why do people have superstitions about days of the week and dates? E.g. Friday 13th, Valentine's Day...

Alice was puzzled. 'In *our* country,' she remarked, 'there's only one day at a time.'

The Red Queen said, 'That's a poor thin way of doing things. Now *here*, we mostly have days and nights two or three at a time, and sometimes in the winter we take as many as five nights together—for warmth, you know.'

'Are five nights warmer than one night, then?' Alice ventured to ask.

'Five times as warm, of course.'

'But they should be five times as *cold*, by the same rule—'

'Just so!' cried the Red Queen. 'Five times as warm, *and* five times as cold—just as I'm five times as rich as you are, *and* five times as clever!'

Alice sighed and gave it up. 'It's exactly like a riddle with no answer!' she thought.

> **Commentary:** A riddle with no answer is rather like the Mad Hatter's riddle in the first book (Carroll L., Gardner M., 1990, p. 256).

> **Discussion point:** Can you think of any riddles with no answers? Invent some of your own...

'Humpty Dumpty saw it too,' the White Queen went on in a low voice, more as if she were talking to herself. 'He came to the door with a corkscrew in his hand—'

'What did he want?' said the Red Queen.

'He said he *would* come in,' the White Queen went on, 'because he was looking for a hippopotamus. Now, as it happened, there wasn't such a thing in the house, that morning.'

'Is there generally?' Alice asked in an astonished tone.

'Well, only on Thursdays,' said the Queen.

'I know what he came for,' said Alice: 'he wanted to punish the fish, because—'

Here the White Queen began again. 'It was *such* a thunderstorm, you can't think!' ('She *never* could, you know,' said the Red Queen.) 'And part of the roof came off, and ever so much thunder got in—and it went rolling round the room in great lumps—and knocking over the tables and things—till I was so frightened, I couldn't remember my own name!'

Alice thought to herself, 'I never should *try* to remember my name in the middle of an accident! Where would be the use of it?' but she did not say this aloud, for fear of hurting the poor Queen's feeling.

'Your Majesty must excuse her,' the Red Queen said to Alice, taking one of the White Queen's hands in her own, and gently stroking it: 'she means well, but she can't help saying foolish things, as a general rule.'

The White Queen looked timidly at Alice, who felt she *ought* to say something kind, but really couldn't think of anything at the moment.

'She never was really well brought up,' the Red Queen went on: 'but it's amazing how good-tempered she is! Pat her on the head, and see how pleased she'll be!' But this was more than Alice had courage to do.

'A little kindness—and putting her hair in papers **(papers around which locks of hair are wound for curling)**—would do wonders with her—'

The White Queen gave a deep sigh, and laid her head on Alice's shoulder. 'I *am* so sleepy?' she moaned.

'She's tired, poor thing!' said the Red Queen. 'Smooth her hair—lend her your nightcap—and sing her a soothing lullaby.'

'I haven't got a nightcap with me,' said Alice, as she tried to obey the first direction: 'and I don't know any soothing lullabies.'

'I must do it myself, then,' said the Red Queen, and she began:

> 'Hush-a-by lady, in Alice's lap!
> Till the feast's ready, we've time for a nap:
> When the feast's over, we'll go to the ball—
> Red Queen, and White Queen, and Alice, and all!

> **Commentary:** this is a mocking tribute to the familiar nursery rhyme:
> Rock-a-bye (sometimes hush-a-by) baby, on the treetop,
> When the wind blows, the cradle will rock,
> When the bough breaks, the cradle will fall,
> And down will come baby, cradle and all.

Discussion point: how and why does Carroll mock this song?

'And now you know the words,' she added, as she put her head down on Alice's other shoulder, 'just sing it through to *me*. I'm getting sleepy, too.' In another moment both Queens were fast asleep, and snoring loud.

'What *am* I to do?' exclaimed Alice, looking about in great perplexity, as first one round head, and then the other, rolled down from her shoulder, and lay like a heavy lump in her lap. 'I don't think it *ever*happened before, that any one had to take care of two Queens asleep at once! No, not in all the History of England—it couldn't, you know, because there never was more than one Queen at a time. Do wake up, you heavy things!' she went on in an impatient tone; but there was no answer but a gentle snoring.

The snoring got more distinct every minute, and sounded more like a tune: at last she could even make out the words, and she listened so eagerly that, when the two great heads vanished from her lap, she hardly missed them.

She was standing before an arched doorway over which were the words QUEEN ALICE in large letters, and on each side of the arch there was a bell-handle; one was marked 'Visitors' Bell,' and the other 'Servants' Bell.'

'I'll wait till the song's over,' thought Alice, 'and then I'll ring—the—*which* bell must I ring?' she went on, very much puzzled by the names. 'I'm not a visitor, and I'm not a servant. There *ought* to be one marked "Queen," you know—'

Just then the door opened a little way, and a creature with a long beak put its head out for a moment and said 'No admittance till the week after next!' and shut the door again with a bang.

Alice knocked and rang in vain for a long time, but at last, a very old Frog, who was sitting under a tree, got up and hobbled slowly towards her: he was dressed in bright yellow, and had enormous boots on.

'What is it, now?' the Frog said in a deep hoarse whisper.

Alice turned round, ready to find fault with anybody. 'Where's the servant whose business it is to answer the door?' she began angrily.

'Which door?' said the Frog.

Alice almost stamped with irritation at the slow drawl in which he spoke. '*This* door, of course!'

The Frog looked at the door with his large dull eyes for a minute: then he went nearer and rubbed it with his thumb, as if he were trying whether the paint would come off; then he looked at Alice.

'To answer the door?' he said. 'What's it been asking of?' He was so hoarse that Alice could scarcely hear him.

Commentary: the frog has a frog in this throat.

Discussion point: why is the phrase to have a 'frog in your throat' used to describe people's voices? Can you think of other imagery which is used to describe people's voices? What is the effect of this imagery?

'I don't know what you mean,' she said.

'I talks English, doesn't I?' the Frog went on. 'Or are you deaf? What did it ask you?'

'Nothing!' Alice said impatiently. 'I've been knocking at it!'

'Shouldn't do that—shouldn't do that—' the Frog muttered. 'Vexes it, you know.' Then he went up and gave the door a kick with one of his great feet. 'You let *it* alone,' he panted out, as he hobbled back to his tree, 'and it'll let *you* alone, you know.'

At this moment the door was flung open, and a shrill voice was heard singing:

'To the Looking-Glass world it was Alice that said,
"I've a sceptre in hand, I've a crown on my head;
Let the Looking-Glass creatures, whatever they be,
Come and dine with the Red Queen, the White Queen, and me."'

And hundreds of voices joined in the chorus:

'Then fill up the glasses as quick as you can,
And sprinkle the table with buttons and bran:
Put cats in the coffee, and mice in the tea—
And welcome Queen Alice with thirty-times-three!'

Then followed a confused noise of cheering, and Alice thought to herself, 'Thirty times three makes ninety. I wonder if any one's counting?' In a minute there was silence again, and the same shrill voice sang another verse;

'"O Looking-Glass creatures," quoth Alice, "draw near!
'Tis an honour to see me, a favour to hear:
'Tis a privilege high to have dinner and tea
Along with the Red Queen, the White Queen, and me!"'

Then came the chorus again:—

'Then fill up the glasses with treacle and ink,
Or anything else that is pleasant to drink:
Mix sand with the cider, and wool with the wine—
And welcome Queen Alice with ninety-times-nine!'

'Ninety times nine!' Alice repeated in despair, 'Oh, that'll never be done! I'd better go in at once—' and there was a dead silence the moment she appeared.

Commentary: this poem is a parody of Sir Walter Scott's song, "Bonny Dundee":

To the **Lords of Convention** 'twas Clavers who spoke.
'Ere the King's crown shall fall there are crowns to be broke;
So let each Cavalier who loves honour and me,
Come follow the bonnet of Bonny Dundee.

Come fill up my cup, come fill up my can,
Come saddle your horses, and call up your men;
*Come open the **West Port** and let me gang free,*
And it's room for the bonnets of Bonny Dundee!

Dundee he is mounted, he rides up the street,

The bells are rung backward,[14] the drums they are beat;
But the **Provost, douce** man, said, "Just e'en let him be,
The Gude Town[15] is weel quit of that Deil of Dundee."

Come fill up my cup, etc.

As he rode down the sanctified bends of the Bow,
Ilk carline was flyting and shaking her **pow**;
But the young plants of grace they looked **couthie** and slee,
Thinking luck to thy bonnet, thou Bonny Dundee!

Come fill up my cup, etc.

With sour-featured **Whigs** the **Grass-market** was crammed,
As if half the West had set tryst to be hanged;
There was spite in each look, there was fear in each e'e,
As they watched for the bonnets of Bonny Dundee.

Come fill up my cup, etc.

These cowls of **Kilmarnock** had spits and had spears,
And lang-hafted **gullies** to kill cavaliers;
But they shrunk to close-heads and the causeway was free,
At the toss of the bonnet of Bonny Dundee.

Come fill up my cup, etc.

He spurred to the foot of the proud **Castle** rock,
And with **the gay Gordon** he gallantly spoke;
"Let **Mons Meg** and her marrows speak twa words or three,
For the love of the bonnet of Bonny Dundee."

Come fill up my cup, etc.

The Gordon demands of him which way he goes?
"Where'er shall direct me the shade of **Montrose**!
Your Grace in short space shall hear tidings of me,
Or that low lies the bonnet of Bonny Dundee.

Come fill up my cup, etc.

"There are hills beyond **Pentland** and lands beyond **Forth**,
If there's lords in the **Lowlands**, there's chiefs in the North;
There are wild **Duniewassals** three thousand times three,
Will *cry hoigh!* for the bonnet of Bonny Dundee.

Come fill up my cup, etc.

"There's brass on the target of barkened bull-hide;
There's steel in the scabbard that dangles beside;
The brass shall be burnished, the steel shall flash free,

At the toss of the bonnet of Bonny Dundee.

Come fill up my cup, etc.

"Away to the hills, to the caves, to the rocks
Ere I own an usurper, I'll couch with the fox;
And tremble, false Whigs, in the midst of your glee,
You have not seen the last of my bonnet and me!"

Come fill up my cup, etc.

He waved his proud hand, the trumpets were blown,
The kettle-drums clashed and the horsemen rode on,
Till on **Ravelston**'s cliffs and on **Clermiston**'s lee
Died away the wild war-notes of Bonny Dundee.

Come fill up my cup, come fill up my can,
Come saddle the horses, and call up the men,
Come open your gates, and let me gae free,
For it's up with the bonnets of Bonny Dundee!

Discussion point: how and why does Carroll parody this poem?

Alice glanced nervously along the table, as she walked up the large hall, and noticed that there were about fifty guests, of all kinds: some were animals, some birds, and there were even a few flowers among them. 'I'm glad they've come without waiting to be asked,' she thought: 'I should never have known who were the right people to invite!'

There were three chairs at the head of the table; the Red and White Queens had already taken two of them, but the middle one was empty. Alice sat down in it, rather uncomfortable in the silence, and longing for some one to speak.

At last the Red Queen began. 'You've missed the soup and fish,' she said. 'Put on the joint!' And the waiters set a leg of mutton before Alice, who looked at it rather anxiously, as she had never had to carve a joint before.

'You look a little shy; let me introduce you to that leg of mutton,' said the Red Queen. 'Alice—Mutton; Mutton—Alice.' The leg of mutton got up in the dish and made a little bow to Alice; and Alice returned the bow, not knowing whether to be frightened or amused.

'May I give you a slice?' she said, taking up the knife and fork, and looking from one Queen to the other.

'Certainly not,' the Red Queen said, very decidedly: 'it isn't etiquette to cut any one you've been introduced to. Remove the joint!' And the waiters carried it off, and brought a large plum-pudding in its place.

Commentary: In Victorian England, "to cut" could mean to ignore someone you know (Carroll L., Gardner M., 1990, p. 262)

Discussion point: why and when do people ignore people they know? How do they do it? What can be the effects of "blanking" people?

'I won't be introduced to the pudding, please,' Alice said rather hastily, 'or we shall get no dinner at all. May I give you some?'

But the Red Queen looked sulky, and growled 'Pudding—Alice; Alice—Pudding. Remove the pudding!' and the waiters took it away so quickly that Alice couldn't return its bow.

However, she didn't see why the Red Queen should be the only one to give orders, so, as an experiment, she called out 'Waiter! Bring back the pudding!' and there it was again in a moment like a conjuring-trick. It was so large that she couldn't help feeling a *little* shy with it, as she had been with the mutton; however, she conquered her shyness by a great effort and cut a slice and handed it to the Red Queen.

'What impertinence!' said the Pudding. 'I wonder how you'd like it, if I were to cut a slice out of *you*, you creature!'

It spoke in a thick, suety sort of voice, and Alice hadn't a word to say in reply: she could only sit and look at it and gasp.

'Make a remark,' said the Red Queen: 'it's ridiculous to leave all the conversation to the pudding!'

'Do you know, I've had such a quantity of poetry repeated to me to-day,' Alice began, a little frightened at finding that, the moment she opened her lips, there was dead silence, and all eyes were fixed upon her; 'and it's a very curious thing, I think—every poem was about fishes in some way. Do you know why they're so fond of fishes, all about here?'

She spoke to the Red Queen, whose answer was a little wide of the mark. 'As to fishes,' she said, very slowly and solemnly, putting her mouth close to Alice's ear, 'her White Majesty knows a lovely riddle—all in poetry—all about fishes. Shall she repeat it?'

'Her Red Majesty's very kind to mention it,' the White Queen murmured into Alice's other ear, in a voice like the cooing of a pigeon. 'It would be *such* a treat! May I?'

'Please do,' Alice said very politely.

The White Queen laughed with delight, and stroked Alice's cheek. Then she began:

> *"First, the fish must be caught."*
> *That is easy: a baby, I think, could have caught it.*
> *"Next, the fish must be bought."*
> *That is easy: a penny, I think, would have bought it.*
>
> *"Now cook me the fish!"*
> *That is easy, and will not take more than a minute.*
> *"Let it lie in a dish!"*
> *That is easy, because it already is in it.*
>
> *"Bring it here! Let me sup!"*
> *It is easy to set such a dish on the table.*
> *"Take the dish-cover up!"*
> *Ah, that is so hard that I fear I'm unable!*

For it holds it like glue—
Holds the lid to the dish, while it lies in the middle:
Which is easiest to do,
Un-dish-cover the fish, or dishcover the riddle?'

> **Commentary:** the answer: an oyster (Carroll L., Gardner M., 1990, p. 264)

> **Discussion point:** what is the effect of this riddle near the end of the book?

'Take a minute to think about it, and then guess,' said the Red Queen. 'Meanwhile, we'll drink your health—Queen Alice's health!' she screamed at the top of her voice, and all the guests began drinking it directly, and very queerly they managed it: some of them put their glasses upon their heads like extinguishers, and drank all that trickled down their faces—others upset the decanters, and drank the wine as it ran off the edges of the table—and three of them (who looked like kangaroos) scrambled into the dish of roast mutton, and began eagerly lapping up the gravy, 'just like pigs in a trough!' thought Alice.

'You ought to return thanks in a neat speech,' the Red Queen said, frowning at Alice as she spoke.

'We must support you, you know,' the White Queen whispered, as Alice got up to do it, very obediently, but a little frightened.

'Thank you very much,' she whispered in reply, 'but I can do quite well without.'

'That wouldn't be at all the thing,' the Red Queen said very decidedly: so Alice tried to submit to it with a good grace.

('And they *did* push so!' she said afterwards, when she was telling her sister the history of the feast. 'You would have thought they wanted to squeeze me flat!')

In fact it was rather difficult for her to keep in her place while she made her speech: the two Queens pushed her so, one on each side, that they nearly lifted her up into the air: 'I rise to return thanks—' Alice began: and she really *did* rise as she spoke, several inches; but she got hold of the edge of the table, and managed to pull herself down again.

'Take care of yourself!' screamed the White Queen, seizing Alice's hair with both her hands. 'Something's going to happen!'

And then (as Alice afterwards described it) all sorts of things happened in a moment. The candles all grew up to the ceiling, looking something like a bed of rushes with fireworks at the top. As to the bottles, they each took a pair of plates, which they hastily fitted on as wings, and so, with forks for legs, went fluttering about in all directions: 'and very like birds they look,' Alice thought to herself, as well as she could in the dreadful confusion that was beginning.

At this moment she heard a hoarse laugh at her side, and turned to see what was the matter with the White Queen; but, instead of the Queen, there was the leg of mutton sitting in the chair. 'Here I am!' cried a voice from the soup tureen, and Alice turned again, just in time to see the Queen's broad good-natured face grinning at her for a moment over the edge of the tureen, before she disappeared into the soup.

> **Commentary:** The White Queen has moved away from Alice to QR6: an illegal move because it does not take the White King out of check (Carroll L., Gardner M., 1990, p. 266).

> **Discussion point:** why does an illegal move happen here?

There was not a moment to be lost. Already several of the guests were lying down in the dishes, and the soup ladle was walking up the table towards Alice's chair, and beckoning to her impatiently to get out of its way.

'I can't stand this any longer!' she cried as she jumped up and seized the table-cloth with both hands: one good pull, and plates, dishes, guests, and candles came crashing down together in a heap on the floor.

'And as for *you*,' she went on, turning fiercely upon the Red Queen, whom she considered as the cause of all the mischief—but the Queen was no longer at her side—she had suddenly dwindled down to the size of a little doll, and was now on the table, merrily running round and round after her own shawl, which was trailing behind her.

At any other time, Alice would have felt surprised at this, but she was far too much excited to be surprised at anything *now*. 'As for *you*,' she repeated, catching hold of the little creature in the very act of jumping over a bottle which had just lighted upon the table, 'I'll shake you into a kitten, that I will!'

> **Commentary:** Alice captures the Red Queen here. It leads to the Red King, who has slept throughout the whole problem without moving, being check-mated (Carroll L., Gardner M., 1990, p. 266).

> **Discussion point:** Is there a moral here? Are the White pieces the 'goodies', and Red pieces the 'baddies'? What do you think?

See the end of Chapter 12 for questions on this chapter.

10 Shaking

Teaching points

Learning objectives: to develop students' knowledge of violence in stories.

Starter activity: what do you think of the representation of violence in stories? Think of violent stories you like and dislike? What violence precisely happens in them? Why is this violence appealing or unappealing?

Main activities: read these short chapters and think about how violence is represented in them. How and why is Alice represented as violent? Where else in the stories is violence depicted? Why and how does Carroll represent violence in the novels? Find some examples of "violent language" (e.g. "off with his head!") and consider its effects upon the readers.

If they have not done so already, students should explore and consider the points raised in the commentaries/discussion points as well as answering the questions at the end of the chapter as best they can.

Plenary: What have you learnt about violence and representations of violence?

The text

She took her off the table as she spoke, and shook her backwards and forwards with all her might.

The Red Queen made no resistance whatever; only her face grew very small, and her eyes got large and green: and still, as Alice went on shaking her, she kept on growing shorter—and fatter—and softer—and rounder—and—

See the end of Chapter 12 for questions on this chapter.

11 Waking

The text

--and it really WAS a kitten, after all.

> **Commentary:** these are two very short chapters; they create yet more surprises in a book full of surprises.

> **Discussion point:** why has Carroll made these two chapters so short? Discuss short stories/poems/films/events that you find interesting and striking, e.g. consider very brief events that have had a big effect on you. You might have met a celebrity for example. Why are some brief events so important?

See the end of Chapter 12 for questions on this chapter.

12 Which Dreamed it?

Teaching points

Learning objectives: to develop students' knowledge of endings of stories.

Starter activity: what makes an effective ending to a story? What are your favourite endings to stories and why?

Main activities: read the chapter, and note down your reactions to the ending of the novel. What is surprising? What is predictable? How does Carroll keep the reader interested in the ending of the story? Have a go at writing an alternative ending to the story, and writing a commentary which explains why you wrote this ending, explaining why you used the language, characters, settings and events that you did, making contrasts and comparisons with Carroll's ending.

If they have not done so already, students should explore and consider the points raised in the commentaries/discussion points as well as answering the questions at the end of the chapter as best they can.

Plenary: What have you learnt about the endings of stories?

The text

'Your majesty shouldn't purr so loud,' Alice said, rubbing her eyes, and addressing the kitten, respectfully, yet with some severity. 'You woke me out of oh! such a nice dream! And you've been along with me, Kitty—all through the Looking-Glass world. Did you know it, dear?'

It is a very inconvenient habit of kittens (Alice had once made the remark) that, whatever you say to them, they *always* purr. 'If they would only purr for "yes" and mew for "no," or any rule of that sort,' she had said, 'so that one could keep up a conversation! But how *can* you talk with a person if they always say the same thing?'

> **Commentary:** This point is central to 'information theory': there is no way to record or transmit information without at least a binary distinction between yes and no, or true and false. In computers, the distinction is handled by the on-off switches of their circuitry (Carroll L., Gardner M., 1990, p. 269).

> **Discussion point:** why is 'information theory' important in the Alice books? Why is it so important in life?

On this occasion the kitten only purred: and it was impossible to guess whether it meant 'yes' or 'no.'

So Alice hunted among the chessmen on the table till she had found the Red Queen: then she went down on her knees on the hearth-rug, and put the kitten and the Queen to look at each other. 'Now, Kitty!' she cried, clapping her hands triumphantly. 'Confess that was what you turned into!'

('But it wouldn't look at it,' she said, when she was explaining the thing afterwards to her sister: 'it turned away its head, and pretended not to see it: but it looked a *little* ashamed of itself, so I think it *must* have been the Red Queen.')

'Sit up a little more stiffly, dear!' Alice cried with a merry laugh. 'And curtsey while you're thinking what to—what to purr. It saves time, remember!' And she caught it up and gave it one little kiss, 'just in honour of having been a Red Queen.'

'Snowdrop, my pet!' she went on, looking over her shoulder at the White Kitten, which was still patiently undergoing its toilet, 'when *will* Dinah have finished with your White Majesty, I wonder? That must be the reason you were so untidy in my dream—Dinah! do you know that you're scrubbing a White Queen? Really, it's most disrespectful of you!'

'And what did *Dinah* turn to, I wonder?' she prattled on, as she settled comfortably down, with one elbow in the rug, and her chin in her hand, to watch the kittens. 'Tell me, Dinah, did you turn to Humpty Dumpty? I *think* you did—however, you'd better not mention it to your friends just yet, for I'm not sure.

'By the way, Kitty, if only you'd been really with me in my dream, there was one thing you *would* have enjoyed—I had such a quantity of poetry said to me, all about fishes! To-morrow morning you shall have a real treat. All the time you're eating your breakfast, I'll repeat "The Walrus and the Carpenter" to you; and then you can make believe it's oysters, dear!

'Now, Kitty, let's consider who it was that dreamed it all. This is a serious question, my dear, and you should *not* go on licking your paw like that—as if Dinah hadn't washed you this morning! You see, Kitty, it *must* have been either me or the Red King. He was part of my dream, of course—but then I was part of his dream, too! *Was* it the Red King, Kitty? You were his wife, my dear, so you ought to know—Oh, Kitty, *do* help to settle it! I'm sure your paw can wait!' But the provoking kitten only began on the other paw, and pretended it hadn't heard the question.

Which do *you* think it was?

——

A boat beneath a sunny sky,
Lingering onward dreamily
In an evening of July—

Children three that nestle near,
Eager eye and willing ear,
Pleased a simple tale to hear—

Long has paled that sunny sky:
Echoes fade and memories die.
Autumn frosts have slain July.

Still she haunts me, phantomwise,
Alice moving under skies
Never seen by waking eyes.

Children yet, the tale to hear,
Eager eye and willing ear,
Lovingly shall nestle near.

In a Wonderland they lie,
Dreaming as the days go by,
Dreaming as the summers die:

Ever drifting down the stream—
Lingering in the golden gleam—
Life, what is it but a dream?

Commentary: Here Carroll remembers the 4th July boating trip when he first told the Alice in Wonderland story to the three Liddell sisters; the poem contains the themes of winter and death that run through the first poem in *Through the Looking-Glass*. The poem is an acrostic, the initial letters of the verses spell Alice's name. The poem echoes the anonymous poem: "Row, row, row your boat/Gently down the stream;/Merrily, merrily, merrily, merrily,/Life is but a dream."

Discussion point: why does Carroll end the books with this poem?

THE END of the books.

Questions/tasks

In your Learning Journal answer these questions and complete these activities:

What happens when Alice realises she is a Queen?
What do the Queens tell Alice she must do to become a Queen?
How does the Red Queen frustrate Alice?
How do people travel in the Looking-Glass world according to the White Queen?
Why is the White Queen so rude according to the Red Queen?
What does the Red Queen's singing cause the White Queen to do?
What words boom out of the door that flies open for Alice when she knocks on it?
What creature is confused by Alice from behind the door?
Why does the Red Queen send the food back at the party?
What happens when Alice rises to give thanks to her guests?
What does Alice do with the tablecloth?
Who does Alice believe is responsible for the chaos?
Who does the Queen turn into and what does Alice realise?
Who does Alice think Snowdrop and Dinah are?
What poetry does Alice tell Kitty about?
Analytical question: How does Carroll make this a thrilling and mysterious climax to the story?
Creative Response: write the Red King's diary for the story, summarising his views of events in a reflective journal entry. Or have a go at an acrostic poem about the stories, you can choose what word you make an acrostic of, it could be, for example, "wonderland" etc.
Textual re-casting: re-write the last chapter as a series of Facebook updates or Tweets.
Devise a flow-chart/spider diagram/storyboard of the major events of the chapter.
Write down in your responses to the characters and situations in the chapter, noting down your thoughts and feelings about the various things that happen. What do you think might happen next if the story were to

continue?

What reading strategies are you using to help you enjoy the book? How could you improve your reading?

See Answers to the questions to mark your own work.

Answers to the questions

IMPORTANT NOTE: the answers to these questions are deliberately very brief; many of them could be much longer, particularly the answers to the creative response/analytical/textual re-casting questions which require argumentative, evaluative and personal responses as well as creative thought.

Questions & answers for *Alice in Wonderland*

Chapter 1

Why is the White Rabbit worried? That he is going to be late.

Why does Alice fall down the rabbit hole? Because she follows the White Rabbit.

What are the sides of the well covered in? Cupboards and shelves.

What is strange about the way Alice falls down the well and what does she do as she is falling? That she goes slowly enough to pick a marmalade jar off a shelf and put it on another one. She speaks aloud, daydreaming about her cat Dinah.

What happens when Alice lands? She is unhurt and sees the White Rabbit disappear around a corner.

What does she discover behind a small curtain? A door.

What happens when Alice drinks a bottle which says "DRINK ME"? She shrinks.

Why is there a problem when she shrinks? She realised she left the key on the table which she can now not reach.

Why is Alice disappointed when she eats the small cake? It does not make her bigger.

Chapter 2

What happens to Alice after eating the cake which says "EAT ME" after some time? She grows to nine foot tall.

What does she do when she grows so tall? She cries.

What does the White Rabbit mutter to himself? That the Duchess is waiting.

Why does Alice think she may not be the person that she once was and who does she think she maybe and why? Because she is so tall, and because she can't remember her lessons. She thinks she may be Mabel because Mabel knows so little.

What does the fanning motion cause to happen? For Alice to shrink.

What happens when she shrinks? She becomes immersed in her own tears.

Who does she ask for help and why does she offend it? She asks a Mouse for help and offends it by talking about her cat and then dogs.

How does Alice manage to get the Mouse to come back? By promising not to talk about cats and dogs.

Who else does Alice meet in the pool of tears? A Duck, a Dodo, a Lory, and an Eagle.

Chapter 3

What history lesson does the Mouse tell the animals and Alice and why? The story of William the Conqueror because it would be the driest thing to do since they need to get dry.

What does the Dodo suggest and why? A Caucus Race to get dry.

What is strange about the Caucus race? There appear to be no rules and Dodo proclaims everyone a winner.

What job does the Dodo give Alice and what does she have to do as a result? She must give out the prizes; she gives out mints.

What is strange about the Mouse's tale? It is in the shape of a tail, and talks about Fury prosecuting a mouse in court.

Why does the Mouse tell off Alice? For not paying attention.

How does Alice frighten off all the animals? By telling them that Dinah eats birds.

What does Alice do when they run off? She cries.

Chapter 4

What is the White Rabbit looking for? His gloves and fan.

Who does the White Rabbit mistake Alice for and what does he ask her to do? He mistakes her for Mary-Ann and orders her to go to the house and fetch his things.

What does Alice do and think? She obeys the rabbit and thinks how strange it is to be ordered about by animals.

What does she find in the house? The Rabbit's white gloves and fan, and a little bottle called "DRINK ME".

What happens when Alice drinks the bottle? She grows quickly, and her foot gets stuck in the chimney, and her arm dangles from a window.

What does Alice think when she is tall? That she is grown up now and will never grow old.

What do the animals threaten to do to Alice? They threaten to burn the house down and throw pebbles at her.

What happens to the pebbles and what does Alice do? The pebbles turn into cakes and Alice eats them, shrinking again.

How and why does Alice run? She runs away from the angry animals.

What two animals does she next encounter? A giant puppy and a caterpillar sitting on top of a giant mushroom.

Chapter 5

What question does the Caterpillar ask Alice and why does she become depressed? The Caterpillar asks who she is and she becomes depressed because the Caterpillar is so hostile, tripping her up when she responds to his questions.

What does the Caterpillar ask Alice to do when she tries to leave? To recite a poem.

Why is the Caterpillar offended by Alice's answer to his question about what size she would like to be? Because she says she finds it wretched being three inches tall, which is his height.

What does the Caterpillar say as he goes off in a huff? That eating one side of the mushroom will make her grow larger and eating the other side will make her grow smaller.

What problems does Alice encounter as she eats the mushroom? Eating one side of the mushroom makes her shrink, while the other makes her neck grow tall.

Why does the Pigeon attack her? Because the Pigeon thinks she is a serpent after his eggs.

What does Alice look for when she grows back to a normal size? The garden.

Why does Alice eat all the mushroom? To shrink small enough to enter the four-foot house.

Chapter 6

How are the fish and frog dressed? In footman's livery, i.e. as servants.

What does the letter delivered by the Fish Footman say? It invites the Duchess to play croquet with the Queen.

What does the Frog Footman say about people answering the door? That no one will come because they are making too much noise to hear knocking.

What does Alice think of the Frog Footman and why? She thinks he is idiotic because he seems not to react when a plate flies out of the house and grazes his nose, and that he has advised her poorly about going into the house.

What and who does Alice encounter when she enters the kitchen? The

Duchess nursing a baby, a grinning cat by the hearth, and Cook at the stove, dumping pepper into a cauldron.

How does the Duchess insult Alice? By saying she doesn't know very much.

What does the Cook throw and at whom? The Cook throws kitchen utensils at the Duchess and the baby.

Why does the Duchess say "chop off her head"? Because she mishears when Alice talks about the earth's axis, believing she is talking about axes.

Why does the Duchess fling the baby at Alice? She needs to go and prepare for the croquet match.

What is the baby really? A pig.

What does the Cheshire Cat reply when Alice asks him where she might go next? He tells her no matter where she goes she will end up somewhere. He tells her to visit the Mad Hatter and the March Hare.

Why does the Cheshire Cat think Alice must be mad? Because everyone is mad in Wonderland.

Where does the Cheshire Cat say he will see Alice again? At the Queen's Croquet match.

What happens to the Cheshire Cat? He disappears, leaving only his grin.

Why does Alice eat more of the Caterpillar's mushroom? To grow smaller in order to fit into the March Hare's house.

Chapter 7

How do the March Hare and Mad Hatter treat the Dormouse? Badly, by putting their elbows on it.

What do the March Hare and the Mad Hatter say to Alice? That there is no room at the table.

What does the March Hare offer Alice and why is this odd? He offers wine but there is none.

What does the Mad Hatter think of Alice's hair? He thinks it needs cutting.

What riddle does the Mad Hatter pose? Why is a raven like a writing desk?

Why does the Mad Hatter become angry? He discovers the March Hare's watch is broken.

How does the March Hare treat the watch? By putting butter on it and dipping it in his tea.

Why does Alice become angry with the Mad Hatter? When she discovers he doesn't know the answer to the riddle either.

Why is Time upset according to the Mad Hatter? Because he was, according to the Queen of Hearts, murdering time when singing a song badly in her presence.

What has happened to Time as a result? Time has stayed fixed at 6 O'clock, which means it is perpetual tea-time.

What story does the Dormouse tell? About three sisters who live in a treacle well, eating and drawing treacle.

Why does Alice walk off? Because the Mad Hatter insults her.

What does she find in the wood? A tree with a door in it.

What happens when she finally open the door? She finds a passageway that leads to the Garden.

Chapter 8

What is strange about the gardeners? They are shaped like playing cards.

What are the gardeners doing and why? They are painting white roses red because they have planted white rose trees and not red roses by mistake and must do this before the Queen of Hearts finds out.

Why does the Queen ask for Alice's head to be chopped off? Because Alice did not respond to her question about why the gardeners are trembling in the right way.

How does Alice save the gardeners from beheading? By hiding them in a flower pot.

What does Alice find out from the White Rabbit? That the Duchess is under sentence for execution for boxing the Queen's ears.

What is odd about the croquet match? The balls are hedgehogs, the mallets are flamingos and the hoops are made from four cards.

Who does Alice see when she tries to get away and what does this creature say? She sees the Cheshire Cat who asks how she is getting on.

Why does the Queen want the Cheshire Cat beheaded? Because the Cat had annoyed the King after refusing to be bullied by the King's taunts.

What do the executioner and the King have a problem with? How to chop off the head of a cat which only has a head.

What advice does Alice give and why? For them to ask the Duchess who owns the Cheshire Cat.

Chapter 9

Why does Alice become uncomfortable in the Duchess's presence? Because the Duchess is holding her so close.

Why does Alice think the Duchess is being nice? Because there is no pepper about.

What does the Queen order? That the Duchess goes away and that Alice plays the croquet game again.

Why do only the King, Alice and the Queen end up playing the croquet game? Everyone else is under the sentence of death.

Why does the Queen end the game? Because there are no soldiers left to act as arches.

What does the Gryphon tell Alice about the Queen? That she never executes anyone.

Why is the Mock Turtle sad? Because he used to be a real turtle once.

Why did the Mock Turtle's lesson become shorter? They were called lessons because they "lessen".

Textual re-casting: Write an "agony aunt/uncle's" response to the Mock

Turtle's problems.

Chapter 10

What is the Lobster-Quadrille? A dance where all the sea animals partner up with lobsters, dance on the seashore and then throw the lobsters into the sea.

What do the Mock Turtle and the Gryphon do for Alice? They dance the Lobster-Quadrille with the Mock Turtle singing a song about a whiting and a snail.

Why, according to the Mock Turtle, is a whiting called a whiting? Because he polishes sea animals' shoes.

What is unwise to do according to the Mock Turtle? To go anywhere without a "porpoise" (purpose).

Why do the Mock Turtle and the Gryphon interrupt Alice's story about her adventures? Because they find it "curious" that Alice got the words to "Father William" wrong.

Why does the Mock Turtle become confused? Because Alice messes up the words of the poem "Tis the Voice of the Sluggard".

What cry does the Gryphon hear? That the trial is about to begin.

Chapter 11

What does Alice find when she enters the courtroom? The King and Queen on their thrones, surrounded by a pack of cards and animals. The Knave is in chains.

Why do the jury have to write their own names? In case they forget them.

What does Bill write with? His finger.

What does the White Rabbit announce? That the Knave of Hearts stole the tarts.

Why won't the Hatter remove his Hat when the King asks him to? Because he does not own the hats, but only sells them.

Why does the Dormouse become upset? Because Alice has grown and is squashing him.

What is the Hatter's mood and behaviour like? Why is he like this? He is very nervous and incapable of following any instructions, partly because of the King's questions and attitude but also because he is mad.

Why does the Dormouse cause a commotion? By saying that the tarts are made of treacle.

Who does the White Rabbit call at the end of the chapter? Alice to the stand.

Chapter 12

How and why does Alice disturb the jury? She knocks over the jury stand.

What does Alice say she knows about the case and what is the King's response to her statement? She claims to know nothing whatsoever; the

King deems this very important.

What does Rule 42 state? "That all persons more than a mile high to leave the court".

What does Alice accuse the King of? Of making up Rule 42.

Why does the King believe the note proves the Knave's guilt? Because an honest man would have signed the note.

What does the poem prove? Nothing, it does not make sense.

Why does Alice criticise the Queen? For calling for a verdict when the evidence is not satisfactory.

How does Alice defeat the Queen and the creatures of Wonderland? By calling them a pack of cards.

Where does Alice find herself when she wakes up? On her sister's lap.

What does Alice's sister imagine and why? All the creatures of Wonderland who she heard about from Alice. She imagines that Alice will one day tell her adventures to her children.

Questions & answers for *Alice Through the Looking Glass*

Chapter 1

Why does Alice tell off the kitten? For unravelling a ball of wool.

Who does Alice imagine Kitty is? She imagines Kitty is the Red Queen in a chess game.

What does she threaten to do to Kitty? She threatens to put Kitty on the other side of the mirror, into what she calls the "Looking-Glass House".

How does Alice enter the Looking-Glass World? She finds herself on the mantelpiece and magically steps into the mirror.

What does she find on the other side of the mirror? She finds a mirror image of the room, but some things are very different. The pictures on the wall seem alive and the clock has a grinning face.

What does she notice in the fireplace? A group of chessmen walking around in the ashes, walking in line two-by-two.

How does Alice appear to the chess pieces? She is invisible.

Why is the White King so surprised? He is manhandled by the invisible Alice, who snatches his notebook from him and writes in it.

What does Alice find strange about the books in the room? All the writing is "mirror writing".

How does Alice manage to read "Jabberwocky"? By looking at it in the mirror.

What happens to Alice when she leaves the room? She finds herself floating down the stairs.

Chapter 2

Why does Alice climb the hill? To get a better look of the house.

What does Alice find frustrating? That the path always leads back to the house.

What is surprising about the flowers? They can talk.

Who protects the flowers and how? A tree which barks at any threats.

How do the Rose and the Violet treat Alice? They insult her.

Who else is in the garden? The Red Queen.

How does Alice manage to reach her and why does she reach her this way? She goes in the opposite direction to her and meets her because she is in the mirror world.

What does the Red Queen say the hill is like and what is Alice's response to this? She says the hill is like a valley. Alice says this is nonsense.

What does Alice realise about the countryside? That it is a huge chessboard.

How does Alice join the game? The Red Queen says she can become a White Pawn by replacing the Tiger-lily.

What is strange about their running? They stay in the same place.

What does the Red Queen explain about the game? That Alice is on the second square and must advance to the eighth square if she wants to become a Queen.

Chapter 3

What do the elephants appear to be doing in the distance? Pollinating flowers and making honey.

Where does Alice suddenly find herself in and what problem does she feel she has? She finds herself in a train and is worried because she does not have a ticket.

Who is in the carriage and what do they say about Alice? A Guard, a man dressed in white paper, a goat, a beetle. They all indicate that it's a problem that she doesn't have a ticket.

Why does the train jump? It goes into the next chess square, over a brook.

What voice does Alice hear in her ear? A gnat's.

What does the Gnat say will happen to Alice when she enters the wood? She will lose her name.

What does happen to Alice when she enters the wood? She forgets the names of everything.

Where does Alice head towards in the wood? Tweedledum and Tweedledee's house.

Chapter 4

How do Tweedledee and Tweedledum stand? Side by side, with their arms around each other.

What does Alice's poem about them describe? How the brothers fight over a rattle and a big crow scares them and causes them to forget about their argument.

What is their response to Alice's questions about how to get out of the wood? They ignore them.

What is the poem "The Walrus and the Carpenter" about? About a walrus and a carpenter who trick some baby oysters to leave their sea bed and come out onto the sands, where they eat them.

Who does Alice prefer in the poem and why? How are her opinions challenged? The Walrus because he has sympathy for the oysters. Tweedledee says that the Walrus ate more oysters than the carpenter.

Who does Alice see sleeping under a tree and what does Tweedledee say about him? She sees the Red King who Tweedledee says is dreaming about her and if he stops dreaming about her, she will disappear.

What do the twins fight over and how are they distracted? A rattle. A crow scares them.

Chapter 5

Who does Alice bump into and why? She bumps into the White Queen because she grabs the shawl the White Queen is chasing after.

What job does the White Queen offer her and what perks does it have? As a maid, it has "twopence a week, jam every other day".

What is going to happen to the King's Messenger according to the White Queen? He will go to prison, have a trial, with his crime coming last.

What happens to the Queen when she crosses the brook? She turns into a sheep.

Where does Alice suddenly find herself and what is odd about this place? She finds herself in a shop which is full of curious items, but whenever she looks directly at a shelf it appears to be empty.

What activity does Alice do with the Sheep and where does she find herself again? She rows a boat, falls over and then finds herself back in the shop when she stands up.

What does Alice pay for and why is this purchase a problem? She pays for an egg which keeps getting further away from her.

Chapter 6

What does the egg grow into? Humpty-Dumpty.

What does Humpty say about Alice's name and why? That it is stupid because all names should mean something and "Alice" means nothing.

How does Alice anger Humpty? By alluding to the nursery rhyme in which he breaks up into pieces.

What is troubling about Humpty's conversation? He turns most points into riddles without any answers.

What is an un-birthday? A day which is not your birthday.

What poem does Humpty explain for Alice and how convincing his explanation? He explains "Jabberwocky" but nothing he says really makes sense.

How does Humpty's poem annoy Alice? It ends abruptly with goodbye.

What noise does Alice hear in the wood? A great crash.

Creative response: write Humpty's story, outlining his thoughts and feelings about Alice, and the things that happen in the nursery rhyme.

Chapter 7

What characters does the King ask Alice? Why does Alice's reply confuse the king? Haigha and Hatta. She says she has seen nobody, who the King takes to be a person.

What discussion do the King and Haigha (the March Hare) have about Nobody? Why is this funny? They discuss how fast Nobody walks. This is funny because they are discussing literally "nobody".

What happens in Alice's rhyme about the Lion and the Unicorn? They fight for a crown, stop to eat bread and butter, and then are drummed out of town.

Why does the White King believe it is pointless for Alice to follow the White Queen? She moves too quickly.

Who does the Unicorn think Alice is? A monster.

What causes Alice to run off in terror? A deafening drumbeat.

Chapter 8

What does Alice wonder as the drum beat dies down? That she is existing in the Red King's dream.

Who comes to Alice's rescue when the Red Knight puts her in "check"? The White Knight.

What news does the White Knight tell Alice? That she will become a Queen when she crosses the next brook.

What is odd about the White Knight and his horse? The fact that he is carrying so many items.

How does Alice offend the White Knight? By questioning his riding ability.

What has the White Knight invented? A new kind of helmet, different ways of jumping a fence, and a new kind of pudding.

How does Alice say goodbye to the Knight? What is the mood here? She waits for him to pass out of sight, waving her handkerchief at him. The mood is quite sad.

What happens when Alice jumps over the brook? She finds herself sitting on a lawn, wearing a crown.

Chapters 9-12

What happens when Alice realises she is a Queen? She finds herself with the Red and the White Queen.

What do the Queens tell Alice she must do to become a Queen? Pass their examinations.

How does the Red Queen frustrate Alice? By correcting her every incorrect answer.

How are taken in the Looking-Glass world according to the White Queen? 2 or 3 at a time.

Why is the White Queen so rude according to the Red Queen? She wasn't brought up properly.

What does the Red Queen's singing cause the White Queen to do? To fall asleep on Alice's shoulder.

What words boom out of the door that flies open for Alice when she knocks on it? "NO ADMITTANCE UNTIL THE WEEK AFTER NEXT!"

What creature is confused by Alice from behind the door? A frog.

Why does the Red Queen send the food back at the party? She says it would be rude to eat the food after making its acquaintance.

What happens when Alice rises to give thanks to her guests? Chaos erupts.

What does Alice do with the tablecloth? Pulls it off the table.

Who does Alice believe is responsible for the chaos? The Red Queen.

Who does the Queen turn into and what does Alice realise? Kitty. Alice realises she has been dreaming.

Who does Alice think Snowdrop and Dinah are? The White Queen and Humpty Dumpty.

What poetry does Alice tell Kitty about? Her fish-themed poetry.

Speaking and Listening Exercises

Work in a group and devise a **chatshow** based on one or either of the books. Make sure that you have an interviewer (chat-show host) who questions the main characters in the novels about their thoughts and feelings regarding what has happened to them. The aim is that students need to show that they understand the storyline and characters by talking in role about the events in the novel. You can include all the animals and inanimate characters such as the Cheshire Cat and the pack of cards.

You could put the Red Queen on **trial** for crimes against the people. Set things up so that you have a prosecuting lawyer who is accusing the Red Queen of the crimes of attempting to execute people for no just cause and for being a brutal, abusive ruler. Have a defence lawyer who argues that there is evidence that the Red Queen should be treated leniently because possibly she is merely obeying the laws of the world she inhabits, and is possibly just part of the Red King's dream or Lewis Carroll's imagination. Call witnesses for the prosecution and defence who are characters from the novel such as Alice, the different kings and queens, the Duchess, the Mad

Hatter etc; or the author; or "made-up" characters such as a psychiatrist who has assessed the Red Queen, her children, and friends etc. Use the trial to explore different views on the novel. Then possibly write it up as a script or review what you have learnt from doing it.

Put the main characters in **therapy:** Alice, the Mad Hatter, the White Rabbit, the kings and queens, and the other chess pieces such as the White Knight. Have them visit a therapist to discuss their problems with him/her. You could do this so that they go into therapy at various stages during the story, i.e. Alice when she first arrives in the different worlds, the Mad Hatter after his Tea Party and imprisonment, and the White Knight before he rescues Alice and afterwards. Write a review of what you have learnt from devising this series of interviews.

Work in a group and devise a **radio drama** of the major parts of the novels. Different groups could work on different sections of the book; e.g. the major incidents in Wonderland and the ones that happened in the Looking Glass World. Make the drama short and punchy. This exercise will help you get to know the text in much more depth: the editing of the novel will help you summarise key points.

How to write top grade essays on the novels

To write a good essay or assignments about the *Alice* novels, you need to understand them in depth. You will need to know what the difficult vocabulary means and be aware of how the text is the product of the world it comes from: nineteenth century England. You will also need to be aware of what the examiners for your question are looking for. For many exams, particularly in England, it appears that most questions are, at the time of writing this guide, "extract based"; you will be given a small extract and asked to consider how the author builds suspense or drama in the extract, or presents the characters or key themes in a particular way. To achieve highly, you will need to answer the question carefully and not simply re-tell the extract; this is something that I have seen many good students do. The A Level and GCSE questions on books like *Alice* are much more like the ones posed in the **essay question section** of this study guide and the analytical questions posed at the end of the chapter questions. Sometimes, you might be asked to compare the novel with other literary texts, depending upon the nature of the task and/or exam board. For A Level, you need to be aware of other literary critics' views on the novel.

You should consider a few key questions:

For extract questions, consider how has the author **built up** to this moment? Think carefully about what the reader already knows before they have read the extract. You will need to know the story well to do this.

What literary devices does the author use to make the passage interesting or to reveal a character in a certain light? Think very carefully about the author's use of language: Carroll's use of descriptions to create a certain atmosphere or paint a sketch of a character/event; his use of dialogue to reveal character and create drama/tension; his use of imagery (metaphors/similes/personification). You will need to pack your essay full of the relevant terminology if you want to aim for higher marks as it appears many mark schemes as a key requirement.

You need to be aware of several different interpretations of the novel. The weblinks below should help you with this.

Finally, you need to provide evidence and analysis to back up your points. As a cornerstone of your essay writing technique, you should be aware of the **PEEL** method of analysing texts: making a Point, providing Evidence, Explaining how your evidence endorses your point, and Linking to a new point.

Writing about the story/narrative

I would strongly advise you to read my section on the **structure and themes of the novel here** before writing about the effects the narrative structure of the books creates. There are many, many things to say about the story of the book, but you should think about your own personal response as well: what did you find the most engaging parts of the novels and why? Look back over the notes you have made while you read the novels and use them to shape an original response. You need to avoid just re-telling the story, which is very easy to do in highly pressurised situations and you're not thinking straight!

Writing about the characterisations

There are many websites which can help you with writing about the characters in the novels, already listed earlier on in this book. A central technique of Carroll's is to make the reader think about how and why characters are similar and different; we are constantly being invited to compare characters in our minds. This is a central way that Carroll generates suspense and drama in the novels; the novel is full striking comparisons and contrasts. Think carefully about how Alice changes throughout the novels both physically and mentally. Consider how the kings and queens in both novels are similar and different. Think about how the animals both share characteristics but also are quite unlike. It may be helpful to draw a visual organiser to help you or a chart, where you can map out how characters are similar and different, and consider why they are.

It is the madness and sanity of the characters which creates much of the humour and suspense: many of them do and say things that are perfectly sane in "real" life but are insane in the context of the stories, such provide riddles which have no answer, draw attention to Alice's strange manners and habits when it is their reactions which are much stranger, pursue past-times which are quite ordinary but insane in the context of the dream worlds.

Task

Look at some character studies online and devise a chart or **visual organiser** which illustrates the similarities and differences between the major characters, exploring the effects that these similarities and differences have upon the reader.

Writing about the settings

Lewis Carroll is an interesting writer because he avoids describing the physical surroundings in depth; instead we gain more of a sense of the place from vividly drawn details and through the dialogue of the characters, and the drawings that often accompany the books. Nevertheless, certain settings play a very important part in the book: the river bank, the rabbit hole, the lawn with the croquet match, the court setting, the chessboard with its brooks, forests and gardens.

You can find more information about settings here:
http://www.alice-in-wonderland.net/resources/analysis/setting/

Task

Look carefully at the use of settings in the novel; what purpose do they serve? Why does Carroll set scenes in particular settings such as the rabbit hole, the lawn of the croquet match, the chessboard and the forest? Think carefully about the time of day that he sets his scenes: how and why is time important in the novels?

Dreams and reality

A central technique of Carroll's is to question what the difference is between dreams and reality: we are constantly confronted with things such as food, games, rituals, ordinary settings, recognizable characters and animals, believable situations which are twisted beyond all recognition in the dream worlds of the novels.

Task

Look back over the novel, and work out what is plausible about the situations in the novels, and what is utterly ridiculous. Devise a visual organiser which charts the moments which contain both dream-like and "believable" elements. If you think carefully, you will realise that this is most parts of both books. For example, the Caucus Race in Chapter 3 of *Wonderland* is an utterly absurd race, but it is based on a very "real" idea that of a "competition"; it becomes absurd in the novel because no one wins. Consider what deeper point Carroll might be making by merging the "real" and the "dream-like": why are animals both like and unlike human beings? What are the effects of turning inanimate figures into live, speaking beings?

Use of language

Above all, you need to analyse the effects of Carroll's language upon the reader; exploring what the language makes the reader think, feel and see.

Task

Devise a chart/visual organiser/notes on the different types of language Carroll uses in the novel, providing quotes and examples for the following types of language:

Descriptive language: language which describes people, places and situations

Imagery: language which makes comparisons

Important dialogue: important quotes that people say that make the plot move on.

Language games which include:

- Puns: one of Carroll's main techniques is to play on the double meanings of words.
- Satire and parodies: Carroll is constantly poking fun at more serious forms of writing and behaviour, parodying serious poems and writing, and satirising serious human behaviour such as court room scenarios.

Useful links

The following websites contain some incisive analysis on the use of language.

This document looks at the language games in the novel, written an academic style:

http://ler.letras.up.pt/uploads/ficheiros/7246.pdf

Other websites cover the main themes, imagery and motifs of the novel, examining the language as well. They are worth looking at but do not copy them, examine them critically, thinking hard about whether you agree:

http://www.sparknotes.com/lit/alice/themes.html

http://www.victorianweb.org/authors/carroll/beckman2.html

https://revistacititordeproza.wordpress.com/2012/10/20/the-use-of-nonsense-in-lewis-carrolls-alice-in-wonderland/
https://www.cliffsnotes.com/literature/a/alices-adventures-in-wonderland/critical-essays/themes-in-alices-adventures-in-wonderland

Possible essay titles

To what extent are the *Alice* novels books for children?

To what extent do both novels explore the theme of identity?

To what extent are both books about different forms of bullying?

To what extent do both novels reflect the morals and values of Victorian society?

'The nonsense in the novels may seem ridiculous on first reading, but paying closer attention to it makes the reader realize there is a serious purpose behind the fun.' To what extent do you agree or disagree with this statement?

Analyse and explore the role dialogue plays in the novels.

'The Alice novels would not be half the books they are without interesting illustrations'. Carry out some research into the different illustrations for the novels, and discuss whether you agree or disagree with this statement.

'Lewis Carroll makes the reader realise that life is a no more than a silly game'. To what extent do you agree or disagree with this statement.

Explore the role dreams play in both novels.

Glossary

adjourn; take a break; break from a meeting or gathering

askance; view with doubt; with suspicion or disapproval

beseech; beg; ask for or request earnestly

bewilderment; total confusion; confusion resulting from failure to understand

brandish; wave (usually a weapon) about in a swaggering, arrogant, proud way; move or swing back and forth

cauldron; a very large pot that is used for boiling

chortle; laugh quietly or with restraint

circumstance; a condition that accompanies some event or activity

coax; influence or urge by gentle urging, caressing, or flattering

contemptuous; expressing extreme scorn

contrariwise; contrary to expectations

demure; affectedly shy especially in a playful or provocative way

devour; eat greedily

diligent; characterized by care and perseverance in carrying out tasks

dismal; causing dejection

distinguish; mark as different

dwindle; become smaller or lose substance

effect; a phenomenon that is caused by some previous phenomenon

etiquette; rules governing socially acceptable behavior

fancy; imagine; conceive of; see in one's mind

falter; speak haltingly, break down

fretful; worrying a lot; habitually complaining

giddy; feeling dizzy; having or causing a whirling sensation; liable to falling

impenetrable; impossible to understand

impertinence; cheekiness; the trait of being rude and inclined to take liberties

imperial; belonging to or befitting a supreme ruler, or referring to an old-fashioned type of measurement

incessantly; never stopping; without interruption

inclined; liking to do things in a certain way; having a preference, disposition, or tendency

indignant; angered at something unjust or wrong

ingenuity; being very clever; the power of creative imagination

insolence; the trait of being rude and impertinent

latitude; an imaginary line around the Earth parallel to the equator

Melancholy; sadness

loll; lie about in a lazy way; be lazy or idle

mischief; naughtiness; reckless or malicious behavior causing annoyance in others

obstinacy; resolute adherence to your own ideas or desires

perplexity; confusion; trouble or confusion resulting from complexity

plaintive; sounding sad; expressing sorrow

ponder; reflect deeply on a subject

prattle; talk in an irrelevant way; speak about unimportant matters rapidly and incessantly

proboscis; a long flexible snout as of an elephant

provoke; annoy continually or chronically

pun; a humorous play on words

pretext; an artificial reason for doing something

relent; give in, as to influence or pressure

reproachful; telling off someone or yourself; expressing reproof especially as a corrective

resolutely; showing firm determination or purpose

saunter; walk leisurely and with no apparent aim

scornful; angry; expressing extreme contempt

severity; excessive sternness

shrill; having or emitting a high-pitched and sharp tone or tones

sluggard; an idle slothful, lazy person

sullen; showing a brooding ill humor

suppressed; held in check with difficulty

toil; productive work, especially physical work done for wages

tremulous; quivering as from weakness or fear

trifle; something of small importance

triumphant; joyful and proud especially because of success

tureen; large deep serving dish with a cover

unfortunate; marked by or resulting in bad luck

vexation; anger produced by some annoying irritation

About the Author

Francis Gilbert is a Lecturer in Education at Goldsmiths, University of London, teaching on the PGCE Secondary English programme and the MA in Children's Literature with Professor Michael Rosen. Previously, he worked for a quarter of a century in various English state schools teaching English and Media Studies to 11-18 year olds. He has also moonlighted as a journalist, novelist and social commentator both in the UK and international media. He is the author of *Teacher On The Run, Yob Nation, Parent Power, Working The System -- How To Get The Very Best State Education for Your Child*, and a novel about school, *The Last Day Of Term*. His first book, *I'm A Teacher, Get Me Out Of Here* was a big hit, becoming a bestseller and being serialised on Radio 4. In his role as an English teacher, he has taught many classic texts over the years and has developed a great many resources to assist readers with understanding, appreciating and responding to them both analytically and creatively. This led him to set up his own small publishing company FGI Publishing (fgipublishing.com) which has published his study guides as well as a number of books by other authors, including Roger Titcombe's *Learning Matters* and Tim Cadman's *The Changes*.

He is the co-founder, with Melissa Benn and Fiona Millar, of The Local Schools Network, **www.localschoolsnetwork.org.uk**, a blog that celebrates non-selective state schools, and also has his own website, **www.francisgilbert.co.uk** and a Mumsnet blog, **www.talesbehindtheclassroomdoor.co.uk**.

He has appeared numerous times on radio and TV, including Newsnight, the Today Programme, Woman's Hour and the Russell Brand Show. In June 2015, he was awarded a PhD in Creative Writing and Education by the University of London.

CPSIA information can be obtained
at www.ICGtesting.com
Printed in the USA
BVHW031707100619
550616BV00001B/25/P

9 781494 758646